MY-TE-FINE MERCHANT

FRED MEYER'S RETAIL REVOLUTION

Fred Leeson

Irvington Press
PORTLAND, OREGON

Book Layout ©2013 BookDesignTemplates.com
Cover design by Courtney Roby-Sage

MY-TE-FINE Merchant/Fred Leeson -- 1st ed.
ISBN 978-0-9960626-0-2

Library of Congress Control Number: 2014905872

Manufactured in the United States of America

In honor of those who worked for, endured and respected Fred G. Meyer, a brilliant and difficult man.

ON THE COVER

Fred Meyer spent little time during his long career personally waiting on customers. Yet he chose the imagery of the grocer's apron when he posed for this publicity photo in 1947, the start of his post-war boom. Meyer was 61 at the time. (Oregon Historical Society Fred Meyer Collection, Box 7)

Table of Contents

CHAPTER ONE

Behind the Bow Tie

An elderly man with a hat pulled low on his head and using a cane to steady his weakened right leg found himself confronted on Southwest First Avenue near Harrison Street in Portland by a young man with long hair and a bedroll strapped to his back. The young man asked for money.

The man with the cane paused. Nearly 70 years earlier, he, too, had been at a similar point in life – footloose, with little money in his pockets and no firm destination in mind. Young and headstrong, he had set out across the country in search of adventure and his own place in the world. Ultimately, after an unsuccessful attempt at getting rich quick, he settled down nearly as far as possible from the New York City neighborhood he fled as a teenager. On the streets of downtown Portland, the old man had built a career over several decades that made him wealthy beyond his dreams and transformed the way shoppers in the Pacific Northwest bought groceries, clothes, drugs and a wide variety of other goods.

The young man had no idea that the old man's name glowed in big red electrified letters over more than five dozen one-stop shopping centers in four states, or that the man in his late 80s possessed a net worth ranging well into tens of millions of dollars. The frail man's route to success had not been direct or speedy; it was a combination of happenstance, intelligence, perseverance and a domineering personality that pushed others to their limits in attempting to earn his praise.

Yet the man who could berate his managers in closed-door meetings for hours at a time seldom showed that side of his personality outside his office. He enjoyed talking to customers in the stores that bore his name. He liked conversations to be simple and direct. Big words, he believed, were a hindrance to communication. He was endlessly curious about what his customers wanted, how best to serve them and ways to cut costs. He showed the same patience and curiosity as he engaged in a brief conversation with the young man seeking money.

Wealthy as he was, the old man had never shown much of a charitable streak. He was in the process of figuring out how to leave his tens of millions in trust for the public benefit, but he'd never been keen about giving away money while he was alive. Now in his late 80s, he was still busy running his big company. His idea of helping people was providing jobs, not handouts. He liked giving underdogs a chance and seeing if they were willing to work hard and make something of themselves. Though ruthlessly shrewd in business, the old man seemed to have an understanding about human frailty; he showed remarkable patience at times with employees suffering from substance abuse or with business tenants who struggled with bookkeeping or managerial problems.

Yet the old man's endless drive for wealth was not for his own earthly pleasure. He lived a simple life. His apartment was sparsely furnished. His closet was mostly empty. He spent almost nothing on personal recreation and seldom socialized with his few friends who knew him well. He believed that many successful entrepreneurs succumbed to infatuation with their own egos and wasted money that could be better spent building their businesses. He had tasted failure more than once in his own life and had seen others' successful businesses fail along the way. True to his simple lifestyle, the old man seldom carried more than $20 in cash with him.

Something in the young panhandler's plea for help – who knows what it was – struck a nerve in the old man. When he opened his wallet that day it contained three one-dollar bills. He handed over all three and waited for the young man to walk away.

The young man gratefully accepted the gift but paused when he noticed that the man's wallet was empty. "Mister," he asked gently, "are you sure you can afford this?" It was a story that Fred G. Meyer told with glee the next day at the sprawling headquarters of Fred Meyer Inc. in Southeast Portland. Yes, Fred Meyer, surely one of the wealthiest men in Oregon, could do without the $3.[1]

Some months later, in February, 1976, the happy din of a capacity banquet crowd of 600 of Oregon's leading business people, public figures and civic boosters filled the ballroom of the Portland Hilton Hotel. Unlike the hippie on First Avenue, everyone in the room recognized the guest of honor. Fred Meyer, who was being honored two weeks short of his 90th birthday, had prepared carefully. With help from his staff, the man who cared little about clothes sat at the head table in a brand new suit and with his feet resting in the most expensive pair of shoes he'd ever worn. Days before, he had sat near the edge of the bathtub in his two-bedroom apartment at Harrison Tower and run hot water past the tops of the new leather Bally dress shoes up to his ankles. Then he drained the water and sloshed around his apartment until the shoes were almost dry. "That's how you break them in, isn't it?" he asked.[2] Meyer topped his banquet regalia with his signature bow tie. It was a clip-on. The man who often worked seven days a week and whose commercial empire had been built on efficiency and standardization no longer wasted time tying cloth strips around his collar.

Of course, Meyer had been the center of attention on several other occasions, notably store openings when he'd greet the anonymous customers to whom his retail career had been devoted. Often he would help serve a huge cake weighing hundreds of pounds and engage in friendly chitchat with customers who were thrilled to shake his hand.

At Christmas, Meyer often would be pictured in the newspapers giving away tons of food and toys to the Salvation Army and the Sunshine Division of the Portland Police Bureau, his two preferred charities. He didn't give cash; always thinking of savings and business first, the food and toys were wholesale and often items that weren't moving quickly off his store shelves.

The evening of February 6, 1976 was an unusual one for Meyer. He might have preferred to be dining at his favorite restaurant – Eve's Buffet at his Burlingame store in Southwest Portland – but on this night Meyer was being honored by the Portland Board of Realtors as Portland's First Citizen, an event with a long history of celebrating success with good food, drinks and pleasant talk. Meyer surely was a deserving honoree. His name was on 63 stores in four Pacific Northwest states; most of them were so-called "one-stop shopping centers" where a customer could find anything from fresh fruits and blue jeans to toys and table saws. As Oregon Gov. Bob Straub said that night, "There are few people in Oregon who have had such an impact on the state for the last 60 years." [3] Others who joined in the praise included: Mayor Neil Goldschmidt, then perhaps at the height of his political popularity; former Gov. Tom McCall, and Meyer's hand-picked successor to lead Fred Meyer Inc. after Meyer's death, Oran B. Robertson.

Robertson described his boss of 31 years as a tough but forgiving task-master. "He says it's all right to make a mistake, but don't make the same mistake more than seven times." [4] Robertson and anyone else who had worked closely with Meyer knew that the first part of the sentence was true. The second part was the punch line. Meyer might look in public like a quiet old relative at a wedding with his wire-rimmed glasses and bow tie, but in the executive offices and board room at Fred Meyer Inc. he was still the dominating tiger who commanded respect and intimidated lesser minds into silence.

As he neared 90, Meyer knew – he always seemed to know so much in advance – that he wasn't going to achieve his dream of living to

100.[5] Just a few years before, he had fended off what he interpreted as an internal coup by executives and corporate directors who thought he was too old to be running a major public corporation and who wanted him to step down. But they underestimated him. Meyer won that battle behind closed doors and the challengers departed quietly, leaving behind few public hints of the rancor. Soon thereafter, Meyer suffered a stroke that would have crippled most people. His doctor told him he'd never walk or work again, but in three weeks Meyer was back at the office, walking with a cane and struggling to get his signature back to readable form for corporate documents.

In the time he had left, Meyer was trying to craft a management team that would succeed him and was making plans for his estate that would amount of tens of millions of dollars – a number that Meyer himself could not quantify during his life. He owned nearly 30 percent of the stock in Fred Meyer Inc., but how much his stake was worth depended on what a willing buyer would pay, and that likely would depend on whether a buyer wanted the entire company or just part of it. In his later years, he had received offers from time to time to buy Fred Meyer Inc. He would listen patiently, and then always say no thanks. Meyer in 1976 couldn't know that his management team would fracture not long after his death, and that his best-laid plans would generate lawsuits involving several of the state's top legal minds for nearly a decade.

Of course, there was other Portland news on that February Friday. State and federal regulators had issued new obstacles to Portland General Electric Co., which was planning to build a natural-gas-fired power plant in Northwest Portland and two nuclear plants in Eastern Oregon, none of which was ever erected. In Seattle the same night, Portland's entry in the National Basketball Association won its seventh straight game, the longest streak in the team's six-year history. Bill Walton, an impressive young center with injury-plagued feet, was starting to show the dominance that would help carry the team to a surprising league championship the following year. But anticipation mounted in the Hilton ballroom as the accolades ended and Fred Meyer stood at the lectern. Three weeks earlier, he had told a Seattle newspaper that he had always preferred Seattle to Portland, and that he had based his empire in Portland because his wife, Eva, who died in 1960, liked Portland better.[6] Meyer had described Seattle as being more cosmopolitan and more business-friendly, with fewer of the nettlesome land-use laws that slowed people who wanted to grow and build. When he discovered that he had hurt some feelings in Portland, Meyer didn't try to claim he was misquoted; instead, he said one wouldn't bother criticizing people or places unless one cared about them. Now, here he was in the same ballroom with two prominent officials he had indirectly criticized: Gov. Straub, who supported the state's new land-use regulations; and former Gov. McCall, whose famed "come visit but don't stay" message grated on Meyer's views about Oregon's future.

Just short of five years earlier, the Oregon Legislature had adopted a comprehensive set of planning guidelines intended to preserve high quality farm land and to prevent Oregon cities from following a pattern of an unplanned, sprawling, inefficient growth that had afflicted many American cities since World War II. In the Portland area, Meyer and his growing network of stores were both a beneficiary and an instigator of urban sprawl. He had recognized back in the 1930s that the automobile would soon dominate American life. His big, one-stop suburban shopping centers with acres of flat, asphalt parking lots were precisely the sort of development that planners hoped to regulate more closely with regional boundaries and regional growth and transportation strategies. To his way of thinking, Meyer had helped every community in which he had built a store. His stores provided new jobs that offered routes for professional growth, and they acted as magnets attracting other businesses that stood to gain from large volumes of traffic lured seven days a week to Meyer's huge stores. It was incomprehensible to him why neighborhoods such as Westmoreland and Oak Hills battled so hard, and successfully, to keep his stores from locating there.

This would not be a night for controversy, however. "I appreciate this more than you realize," Meyer began. Referring to those who had lauded him, he said, "You should discount some of the things they have said." The outline of his story was well-known: a pioneer in the evolution of self-service retailing and an early proponent of merging full-scale food sales with a variety of other goods, a concept that came to be known in America as a "one-stop shopping center" and in Europe as a hypermarket. Parts of Meyer's quick story line as repeated numerous times in newspapers in the final decades of his life weren't entirely factual, however, and Meyer never bothered to correct the record. Perhaps there was no need; his success and the big red "Fred Meyer" signs throughout the region spoke for themselves.

"Being 90 is better than being 65 or 70 because then they ask you to retire and chase a little while ball on the green," he told the audience. Maybe it was a just a joke; maybe it was a backhanded slap at a former business partner of the 1920s, Robert A. Hudson, who had become known in Oregon as "Mr. Golf" before Hudson's own business empire imploded in the early 1970s. At 90, Meyer added, people are surprised that one is still lucid from time to time. Forgetfulness was an acceptable excuse if one neglected to attend some meeting or other. "The best thing you can do is relax without misgivings," he said. "So you see, life really begins at 90."[7]

The jokes about not retiring and being lucid at 90 and still running a major corporation were proof of Meyer's distinctive abilities. And not just for those reasons. He would work seven days a week at the office, and sometimes wonder why his top executives were not there with him on Sundays. He could do arithmetic calculations in his head almost as fast as a computer. He cared little about clothes and his closet was mostly empty; as soon as his wife, Eva, bought him something new, he'd send the old item to the Salvation Army. Often, he seemed to know what people were going to say before they said it. He had no hobbies other than reading and listening to music. His few friends all involved links to his business. He could easily turn his back on his few blood relatives, in-laws, and businessmen like Hudson if Meyer felt wronged. Few people knew it, but there were three brothers living in Portland who were born into the Grubmeyer family from Brooklyn. All arrived in Portland as young men. All spent their careers in the retail food business, in a sense competing with one another. Fred Meyer refused to see or talk with Henry Meyer after a business dispute dating to the late 1920s. If his relations with William Grubmeyer, who retained the family's original surname throughout his life, were any more cordial, Fred Meyer's close associates were unaware of it. Fred Meyer had no children of his own. Instead, he developed what seemed like father-daughter and father-son relationships with two employees who came to work for him.

Meyer was a man with an elementary-school education who read voraciously. He could quote Shakespeare and Goethe at length; his knowledge of music, from the baroque and classic eras to Gershwin and the big bands, was extensive. He was a man who never attended church, but believed deeply in the Rosicrucian Fellowship, an occult ideology laid atop a foundation of biblical Christianity. He made monthly donations to the California-based fellowship and gave close associates Rosicrucian books that had impressed him so intensely, but he never proselytized or followed up to determine whether any recipients bothered reading them.

Although he never bought a house during his life in Portland, Meyer had a special sense for commercial real estate and future urban growth patterns. Working through surrogates, he bought farmland on the fringes of the city and waited as long as 20 years to develop the parcels into large shopping venues. Almost a decade before the famed New York planner Robert Moses visited Portland and started drawing potential freeway routes on maps, Meyer, in the mid-1930s, told associates where he thought freeways would go. He was mostly right. While streetcars were still the primary mode of transportation in Portland, he anticipated the future dominance of the automobile and the need for customer parking. Where could cars go in the heavily developed existing neighborhoods? Why not the roof? It was empty space crying to be used. The idea occurred to him in the mid-1930s. World War II intervened, but then he built stores at Rose City and Hollywood and Hawthorne with roof-top parking.

Appealing to customers' needs was always his motivation. How could he cut costs? How could his stores be more efficient? What steps in a process could be eliminated or compressed? What procedures or

Two of the most recognizable faces in Portland in the 1970s belonged to Fred Meyer and Portland City Commissioner Mildred Schwab, on the dais here at the 1976 First Citizen banquet. (Oregonian)

physical devices or aisles could be standardized? He battled in court when some of his practices that led to lower prices were challenged; sometimes he won, sometimes he lost. He lectured his advertising staff on ways to make his print ads simple yet descriptive. If he saw staff behavior he didn't like in a store, he didn't hesitate to upbraid even lowly employees. He knew most of his customers were women. Soon after his first Stadium store opened late in 1939, he saw merchandise stacked on top of a high rack. He took his cane and knocked items to the floor. When a supervisor came running, Meyer hotly explained that the average height of his customers was five foot two, and they couldn't buy items if they couldn't reach them. Lesson learned.

Teaching and learning were always in the back of his mind. When associates invited Meyer out to dinner, he'd ask, "Where can we go? What can we learn?" When his managers traveled or visited competing stores, he'd ask, "What did you see?" They quickly learned that "Nothing" was not an acceptable answer; they needed to find something, whether it be about the floor covering or ceiling tiles, check-out system or signs, displays or aisle arrangement, parking or methods for dealing with irksome trash receptacles outside. He was always open to new technology if it could save time or money. He installed the first microwave ovens in his commercial kitchen in the 1950s, even though they were big as refrigerators and each weighed 750 pounds. With the advent of electronic cash registers – long before computers – he figured there must be a way that all his registers could be attached to a machine that would give him daily sales totals from all his dozens of stores.

Meyer was toughest on his executive committee, a group of approximately 10 top managers that included his wife, Eva, who met early on Tuesday mornings. Meyer would lock the door, making it impossible for a late-comer to slip in unobtrusively. It came to be known out of Meyer's presence as "fish-in-the-barrel" day. Often as not, Meyer would select one person for intensive questioning or criticism. He wanted brief, direct answers. No excuses, no big words. He would become persistent, impatient, even abrasive, thrumming his fingers impatiently on the table and calling people or their ideas "stupid." No one was exempt. "Dummy," was his favored descriptor for those less smart than he, or who couldn't come up with answers he wanted to hear. There were times when he drove his own wife, the woman he professed to love and adore, to tears in front of the others. Newcomers never forgot their first "fish-in-the-barrel" experience. For Meyer, making others feel inferior had a purpose. It made them work harder to earn approval that never seemed to follow.

Yet if someone was able to fight back in those meetings, fact by fact, with conviction and clarity, even with raised voice, Meyer would listen. He liked hearing all sides of an issue. He wanted to know as much as he could about any problem before making a decision. Critical as he often was, outbursts in the office stayed in the office. "No, we respected him so much," Robertson said after Meyer's death. "You wouldn't let anybody else say a bad word about Fred Meyer."[8]

Corporate titles meant little. Meyer was the boss. He made the decisions. There was a dramatic exception in the mid-1960s, when two executives, acting behind Meyer's back, upgraded interior design and colors at three stores without his permission. They risked their jobs doing it, and Meyer was angry when he walked into a new store on Foster Road and saw the changes first-hand. But his ire was quickly tempered by increased sales and by happy employees who liked working in more pleasant surroundings. Indeed, the change in philosophy may have saved the entire Fred Meyer chain from looking outdated and rundown. Oran Robertson and Rollin Killoran expected no kudos for their daring exploit, however. They knew that at Fred Meyer Inc., all good ideas belonged to Fred Meyer. Failures belonged to others.

For all his abrasiveness, Meyer's closest associates, many of whom stayed with the company for decades, realized that Meyer's tactics were intended to instruct them. On the plus side, the strong-willed boss didn't hold grudges. When he next saw those whom he had berated, be it the next day or the next week, it was like all was forgotten. On more than one occasion, top managers got so angry they declared they were quitting and stormed out. But when they returned later to clean out their desks, it seemed as if all was forgotten, or maybe forgiven. So they stayed.

Meyer valued loyalty and always looked at promoting from within as the first option in filling vacancies. Ironically, perhaps, he was reluctant to fire employees. He had a more gradual but equally effective way of replacing people in his inner circle: If he didn't want them around, he made their work lives so unpleasant, they chose to quit.

Meyer liked to see employees grow in their careers. He had a knack for sizing up bright, hard-working people quickly, regardless of schooling or background. College degrees meant nothing to him; many of his top managers had started as box boys stocking shelves or in similar entry-level jobs. Though many went on to earn college degrees at night schools or as part-time students, employees proved their value through performance, not formal education. Indeed, the best educated was Meyer's stepson, Earle A. Chiles. He, too, started with his stepfather as a high school student and graduated from the University of Oregon and earned a master's in business administration from Harvard University. Chiles ultimately held the title of corporate president and took a seat at executive committee meetings along with his mother, Eva Chiles Meyer, but Meyer largely ignored him or cut him down verbally. Earle Chiles, a gentle soul in the eyes of those who knew him well, eventually stopped offering suggestions. He made the best of the situation by representing the company in trade associations. He also stepped out front occasionally by issuing public statements to the newspapers when the corporate need arose.

Meyer's long working life was devoted to making money. At age 74, long after most people have retired, Meyer launched his era of most aggressive expansion, buying stores, building new ones and expanding his product lines. A carefully-crafted bonus policy was designed to reward employees for successful performance; the bottom line was always the measure. Yet Meyer's drive to earn profits was not for his own gratification; he lived simply and planned to give away his estate. Growing the business was his way of improving communities and providing opportunity.

What motivated him to work so hard, and work so hard for so long? It may have been his Germanic roots, or the fact that his formal education ended with elementary school. He once admitted to having an inferiority complex. "And that's been one of my motivating forces," he told Jack Crocker, one of his executives. "Remember that an inferiority complex can be a great motivating force because it's people who really lack that confidence who constantly strive to improve themselves and be better."[9]

If there were any commonalities among Meyer's inner circle over the years, those threads were family and economic backgrounds. Many were from small towns or rural areas and had experienced economic or familial hardships as children or young adults, a common experience for Meyer's first generation of workers who lived through the Great Depression. They earned Meyer's respect with their diligence and successful performance. He earned their respect with his business acumen and raw intelligence. Even among those who worked closely with him for decades, he was always "Mr. Meyer." Out of his presence, his wife, Eva, didn't refer to him by his first name, but rather, "Mr. Meyer." After his death, an ad agency came up with a new slogan: "You'll find it at Freddy's," recognizing the informal name that many customers used in referring to the Meyer stores. It struck some of the veterans as disrespectful.[10] To them, he was never Fred, let alone Freddy. He was always Mr. Meyer.

Before her death in 1960, Eva Meyer would make the rounds of the corporate offices after especially difficult meetings with her husband. To many of the corporate insiders she earned the informal nickname of "Mama," the person who offered comforting words and a knowing smile after an abrasive session with the boss.[11] Still, there were times when the top managers wondered out loud – in private, of course– why they stayed with the company. During the Great Depression, some held on in the face of Meyer's abrasiveness simply because having any job was a blessing, and finding another one would be too risky. Later on, several realized that given their abilities and experience, they could find better paying jobs and more congenial conditions elsewhere. So why stay at Fred Meyer?

They relied on their own experiences to arrive at answers that boiled down to the same conclusion: How often do you have the chance to work for a genius?[12]

---

[1] Robertson, Oran, OHS sound recording 1312, Feb. 2, 1989.
[2] Sadis, Jerry, OHS sound recording 1313, April 20, 1989
[3] *Oregon Journal,* Feb. 7, 1976.
[4] *Ibid.*
[5] Sadis, *op cit.*
[6] *Oregonian,* Jan. 18, 1976, p. E1.
[7] *Oregon Journal,* op cit.
[8] Robertson, *op. cit.,* Oct. 25, 1989.
[9] Crocker, Jack, OHS sound recording 1304, June 1, 1989.
[10] Lawrence, Pauline, OHS sound recording 1309, May 25, 1989.
[11] Robertson, *op cit.,* Dec. 8, 1988.
[12] *Ibid.*

CHAPTER TWO

The Road to Yamhill Street

In the final weeks of his life, Fred G. Meyer asked his secretary, Jean Webb, to bring papers from six short file cabinets located under the window of his small office in the sprawling Fred Meyer Inc. headquarters in Southeast Portland to his apartment on the 19th floor of the Harrison Tower near downtown. There were impressive views from his windows to the east and south, but his attention was focused on the files Webb delivered. At age 92 and knowing that his death was imminent, Meyer systematically removed items about his personal life and destroyed them. Documents, newspaper clippings and photographs relating to the giant retailing company he had built over the prior five decades were another matter. He left those intact.

Meyer's reason for destroying information about his personal past died with him. Perhaps it was because he had spent his life looking ahead, never backward, always interested in new technology, new merchandising trends and new expansion possibilities. Perhaps he thought no one would be interested in details of his personal life outside of Fred Meyer Inc. Or perhaps there were episodes in his life that he didn't want anyone to dwell on. Those could have been his German roots, his failed attempt at mining gold in Alaska, his name change at age 34, the disputes with two brothers in Portland with whom he had cut off communications in the 1920s, and perhaps a bout of mental instability in the 1930s. Possibly he thought that other businessmen with whom he had associated early in his Portland career were not worthy of mention. He may well have been satisfied with the brief but sketchy corporate biography, which in just a few sentences traced a direct route from his start in Portland as an itinerant merchant with a horse-drawn coffee cart to his success as a multi-state mega-store retailer with nearly $1 billion in sales. Those who knew him well never recognized Meyer in middle age as being egotistical or vain. But it also was true that he enjoyed the attention that came his way late in life acknowledging his outstanding success. In recognition of his ability and age, top-ranking Fred Meyer executives made sure that appropriate limelight would fall on him, not them. It would be realistic, perhaps, for a highly successful and often-domineering merchandising entrepreneur to package his own story as he saw fit.

Despite his efforts, however, Meyer could not eliminate all traces of his early life and interests. The surviving evidence shows that his route to ultimate success was neither short nor direct. After his arrival in Portland in 1909, he worked with several businessmen under several business names before incorporating in 1927 as "Meyer, Fred Inc." and putting the name "Fred Meyer" on a tobacco shop. Most of his work focused on food and retailing, but not directly with consumers. In those intervening years, Fred Grubmeyer worked successfully as a landlord, renting market stalls to vendors on the popular Yamhill Street public markets. For a time he operated from an office high in the Pacific Building, one of the city's nicest new office structures, sold corporate shares in a new grocery chain called Piggly Wiggly Stores, and partnered with Robert A. Hudson, who became a major wholesale food processing and distribution entrepreneur. Just before the crushing Depression of 1929, Meyer built a major downtown retail and office building from the steel-frame carcass of the old Pantages Theater, where he installed an innovative self-service toiletries and over-the-counter drug store. Though exact dates are difficult to pinpoint, it was not until the late 1920s that Meyer focused exclusively on his retail businesses, and not until 1931 that he opened his first real "one-stop shopping center," the concept on which his ultimate success and fame was based. That was the year he turned 45.

In the spring of 1886, Conrad Grubmeyer and his wife, Sophie Dorothea Vorverk Grubmeyer, both 31, boarded an ocean liner docked in Bremen, called the Ems, a 4,700-ton liner operated by the North German Lloyd shipping line. The two-year-old vessel was one of several speedier liners the big international shipping company had built that was capable crossing the Atlantic in eight days. The Grubmeyer parents had with them their two sons, William, 4, and Fritz (Fred), 2. The family arrived in Southampton, N.Y., on May 7. Conrad Grubmeyer had listed Chicago as the family's destination, but they settled, instead, in Brooklyn, perhaps to be near his older brother, Henry Grubmeyer. Henry, who had arrived in New York from Germany a decade before, operated a small grocery store in Brooklyn. In an 1892 census, Conrad Grubmeyer listed his occupation as a varnisher, but shortly thereafter he, too, was engaged in running a small neighborhood grocery.

Conrad and Sophie Grubmeyer were far from finished growing their family. Daughters Sophie, Minnie and Marie were born in 1891, 1892 and 1895, respectively, followed by sons Henry, Charles and Carl in 1896, 1898 and 1900. William and Henry joined their brother, Fred, in Portland after 1910. Like Fred, Henry shortened his last name to Meyer, while William retained the original Grubmeyer surname throughout his life. William Grubmeyer and Henry Meyer spent the rest of their lives living and working in Portland. For reasons related to business dealings, Fred Meyer had little or no contact with either brother after the late 1920s.

The young Grubmeyer family settled in western Brooklyn,

midway between one of the borough's best attractions, Prospect Park, and one of its worst sites, the Gowanus Canal. The 585-acre park included nearly 300 acres of deciduous forest in addition to lawns, playgrounds, monuments and public gathering spots. It had been designed in the 1860s by Frederick Law Olmsted and his partner Carl Vaux, who only a few years earlier had won a design competition for Central Park in Manhattan. The pioneering landscape architects recognized that the burgeoning population, fueled heavily by immigrants like the Grubmeyers from Central and Eastern Europe, needed the respite of open space and outdoor recreation in the densely-urban vicinity.

But closer yet to the Grubmeyers was the smelly canal only a few blocks to the west. The channel of a once-minor creek had been widened in 1869 into a mile-and-a-half dead-end canal intended to provide shipping access from the Upper New York Bay to businesses in the largely industrial Gowanus neighborhood. However, budget cuts prevented completion of the project as originally designed, and tides from the Upper Bay proved unable to flush the canal daily as planned. Its waters gradually lost enough oxygen to support living organisms, and shippers found more modern modes of transportation. The canal became a dark, smelly eyesore used for dumping garbage and as a sewage outlet when storms overloaded the nearby sewer system. Later, the canal became a rumored dumping site for Mafia victims and weapons. Even by the time the Grubmeyers arrived, the canal was a place to avoid. At times, given certain temperatures and wind patterns, its odors would have been unavoidable.

The family's survival depended on Conrad Grubmeyer's small grocery store. Like countless small stores around the country, it amounted to no more than a few hundred square feet. Most groceries of the era arrived in bulk, such as 100-pound bags for flour and sugar and 50-pound bags for salt. Shoppers generally went to more than one small store to meet a family's food needs; a grocery such as the Grubmeyer's for dry staples; a meat market; and a green-grocer's for fresh fruits and vegetables. A customer entering the Grubmeyer store, for example, would see the store's inventory on shelves behind counters. The customer would order certain amounts of the bulk items and the merchant would measure the quantities into small bags using a scale or measuring cups of varying sizes. The parcels would be wrapped and the customer would pay at a cash register or the merchant would make change from his apron. Likewise, canned goods were stored on shelves behind the counter. A customer seeking a tin of this or that would ask for it and the merchant would fetch it to the counter. With the advent of telephones, many customers phoned in their orders as often as they wished. The merchant then prepared the parcels for delivery, sometimes by horse and cart or later by bicycle. The merchant kept a tab on each customer's purchases and prepared bills that were generally paid monthly.

Of course, the young Fred Grubmeyer learned store operations from an early age. He attended Public School 19 in Brooklyn through the fifth grade, but then, given the economic pressures of the growing Grubmeyer family, he was pressed into full-time work at the store, helping behind the counter with his father and making deliveries. By his late teens, Fred Grubmeyer had had enough. He knew there was more to the world than Brooklyn. At age 19, in 1905, he was curious about the big hurricane that had almost destroyed Galveston, Texas, five years before. But rather than wait for a passenger ship to the Gulf Coast, Meyer changed his mind and caught a train to Chicago. There were plenty of younger Grubmeyers to help in the family store. Fred Grubmeyer set off to seek his fortune.

According to an account he gave years later,[1] Grubmeyer couldn't tolerate the smell of Chicago's stockyards, so he kept heading west. One of his stops was in Butte, Montana, then the center of a thriving copper mining industry. He looked for opportunities in Butte, and decided to keep moving westward. He had reached the Pacific Northwest when he heard of yet another gold strike in Alaska, and he turned north to Nome. Alaska had been the scene of several gold rushes in different locations for more than a half a century. New reports of gold found on old beaches above sea level led to the second so-called "Nome gold rush," the first having occurred in 1899.[2] Although the population of Nome swelled to 20,000 at the peak of the rush, few of the miners found riches. The people who made money were entrepreneurs who sold them essential goods, entertainment and, often, alcohol. Young Grubmeyer found himself no exception to the general rule.

"There was gold there for the digging, all right," he said much later. "But I took a long look at that mountain of dirt and it looked awful big alongside the little shovel in my hands." There was another surprise. "When we got to the gold fields, we found that water was worth more than gold. Some smart operators had cornered all the water needed for washing gold."[3] Although he never mentioned his Nome experience in detail, on another occasion Meyer later admitted that he had been sold a "sucker" claim on a creek that periodically went dry. It was called a "sucker" claim because it had been sold repeatedly to unknowing prospectors. "I learned then and there not to be a sucker, and decided there probably was more gold in the U.S., anyway."[4]

Grubmeyer's dislike for Alaska was not easily erased. When his big merchandising empire was in expansion mode late in his life, he had to be talked into buying his first Alaska outlet. "He had spent some of his youth mining for gold and he had a bad taste in his mouth for Alaska," recalled Oran B. Robertson much later.[5] Once that resistance was overcome, the company went on to establish five successful Fred Meyer outlets in the state.

Arriving in Seattle in 1906 after his unsuccessful mining experience, the 20-year-old Grubmeyer turned to the business he had grown up in to start supporting himself. He hired on as a driver for Leahy Brothers, a small grocery located on Second Avenue, and later as a clerk for Grand Union Tea Co. He lived in the Seattle Y.M.C.A. in 1907, just blocks from the Pike Place Market that opened the same year. The public market was intended to let customers buy fresh produce directly from producers and eliminate the costs of intermediate handlers.[6] It was a success from the start. The same issues of freshness and price arose in Portland, where John F. Carroll, editor of the Portland *Telegram*, an afternoon newspaper, editorialized often for the creation of a similar public market in Portland.

Spurred by Carroll, a private group called the Producers and Consumers Public Market Association opened a small open-air market near Southwest First and Yamhill Street in Portland in May, 1914. It was mobbed by customers from the first day, and the Portland City Council responded just two months later by adopting ordinances to regulate the market, provide stalls and umbrellas and a city-paid market manager to oversee the operation. The Carroll Market, as it was known, eventually provided spaces for 400 vendors along the curbs on both sides of Yamhill between First and Fifth Avenues. Two-way automobile traffic crept through the middle of the street. The market manager rented stalls and, surprising as it sounds today, set prices for fresh produce being sold by farmers from the Portland area.[7] Like the successful Pike Street Market in Seattle, the Carroll Market drew tens of thousands of shoppers daily. During the 20 years that the Carroll Market operated on Yamhill Street, some buildings fronting on Yamhill were remodeled or built with open-air store fronts that also provided small stalls rented by vendors. Yamhill Street would play a major role in the life of Fred Grubmeyer after he returned to Portland with a wife and a shortened name.

For a young man still wrestling with the big questions about life, Grubmeyer's Seattle days were notable for his introduction to Max Heindel, a Danish-born Christian mystic who was trying to use modern science to explain the mysteries of Christianity, human evolution and life after death. Heindel had been born Carl Louis Van Grasshoff to a German father and Danish mother, but his father died when the lad was 6. At 16, he moved to Glasgow, Scotland, to learn engineering in the shipping industry. Van Grasshoff assumed the name Max Heindel when he arrived in New York in 1901.

In his own quest to understand humanity and the universe, Heindel moved to Los Angeles in 1903 to join the Theosophical Society. Heart problems left him near death for a substantial portion of 1905, which only deepened his search for religious truth. He launched a West Coast lecture tour in 1906 and 1907, where, in the latter year, he crossed paths with Fred Grubmeyer. The extent of their personal interaction is not known, but it went beyond Grubmeyer's attendance at lectures. The two men, who likely met through the Y.M.C.A., were involved in a small reading group that would read a specific book and then meet to talk about it. Religion was one of their primary topics. How were the world's major religions similar? How were they different? Heindel, with his deeper travel, philosophical and near-death experiences, clearly impressed the younger Grubmeyer. In his will, opened after his death in 1978, Fred Meyer requested the trustees of the charitable trust to promote Rosicrucian philosophy as expounded by Heindel. "I had a personal relationship with its founder, Max Heindel, and go along with his interpretations and exposition of Christian philosophy," Meyer wrote. "I recommend it be made available to such people as seek this philosophy, but that there be no proselyting (sic) of it."[8]

MAX HEINDEL

(Rosicrucian Fellowship, Oceanside, Cal.)

An aspect that caught Meyer's attention was Heindel's theory of reincarnation.[9]

In 1907 when his path crossed with Grubmeyer, Heindel was on the verge of writing his seminal work that became the basis of the Rosicrucian Fellowship, a volume first issued in 1909 called *The Rosicrucian Cosmo-Conception or Mystic Christianity.* The thick volume was filled with charts and diagrams, including lengthy discussions of modern scientific developments. The book purported to be no less than a treatise on "mans evolution, present constitution and future development."

In Heindel's mind, an occultist was someone who used science to study spiritual reality. He used the term "mystic" on occasion, but to Heindel a mystic was a person who waited for spiritual inspiration rather than pursuing scientific means. He believed that Americans were pragmatists by nature and preferred straightforward explanations. In the 12 years before his death in 1919, Heindel published a dozen books outlining modern Rosicrucian theory and beliefs.

Key elements of Rosicrucian belief included a view that people returned to the earth many times during the course of their personal evolution, and that some eternal "heaven" was not the final destination for a well-lived life. Indeed, the purpose of a good life was to return to the earth and to continue making the earth a better place for others.

> Man is also in school—the school of experience. He must return many times before he can hope to master all the knowledge in the world of sense. No one earth life, however rich in experience, could furnish the knowledge, so nature decrees that he must return to Earth, after intervals of rest, to take up his work where he dropped it, exactly as a child takes up its work in school each day, after the intervening sleep of night...
>
> Again, if there were no return to Earth, what is the use of living? Why strive for anything? Why should a life of

> happiness in an eternal heaven be the reward for a good life? What benefit could come from a good life in a heaven where everybody is already happy? [10]

Oran Robertson, who worked with Meyer on a daily basis from 1945 until Meyer's death in 1978, once asked Meyer what influence his Rosicrucian beliefs had on his business life. Meyer replied that he kept his religious beliefs separated from his business practices.[11] Yet it is clear that Meyer followed several precepts written by Heindel, and his personal life could not be completely divorced from his business life. Some examples:

- "The occult scientist uses concentration in preference to prayer, because the former is accomplished by the aid of the mind, which is cold and unfeeling, whereas prayer is usually dictated by emotion," Heindel wrote.[12] While building his retail empire later, Meyer often would lie fully clothed on his back on a conference table with eyes closed after lunch. Some employees assumed he was napping. More likely, it was a form of meditation, in which Meyer was concentrating on a single thought or problem and freeing his brain from other matters.[13] As an entrepreneur, Meyer made decisions based on facts, not hunches. He often told his executives that business was not a place for emotions. He wanted clear, direct answers and he would not tolerate wordy, pompous or unclear responses. "If you were not dealing with the facts, the discussion ended abruptly," said Rollin Killoran, one of the few executives who once left the Meyer empire and later rejoined it.[14]
- According to Heindel, "Neither is the imagination of the budding occult scientist correct at first. The only way to make it true is by uninterrupted practice, day after day, exercising the will to keep the thought focused upon one subject, object, or idea, exclusive of all else. Thought is a great power which we have been accustomed to waste."[15] Whether he learned it from Heindel or on his own, Mey-

er relentlessly pursued his ideas until they achieved success or until he decided to drop them. "He was a great guy to get competent counsel," Killoran said. "He'd ask anybody anything. He didn't always accept their plan, but he got everybody thinking before he got into something."[16] Meyer's retail career offers several examples, such as gas stations, two forays into major appliances and catalog sales, where his ideas proved unsuccessful. He quickly cut his losses and moved forward. His associates learned not to bother Meyer if he appeared to be deep in thought. Before approaching Meyer personally, many associates would stop and ask Jean Webb, Meyer's secretary, if it seemed like a good time to talk to him. If not, they would try again later.[17]

- "Constructive criticism, which points out defects and the means of remedying them, is the basis of progress; but destructive criticism, which vandalistically demolishes good and bad alike without aiming at any higher attainment, is an ulcer on the character and must be eradicated."[18] Meyer strove during weekly executive meetings to instruct and teach his managers successful business practices. His methods often were not constructive, however. His interrogations were aggressive and unpleasant for the targets of his inquiries. There were times when he drove his own wife to tears.[19] However, Meyer apparently did not see his educational tactics as rough; he seemed to hold no lasting grudges for the employees who suffered his disparagement. "And you'd just sit there and take it for a couple of hours," Robertson recalled. "We got so we could shrug that off and laugh about it. I'll still go back and say that every one of those was a teaching process. They really were. It was a learning curve, if you will." Jerry Sadis, the youngest member of the management team late in Meyer's life, joined the company in October 1971. He was exposed quickly to Meyer's aggressive tactics. "In today's modern management, Fred Meyer would not be considered a good manager," Sadis noted. But there was an unmistakable upside to Meyer's approach: No one ever forgot the messages that Meyer imparted.[20]

- Heindel on wealth: "It may be hard to fight poverty and hunger, but from the standpoint of the soul it is infinitely preferable to a life of idle luxury. Where wealth is nothing more than a handmaid of well thought out philanthropy, which helps man in such a way as to really uplift him, it may be a very great blessing and a means of growth for its possessor, but when used for selfish purposes and oppression, it cannot be regarded as other than an unmitigated curse."[21]

The big-spender, to the extent there was one in the Meyer household, was Eva Meyer, the woman he married in 1919. She liked good clothes, she liked to travel, and she played the major role in the couple's social life, limited as it was. After her death in 1960, Fred Meyer's single, unbroken focus for the next 18 years was expanding Fred Meyer Inc., and planning his strategy for philanthropy after his death.

Meyer's interest as a Rosicrucian continued throughout his life. He made monthly contributions to the Rosicrucian Fellowship for decades. In his will, Meyer gave the fellowship $200,000 and made special mention of it in the written guidance he left for trustees of the charitable trust he established with the wealth of his estate.

The reason for Fred Grubmeyer's arrival in Portland from Seattle is difficult to pinpoint. An unverified account[22] suggests that he bought a market stall from someone in Seattle, only to find after his arrival that the location near Portland's Union Station railroad depot was no longer a viable retail location. By the time of his arrival in 1909, the city was far beyond its pioneer village days. Thanks to the abundant nearby forests and success of the 1905 Lewis & Clark Centennial Exposition, the city had already grown to the largest in the Pacific Northwest with a population in excess of 220,000 and growing quickly. Lumber mills in the region were producing two million board feet per day in 1909; Portland's harbor was the nation's largest lumber-shipping port, and the second largest exporting wheat. It was the largest livestock market west of Denver, and some 2,000 manufacturing plants employed approximately 30,000 workers.

The early wooden buildings of the pioneer town had given way to cast iron and then to brick; in 1907, Wells Fargo erected the city's first steel-framed tower of 11 stories, and several more soon followed. City residents had access to 230 miles of streetcar lines and could ride electric-powered interurban routes of 12 miles each to Gresham and Oregon City and 15 miles to Fairview; weightier electric trains travelled 50 miles to Salem and 26 miles to Forest Grove. Steam-powered trains serving the city were run by the Northern Pacific, Great Northern, Union Pacific, Southern Pacific, Burlington and Canadian Pacific. Portland's public school system already stood at 45 buildings. Portlanders had their choice of six daily newspapers, including one published in Japanese.

Grubmeyer's first partner in Portland was candy maker George Menne; the pair worked in a building in the 900 block of Northeast Union Avenue, now Martin Luther King Jr. Boulevard. A year later, William Grubmeyer, Fred's older brother, arrived in Portland, likely at the suggestion of the younger brother. The Pacific Northwest was such a different place than the Grubmeyers had been used to. As Fred Meyer recalled much later, "We liked the fishing and we liked the countryside and it was a pleasant place to live after crowded New York."[23] William Grubmeyer had married in New York and brought his wife, Nellie, and two young children, Mary and Charles, with him. In 1910, William Grubmeyer was listed as manager of Mission Tea Co., which rented a stall in a two-story brick building at Southwest First Avenue and Washington Street known as the City Public Market. The firm included Fred Grubmeyer and Henry Hennings, who a couple years later helped found the Albina Business Men's Club in Northeast Portland.[24] The owners of the City Public Market were losing money at the time, and offered Fred Grubmeyer a chance to manage the building on a salary. Instead, the young entrepreneur offered to manage it in return for half of any profits he made. As a result of inexpensive improvements and his salesmanship in landing new tenants, Grubmeyer soon was earning a princely sum of 1,000 per month. Hennings and Fred Grubmeyer also operated a stall in 1910 on North Russell Street near Williams Avenue in the Albina commercial district. Given Grubmeyer's success at the City Public Market, the building owners found means to rescind the contract.[25]

The heart of Portland's public food market, however, had moved south to Yamhill Street, where it would thrive until into the 1940s. Rather than waiting for business to come to him, Fred Grubmeyer used a horse-drawn cart to take business to customers. He soon gave up the horse in favor of an early, small Ford truck. He built home delivery routes for coffee and tea buyers, and delivered bulk staples to logging camps in the Portland vicinity and to ships arriving at the city's busy docks. His prices for home-delivered coffee were a cent or two higher than what was available in stores, so he offered small, inexpensive premiums to the housewives who were his primary customers. The more coffee one bought, the better the "free" trinket. It was a gimmick he never forgot, and years later he aggressively lobbied suppliers for free merchandise to give away during grand openings. Grubmeyer had no desire to spend his life driving delivery routes, however. As soon as his coffee routes were established, he sold them to others.[26]

During his early years in Portland, Grubmeyer lived at the Y.M.C.A. and then with his brother, William, and sister-in-law, Nellie, in houses on Northeast 21st Avenue and later Northeast Sacramento Street. By 1911, Fred Grubmeyer was listed as manager of Mission Tea, while his older brother assumed the roles of clerk and treasurer. The rift between the brothers evidently occurred in this period; by 1915, Fred Grubmeyer had moved back to the Y.M.C.A. and was doing business with a new partner, John S. Hoggan, and under a new name, Java Coffee Co. Hoggan would surface again approximately a decade later in the early stages of Fred Meyer Inc.

William Grubmeyer operated at varying times a coffee stall and a small lunch counter on Yamhill Street across the street from Fred Grubmeyer's office, and years later operated a small eatery in suburban Portland until his retirement in 1942. He died in 1965,[27] possibly never having spoken to his brother again. William and Nellie Grubmeyer's daughter, Mary, worked in her father's businesses early in her life and later operated her own florist shop. She was one of only two blood relatives who received bequests from Fred G. Meyer after his death in 1978.

An early picture shows Fred Meyer at a coffee stall on Washington Street, approximately 1911. The photo was retouched for newspaper reproduction. (Oregonian)

In 1911, another person arrived in Portland who would play a huge role in the life and business of the man who was still known as Fred Grubmeyer, Eva Chatfield. She was a single mother who had come to Portland to start a new life. A native of Muskegon, Michigan, Eva Chatfield moved with her parents to Baker City when she was still a child. Her parents, Mary and James Chatfield, started a laundry business in their home, and later erected a two-story building to house their successful enterprise. Eva Chatfield married Ira G. Chiles, a railway clerk, on April 10, 1904, in Baker. City, when she was 18. The couple had a son, Earle Arden Chiles, in 1905. Ira Chiles quit his railroad job to work as a driver for the Chatfields at their family business, the XL Steam Laundry. Eva Chiles was the company bookkeeper. The marriage was short-lived, however. Eva Chiles learned about an adulterous relationship involving her husband that had occurred in February, 1907, and she filed for divorce. The Baker County Circuit Court decree signed on Oct. 8, 1908, dissolved her marriage and awarded Eva Chiles custody of her son, Earle Chiles. Ira Chiles, the court found, "is not a fit and proper person to have care and custody." The decree ordered Ira Chiles to pay costs of the case, but mentioned nothing about on-going child support.[28] While the divorce was pending, Eva Chiles and her sister, Mary Chatfield, visited Portland in the summer of 1908, very likely scouting opportunities to start a new life.[29] Ira Chiles quickly moved from Baker and played no further role in the life of his son, Earle. After living briefly in a boarding house in Baker, Eva Chatfield Chiles headed to Portland. Her parents sold their building and business and along with their son, Everett, moved to Portland with her.

Eva Chiles was a hard worker with a good head for business. In 1912 she operated a delicatessen on Southeast 12th Avenue, and a couple years later moved across town to run a delicatessen near Southwest 13th Avenue and Jefferson Street. Her father worked in Portland for one year as a laundryman, then joined his daughter for the next five years in the deli business. Fred Grubmeyer and Eva Chatfield Chiles first met at her deli, mostly likely the one on Southeast 12th Avenue, where Grubmeyer would spread out his receipts and do his bookkeeping when he was building his coffee routes in what was then considered "suburban" Portland. [30]

By 1914, Eva Chiles had moved her residence and business across the Willamette River to a location near Southwest 11th Avenue and its intersection with Burnside. Her friendship with Fred Grubmeyer was solid enough that by February 1917, Eva Chiles had decided to quit the deli business. She relied upon a good friend to sell it for her. A small classified newspaper advertisement under "Business Opportunities," read: "DELICATESSEN and grocery, central West Side apartment neighborhood, all cash trade and no deliveries, clearing over $200 a month, for sale at invoice; $1800 needed; no trades. For further particulars, see Fred Grubmeyer, 291 Yamhill st."[31]

The late teens were busy and successful years for Grubmeyer. He was still operating Java Coffee Co., but a bigger part of his income came from renting market stalls among the popular Southwest Yamhill Street public markets. Many storefronts on both sides of Yamhill between Front and Fifth Avenues opened to the public sidewalk by means of roll-up canvas curtains, and farmers, butchers, bakers, fishmongers, tobacconists, candy makers and other merchants rented stalls to sell their goods in these buildings while canvas-covered stalls lined both sides of Yamhill at the curbs. Grubmeyer bought up leases from vendors who went broke or left for other reasons and then recruited new vendors to take their places. He first controlled the Vista Market on the north side of Yamhill between Third and Fourth Avenues, and later the Central Market on the south side of the street between Fourth and Fifth Avenues and even later the Liberty Market on the southeast corner of Fifth and Yamhill. Business was good for Grubmeyer; by 1917 he had changed his residence from the Y.M.C.A. to the Multnomah Hotel, easily Portland's largest and fanciest of the era.

As a consequence of the United States entering World War I, Congress in 1917 passed the first Selective Service Act, requiring all men between the ages of 21 and 30 to register. The next year, Congress amended the act to require registration of all men between 18 and 45. Grubmeyer dutifully filled out the small, double-sided card: He was Fred Henry Grubmeyer, age 32, manager of First Investment Co., located on Yamhill Street in Portland; his address was the Multnomah Hotel; he had blue eyes and light hair, medium height and medium build. Born in Germany, he was a naturalized citizen because his father had become a U.S. citizen before Fred Grubmeyer reached maturity; his nearest relative was his brother, William.[32] The war ended within weeks of Grubmeyer's registration, so he was never called to serve. Oddly, the 1920 U.S. Census lists the birth place of Fred G. Meyer, the name he had by then adopted, as Illinois. He listed his employment as an office broker.[33] Ten years later, the census listed his birthplace as Missouri.[34] If these were scriveners' errors and not his, the man who always insisted on facts from his associates would have been displeased; the census interviewers never got it wrong with Eva C. Meyer.

In the summer of 1919, Fred Grubmeyer spent nine weeks driving around the country. All the places he went are not known; nor is it known whether Eva Chiles accompanied him. Later in his life, Fred Meyer was not especially fond of travel; Eva was, which suggests maybe she was the impetus for this lengthy jaunt in 1919. On this trip – like many others in his life – Grubmeyer kept his business eyes wide open. "Housewives of Portland would faint if they saw conditions in Portland markets that prevail in Eastern cities," he told a newspaper reporter after his return. "Meats, fruit, fish and other commodities are exposed to flies and heat. Regulations on handling of produce are lax as compared with Portland's."[35]

Later the same year, Grubmeyer signed a 10-year lease on the Central Market, which held down the vital south side of Yamhill Street between Southwest Fourth and Fifth Avenues. In the next decade, there would be intense battles over the strategic southeast corner of Fifth and Yamhill. It would prove to be a key element in the future of Fred Meyer Inc. But for now, Fred Grubmeyer and Eva Chiles headed to Seattle, where they became Mr. and Mrs. Fred G. Meyer. Fred Meyer never explained the reason for the name change, but it is likely that he felt the sting of anti-German sentiment that was rife during the Great War, which later came to be known as World War I. The name change may have eliminated the stigma, if there was one, of his Germanic heritage, but it created another effect that sometimes either puzzled or bothered Meyer. Many people believed that he was Jewish.[36] Meyer never spoke publicly about his personal involvement with the Rosicrucian Fellowship; aside from a few company officials he mentioned it to over the years, the filing of his will in Multnomah County Probate Court in 1978 was the first public mention of his religious leanings.

Whether the couple eloped to Seattle or intended to remain there is not known. Late in his life, Fred Meyer said he preferred Seattle to Portland, but that Eva preferred Portland.[37] Perhaps that was an early concession on his part. His ties to Portland were not going to end, in any event. In November of 1919 a brief newspaper item suggested a longer-lasting tie. "Fred Grubmeyer, formerly operator of the Vista market in this city and now located in Seattle, last week leased the Central Market building from the Brooke estate for a 10-year period. The building is located at the corner of Fourth and Yamhill streets. The lease was acquired as an investment, it is announced, and few changes among the 20 tenants of the building are contemplated." [38]

The Meyers' marriage lasted close to 41 years, until Eva's unexpected death in 1960. Throughout that time, she worked side-by-side with Fred Meyer and provided a tempering influence to his aggressive and often abrasive management style. Indeed, there were many outside the company who thought that Eva Meyer may have been the brains behind the remarkable innovations and expansions ahead. Those who attended the closed-door meetings where Fred Meyer practiced his style of relentless questioning and, at times, stinging personal attacks, agreed that the decisions were all his, not hers. At times, Eva Meyer faced the same hard criticism and accusations of stupidity that Meyer routinely leveled against his other key managers.

"I think in some ways he had a very short fuse," recalled Glen Day, who started at a Fred Meyer laundry counter in 1932 and later rose to Fred Meyer's personal assistant and finally to vice president in charge of warehousing and manufacturing. "He was rough on Mrs. Meyer. Extremely rough. Far more than you would think, because to all outward appearances, at least, and I think it was true, they had a very good relationship. I've never been able to figure it out. If my wife and I worked together in an organization and she did something that displeased me, I think we would discuss it when we left the office or were alone. I don't think I would make an issue of in front of 10 or 12 or 14 executives of the company. It did happen. It happened quite often."[39]

Pauline Lawrence knew Eva Meyer for the last 15 years of Eva's life, including the last eight years as a Fred Meyer employee. She witnessed Fred Meyer's behavior and his wife's responses firsthand. "I saw them as very devoted to each other," Lawrence said. "She was so devoted to him; and I saw her having a pretty big job trying to take care of him because he wanted to do what he wanted to do, you know. That's what I saw. She acted like she worshiped the man and he was sometimes very cruel to her." Lawrence once told Eva Meyer that she was puzzled by Fred Meyer's harsh behavior. Eva Meyer replied, "He's not half as bad as he sounds."[40] Executives who saw Meyer's harsh treatment of his wife pondered possible explanations. Did he expect more from her because they were so close? Did he focus so intensely on business matters at hand that he saw her as just another employee and not his wife? It was a puzzle never solved in their 41 years of marriage.

Eva Meyer once said she planned on being a full-time housewife after her marriage to Fred Meyer, but he never got home until 8 or 9 p.m. So she decided that, if she was going to have time with him, she would work at the office, too.[41] Her desk sat close to his in an open office landscape intended to allow easy communication and to create a spirit of equality. She held managerial responsibilities from the earliest days of Fred Meyer Inc., and came to recognize and know department heads in their growing empire of stores better than her husband.

Though her husband ruled their business life, their business success allowed Eva Meyer to indulge in things she enjoyed. "She loved to go places, she loved to travel, she loved luxury, she loved he nice things," recalled Lawrence, who used to shop for clothes with Eva Meyer. "She wanted to live in the nicest place; she wanted the nicest things."[42] In the teeth of the Great Depression, the couple bought a weekend getaway near Welches close to the Salmon River that included a house and smaller cabins. The couple added a swimming pool. There were gardens and flowers. The Meyers spent most of their weekends and often held company meetings at what became known as "Eva's Eden." During the last 16 years of her life, the couple rented penthouse suites at two of Portland's fanciest apartment buildings, first at The Envoy and later at the Vista St. Clair. Eva Meyer earned her share of the rewards.

Their long marriage produced no children. By the time they married in 1919, Eva's son Earle A. Chiles was attending Lincoln High School, and perhaps Eva Meyer was not interested in more children in her middle 30s. The odds are strong that her husband wasn't interested in having children, given his intense focus on business. Having grown

MULTNOMAH COLLEGE'S

Men of Success

FRED G. MEYER, *President*
Fred Meyer, Inc.

I have been happy for the training and experience received at Multnomah College in those early days when I was studying to get a background of accountancy and kindred subjects. What I learned has stood me in excellent stead and has been a great aid when applied to the solution of the many problems that arise each day. Due to the good fellowship and the excellent teaching staff I found at the college during my studies there, I have always held a warm regard and approval for its good work.

(Signed)
Fred G. Meyer

Arts and Science

Biology
Chemistry
Economics
English
General Science
History
Journalism
Literature
Mathematics
Modern Language
Philosophy
Physics
Political Science
Psychology
Sociology
Speech

Business

Accounting
Advertising
Business English
Business Law
Business Machines
Business Mathematics
Cost Accounting
Income Tax
Life Insurance
Broadcasting
Retailing
Shorthand
Salesmanship
Typewriting

Technical

Auto Mechanics
Airplane Engines
Aircraft Mechanics
Architectural Drawing
Descriptive Geometry
Electricity
Engineering Problems
Machine Shop Practice
Mechanical Drawing
Mechanics
Radio
Surveying
Television

School of Music

Preparatory Department
Bachelor of Music Degree
Layman Music

Multnomah College has much to offer students:

. . . it is located in downtown Portland where there are many opportunities for employment while the student continues his education. In addition, there are both day and evening classes giving greater opportunity to fit a class schedule with a work program.

. . . it is a fully accredited two-year college offering training in business, technical and liberal arts fields, as preparation for continued study in a standard four-year college or university, or as a step to entering the industrial or business world.

MULTNOMAH COLLEGE

Business - Technical - Arts and Science - Music
Day and Evening Classes

819 S. W. 6th Avenue
Portland 4, Oregon
ATwater 7317

PORTLAND'S COMMUNITY COLLEGE

Though his early schooling ended with grammar school, Fred Meyer took business classes at a junior college in Portland, as this 1955 advertisement attests (Oregonian)

up with six younger siblings in Brooklyn, it is also possible that Meyer had had his fill of dealing with small children. In any event, the subject of having children was never mentioned by Fred and Eva Meyer to their close associates, even those who worked with them for decades. Likewise, there was never any hint of infidelity in the Meyer marriage. After after Eva's death in 1960, Fred Meyer showed no interest in another steady relationship. It is possible that Meyer's Rosicrucian Fellowship beliefs played a role in his outlook towards women; in Max Heindel's view, acts of sex were reserved for procreation.[43]

---

[1] Richards, Leverett G., *Introducing the Man Nobody Knows*, The *Oregonian* Magazine, Nov. 11, 1949, p. 6.

[2] *Northwest and Arctic GOLD, 1987 to 1920,* Alaska History and Cultural Studies, http://www.akhistorycourse.org/articles, accessed March 23, 2013.

[3] *Oregonian*, 11-13-49.

[4] Newkirk, Lamar, an *Oregon Journal* business reporter who was a Portland correspondent for Time Magazine, in an account dated Sept. 9, 1953, sent to the magazine. "This has been a toughie," Newkirk told the magazine editors, referring to his interview with Meyer. He found Meyer "not much interested in anything but the future," and not clear about past dates. Oregon Historical Society, Fred Meyer Collection 199, OSD 2/6.

[5] Robertson, Oran B., OHS sound recording 1312, 1989. March, 28, 1989.

[6] http://pikeplacemarket.org/visitor_info/market_history, accessed April 15, 2013.

[7] Eigo, George, *A Market for the City: The History of Public Markets in Portland,* Oregon Historical Society, 2002, p. 12.

[8] Will of Fred G. Meyer, March 29, 1976, Multnomah County Circuit Court.

[9] Many years later, Meyer told an associate, Virgil Campbell, that he learned about reincarnation during his time in Seattle. Author interview with Campbell, Aug. 19, 2013.

[10] Heindel, p. 132, 133.

[11] Robertson, *op. cit.*

[12] Heindel , p. 463

[13] Killoran, Rollin, OHS sound recording 1308, Sept. 22, 1988.

[14] *Ibid.*

[15] Heindel, p. 486

[16] Killoran, *ibid.*

[17] Webb , Jean S., Oregon Historical Society, sound recording 1316, 1989

[18] Heindel, p. 493

[19] Robertson, OHS sound recording 1312, Dec. 8, 1988.

[20] Sadis, Jerry, Oregon Historical Society sound recording 1313, 1989.

[21] Heindel , p. 432.

[22] Associated Press News Archive, Oct. 20, 1998, accessed at www.apnewsarchive.com

[23] Meyer, Fred, oral interview, OHS sound recording 9474, Aug. 8, 1970.

[24] *Oregonian*, Jan. 1, 1914.

[25] Newkirk, *op. cit.*

[26] *Oregonian*, Nov. 13, 1949.

[27] *Oregonian*, Jan. 13, 1965.

[28] *Eva Chiles v. Ira Chiles,* Baker County Circuit Court Journal, September Term, Oct. 8, 1908.

[29] *Oregonian,* July 19, 1908, p. 7.

[30] *Wall Street Journal,* June 11, 1975.

[31] *Oregonian*, Feb. 9, 1917.

[32] Military Registration Card, 1918, accessed in March, 2013 at www.ancestry.com

[33] 1920 U.S. Census, accessed in March 2013 at www.ancestry.com

[34] 1930 U.S. Census, accessed in March 2013 at www.ancestry.com

[35] *Oregonian*, August 20, 1919, p. 11.

[36] Fred Meyer Collection, OHS, box 7, folder 8, contains a newspaper clipping written by Doug Baker, an *Oregon Journal* columnist, in which Baker says that after a 1960 interview with Meyer, a company spokesman called Baker and said, "Mr. Meyer would like to ask you a favor. He would like to make it clear that he is not of the Jewish faith."

[37] *Oregonian*, Jan. 18, 1976.

[38] *Oregonian*, Nov. 16, 1919.

[39] Day, Glen, OHS sound recording 1306, June 27, 1989.

[40] Lawrence, Pauline, OHS sound recording 1309, Oct. 25, 1988.

[41] Killoran, Rollin, *op. cit.,* Sept. 29, 1988.

[42] Lawrence, *op. cit.*

[43] Heindel , p. 492.

CHAPTER THREE

Help Yourself

America's grocery buying habits underwent dramatic changes between 1915 and 1930. Terms like "cash and carry" and "self-service" and "grocery chains" entered the American lexicon. The upshot tended to be lower prices for customers as well as some loudly-voiced opposition to the new ways of business. Once self-service finally grabbed hold of the grocery business, however, there was no turning back. Fred G. Meyer was not the first entrepreneur in Portland to enter the realm of self-service grocery shopping, but once he saw the trend unfolding he became one of its most aggressive and successful proponents. Seemingly more by happenstance than intent, Meyer also began to see advantages of coupling groceries with non-food items such as clothes, toiletries and variety goods under the same roof, making him a pioneer in the new realm of "one-stop" shopping.

Changes in grocery retailing likely can be traced to the 1893 World's Columbian Exposition in Chicago. More than 27 million visitors were thrilled by such innovations as electric streetlights, the first Ferris wheel and the "White City" classical revival architecture that set a trend in American urban planning and building design for nearly 40 years. Many of those visitors saw or bought meals at John Kruger's

"Cafeteria," an eating establishment where diners selected items that were already prepared, paid a cashier at the end of the line and carried their food to tables where they sat down to eat. Diners could select as much or as little food as they wished; Kruger was spared the expense of paying for servers. The concept was based on smorgasbords Kruger had seen while traveling in Sweden. He named his enterprise cafeteria after the Spanish word for coffee shop. Five years later, the Childs Cafeteria in New York City added the quickly-emulated system of sliding trays upon which customers could set several items on their way to the check-out register.[1]

The cafeteria concept led more than one grocery retailer around the United States to ponder whether the idea could be adapted to retail grocery sales. At the time, canned goods, meats and staples at small neighborhood stores were all located in glass-topped counters or on shelves behind the counters. A customer would tell the grocer what items were desired; the grocer or a clerk would find the items, wrap them in bundles and deliver them to the customer in person, or deliver them via horse cart, handcart or bicycle to the customer's abode. With the increasing spread of telephone service, a customer could simply phone in her order, and never set foot in the store.

Some of Fred Meyer's early employees had grown up in stores run the old way. Ray Chirgwin, who joined Fred Meyer Inc. for seven years in the Great Depression, worked part-time in a Twentieth Century store before his graduation from Franklin High School in 1929. It was the end of an era. "In those days, the customer comes in and she hands you her list or she verbally tells you what she wants. You go gather it up. That was the old days when we bagged everything and sold everything by the pound and wrapped everything for the customer. It wasn't self-service. So we wrapped, tied and roped string across the package. Whatever it was, you reached in and got it out of the case or if it was beans or rice, you scooped it up for them and packaged it up.

Before the self-service era, grocery stores looked much like this 1914 photograph of the W.S. Cutler & Son store in Northeast Portland, where almost all inventory was out of reach by customers. (City of Portland Archives, Oregon, A2004-002.6801)

"We used to have cereal, light stuff, way up high toward the ceiling. And we had a ladder that ran across on a rail, and you climb the ladder or you'd take a long stick with a grabbing instrument on the end of it; fork it all down off the stop and fill the orders." The neighborhood markets were small, in the range of 1,000 square feet or fewer. "The smallest pop-and-momma today is a big market in those days," Chirgwin said in 1988. "So you wouldn't have too many customers at a time, but you have a few customers in the store and enough clerks to take care of them." [2]

If a grocery customer was willing to select the desired items and take them to a cash register without assistance, like selecting courses of a meal in a cafeteria, couldn't a grocer eliminate several clerks and reduce overhead? And what if a customer carried groceries home without delivery service? Wouldn't that cut costs even further? The ideas were tempting, but trying them out would be risky. First, the inside of a store would have to be re-designed to give shoppers access to the inventory. Since the shopper would have fewer helpers to assist, prices for the items would have to be marked on individual items or perhaps on the shelves where the items were stocked. The customer would need some method to carry the items, perhaps in a basket or some sort of cart. What about staples such as flour, sugar and salt that traditionally came in large sacks, requiring clerks to measure or weigh consumer-sized purchases? Would women, who composed most of the clientele, be willing to select items themselves without their usual banter with the clerks? Would shopping be a more difficult and less-pleasant experience, meaning that the customer might not patronize a self-service grocery?

The person who often claimed to be the first to apply the self-service concept to grocery sales was Clarence Saunders, a Memphis, Tennessee, grocer who patented his idea in 1917 and promoted it under the name of Piggly Wiggly Stores. His invention was described as follows in the formal language of the U.S. Patent Office: "The object of my said invention is to provide a store equipment (sic) by which the customer will be enabled to serve himself, and, in doing so, will be required to view the entire assortment of goods carried in stock, conveniently and attractively displayed, and after selecting the list of goods desired, will be required to pass a checking and paying station at which the goods selected may be billed, packed, and settled before retiring from the store, thus relieving the store of a large proportion of the usual incidental expenses, or overhead charges, required to operate it..." [3]

Saunders' illustrations accompanying the patent showed a narrow storefront, typical of his era. The square footage was roughly the equivalent of a modern convenience store. A shopper would enter a front door into a small lobby with an entrance gate on the left. After passing the gate, the shopper would be led through a series of maze-like aisles in which there would be only one direction leading to the check-out stand near the front of the store on the opposite side from the entry gate. A person wanting to buy only one or two items would have to traverse all aisles to get to the check-out. "One purpose of the invention is to provide an arrangement for distributing the merchandise of a store in such a manner that the goods may be selected and taken by the customers themselves while taking a circuitous path through the store; and whereby a large number of customers may be accommodated at the same time, without confusion and in an expeditious manner," the patent states.

It is not uncommon, however, for more than one person to arrive at a comparable idea. An earlier venture into a self-service grocery occurred in Butte, Montana, where the Lutey Brothers opened a store in 1912 featuring self-service adjacent to an existing Lutey Brothers outlet that retained the older format. Years later, long after the Lutey Brothers went out of business, evidence surfaced that Saunders may have seen the Butte store before returning to Memphis and patenting his Piggly Wiggly layout. The Lutey Brothers also ventured to the U.S. Patent Office, where they trademarked the term "Marketeria" as a brand name for an extensive variety of canned, packaged and fresh foods. "The trade mark is usually applied to receptacles containing the goods by placing thereon printed labels upon which the trade mark is shown," according to the registration.[4]

William J. Lutey issued a pamphlet in 1911 called "Cutting Out the Frills" in which he laid out the rationale for his Marketeria. He explained that it expanded on the cafeteria concept and offered lower prices because of customers serving themselves and paying in cash rather than on credit.[5] Instead of forcing shoppers to traverse every aisle in the store like Saunders' Piggly Wiggly format, photographs show the

Lutey's Marketeria stocked with customer-accessible shelves on the side and rear walls with free-standing displays in the middle of the store. Given a steep recession in Butte's mining industry after World War I and managerial difficulties in the Lutey family, their stores closed in 1924 – perhaps why the Marketeria's role in self-service history was largely forgotten.

Two phrases captured the essence of the evolution in the grocery business. "Self service" meant exactly that; customers selected their own products from open shelves instead of requesting items and having them delivered by a clerk behind a counter. "Cash and carry" meant no monthly credit and no home delivery; shoppers paid cash at the check stand and toted their own groceries home. These two changes in business format and operations did not have to occur simultaneously, however. There were "cash and carry" stores that were not yet self-service.

Once the cash-and carry trend started to take hold, proprietors could eliminate delivery employees and reduce prices. Lower costs led to lower prices and greater risks for stores still offering credit. Rollin Killoran, who started working for Fred Meyer in the early 1930s, had grown up the son of a small-town grocer in rural Emmett, Idaho. His father tried to continue running an old-fashioned delivery-and-credit store in the face of new competition from a cash-and-carry operation. Killoran said mill workers in Emmett spent their cash at the cash-and-carry, and returned to his father's store when their paychecks fell short before their next paydays. [6] His father was driven out of business by uncollectable accounts, and the family moved to Portland to find work.

World War I also provided an unexpected push for cash-and-carry. In 1917, President Woodrow Wilson appointed a successful young engineer named Herbert Hoover to head the U.S. Food Administration, an agency charged with conserving food resources during the war. One of Hoover's initiatives was aimed at encouraging cash-and-carry grocery stores as a means of freeing up healthy young delivery men for military service. The national recommendation to reduce or eliminate home delivery drew praise from Portland merchants in August 1917. "Retail merchants of Portland will cooperate with the National Defense Council by curtailing and ending other unnecessary service so that men and material may be used in defense of the country. Representatives from almost every channel of retail business met at the Chamber of Commerce yesterday afternoon and adopted resolutions pledging themselves to inaugurate the expense-cutting plan at the earliest opportunity."[7]

Retailers including Portland's major department stores encouraged cash-and-carry for more than patriotic reasons. Many of them had calculated down to the penny or fraction of a cent how much deliveries were costing them, plus additional handling and restocking costs when buyers who had placed orders refused goods delivered on the cash-on-delivery basis. Some retailers also responded to the defense policy by selling reusable cloth shopping bags. However, the cash-and-carry guidelines were not mandatory, and many stores still offered deliveries on a limited basis.

People's Market, one of the era's larger grocery chains with a handful of outlets, opened a straight cash-and-carry store in the Vista Market on Yamhill Street in 1918. "Prompted by the Government's motive of conservation in promoting the recent 'Carry Your Own' campaign, we have gone one step further in opening this People's CASH AND CARRY Grocery," its advertisement proclaimed. "There will be no telephone orders taken – no deliveries – everything strictly cash – and every cent we save by not giving that extra service will go right into your pocketbook – your groceries will be sold to you for that much less."8 When the war ended later that year, however, several retailers reverted to their former delivery systems. Near year's end, the People's Market notified customers that their shopping lives would return to normal. "In the coming year, we would like you to forget the inconvenience you have suffered....We deliver from the People's Market in both East and West Portland."[9]

The gradual evolution towards self-service and cash-and-carry in the grocery business was occurring when businesses of many sorts also were taking major steps to improve efficiency. Herbert Hoover, who served as U.S. Commerce secretary from 1920 to 1928, made national goals of improving efficiency and reducing waste in all business realms. He believed that increased efficiency would smooth out the booms and busts of the economic cycle, and generate increased income for managers and workers alike. During his tenure at Commerce, Hoover worked with more than 100 industries, encouraging standardization in areas including tools, automobile parts, hardware and building materials. At the same time, a new field called industrial engineering conducted research into time and motion studies designed to find the fastest, most efficient means of performing human tasks. Frederick W. Taylor's pioneering work, *The Principles of Scientific Management,* created a new field of management consulting aimed at improving efficiency of industrial and manufacturing processes. Harrington Emerson's chief work, *The Twelve Principles of Efficiency,* suggested more generalized strategies that could be applied to any enterprise.

Fred Meyer, a voracious reader, knew about Hoover's advocacy for efficiency in general and about Emerson's Twelve Principles in specific.[10] While Meyer blithely denied any influence of Max Heindel on his business practices, there could be no denying the effect of Emerson – even though some of Emerson's principles were substantially the same as Heindel's. Both men, for example, stressed discipline, fair dealing and competent counsel. Other principles on Emerson's list that would recur often in the Fred Meyer business empire included clearly defined ideals, common sense, reliable and accurate records, standards and schedules, standardized conditions, standardized operations, and written standard-practice procedures. Rollin Killoran, who had discussed Emerson's principles with Meyer in the 1930s, once left Fred Meyer Inc. because he felt he wasn't paid adequately for his performance. He questioned Meyer at the time as to why he did not follow Emerson's final principle, which addressed "reward" for efficient performance. Meyer did not respond.[11]

Fred Meyer started applying efficiency principles even before he started his retail operations. Returning to Portland after his brief sojourn to Seattle in 1919, he had yet to commit himself to building a company under his own name devoted to retail sales. Fred and Eva Meyer established their residence in an apartment at Southwest Market Street and 14th Avenue in a building that would be torn down decades later for a freeway ramp. Throughout most of the 1920s, his primary business involved renting market stalls to vendors along Yamhill Street in buildings where Meyer controlled the master leases. To convince vendors that their aisles were wider than necessary and that their tables were too wide for efficient operations, Meyer began renting space by square inches rather than by square feet. This strategy encouraged vendors to squeeze out unnecessary space, and it allowed Meyer to increase the number of rentable stalls.[12] He concluded that aisles in the crowded stalls need be no wider than two feet.

Late in his life, Fred Meyer suggested another influence on the gradual change in grocery sales. "Public libraries invented self service, not retailers." [13] Indeed, Andrew Carnegie, who built a massive financial empire from steel manufacturing, started giving away millions of dollars to build more than 2,500 public libraries in the United States, Canada and Great Britain in the first two decades of the 20th Century. An early proponent of the efficiency movement, Carnegie insisted that books be placed on open shelves and that a single librarian sitting near the front door would check them out – a revolution in the library world. Carnegie money paid for seven branch libraries in Portland. The first two, East Portland, built in 1911 and Albina, added in 1912, were in neighborhoods where Meyer lived and worked in his early Portland years. On other occasions, Meyer mentioned another experience that contributed to his belief in self-service grocery sales. He said that when his father was recovering from an injury at his tiny store in Brooklyn, he directed customers to select their own items from shelves behind the counter and to bring their money to him.[14]

In June of 1920, Meyer joined in the formation of Evans Hudson & Meyer,[15] an insurance, lending and investment firm that settled into three offices in the U.S. National Bank Building. Meyer was president, Robert A. Hudson vice president and William M. Evans treasurer. Meyer's association with the firm was short-lived; at some point he had

A wet day at the Yamhill Street open markets in 1925. The building on the right corner is the Mybros Public Market, operated by Fred and Henry Meyer. (OHS folder 1633)

a falling-out with Hudson, who went on to build a large regional food-processing, wholesale supply and retail firm. The nature of their dispute was never revealed in detail by Meyer. He told one associate decades later that he felt Hudson had cheated him, or at least tried to cheat him, in some way.[16] Chirgwin, a later Meyer employee who was an avid golfer as was Hudson, once met Hudson in golf circles. "He sat and bragged about how he browbeat Meyer down, you know," Chirgwin recalled.[17] The dispute most likely involved Portland's first Piggly Wiggly grocery store, which led to a legal squabble among Fred Meyer and his younger brother, Henry, and Hudson in 1928. Hudson was a third partner in the Piggly Wiggly venture, and Henry Meyer cast his lot with Hudson rather than with his brother. However the ouster of Fred Meyer occurred, it likely had no formal impropriety about it. As history would show, Fred Meyer knew good lawyers and was not reluctant to use them. Although he did go on to file suit against Hudson and Henry Meyer, the complaint was about his access as a stockholder to Piggly Wiggly financial records, and not about his removal as an officer and corporate director.

A year after the incorporation of Evans Hudson & Meyer, Fred Meyer was back on Yamhill Street where he and Eva Meyer listed their business as "real estate." They continued leasing stalls to small-volume merchants who sold their goods or fresh produce in open-air markets operating under names such as Vista Market and Central Market. These open markets were migrating away from Front and First Avenues at this time, westward to Fourth and Fifth Avenues. During the rest of the 1920s those intersections amounted to the heart of Portland's downtown food trade, and Fred Meyer's fingers were all over it, first as a lessor and then late in the decade as a merchant himself.

Henry Grubmeyer, Fred Meyer's younger brother by 10 years, also decided to settle in Portland by the early 1920s. He went to work first with his oldest brother, William Grubmeyer, at a stall selling lunches and teas at the Central Public Market on Yamhill Street. Henry also resided for a time with William and Nellie Grubmeyer at their home on Southeast 53rd Avenue. In 1922, Henry, who assumed the same shortened last name "Meyer" as had Fred Meyer, showed more entrepreneurial spirit than their older brother, William, and joined forces with Fred Meyer. Henry and Fred Meyer were involved together in four corporations in the middle 1920s. Two, incorporated in November 1923, bore the name Mybros, obviously a shortened version of "Meyer Brothers." One, Mybros Meat Market, was a wholesale and retail meat company.[18] The other, Mybros Inc., is the entity that became Fred Meyer Inc. four years later.[19] Directors of both Mybros firms were Fred and Henry Meyer and Blanche Wollett, the daughter of a North Portland barber who worked as a secretary in Fred Meyer's office before marrying and leaving Portland about 1930. Wollett owned no stock; she was listed as a director because state regulations required at least three directors. Fred Meyer's other dealings with his brother Henry included the Pioneer Market Co., a firm that acted as a landlord leasing space to vendors in buildings along Yamhill Street. The fourth was Oregon Piggly Wiggly Inc., which led to the lifetime break in relations between them.

The southeast corner of Yamhill Street and Fifth Avenue gained increasing prominence in the Portland food world with the opening of William Constantine's Liberty Market in 1918, and the new Piggly Wiggly store that rented space inside the market building in 1921. Constantine, a butcher who had operated a market earlier at Southwest First and Alder Street, announced plans in January, 1918, to remodel a two-story building on the Yamhill corner that was being vacated by Portland Gas & Coke Co.20 Opened seven months later, the L-shaped structure had open-air entrances on both Yamhill and Fifth Avenue. The building, long-since torn down, is notable because it is the location where Fred Meyer Inc. subsequently claimed its business was started in 1922.[21] Meyer, operating under the name of Pioneer Market Co., took over leasing of the Liberty Market in 1921. Constantine had sold fixtures he had installed when he remodeled the building in 1918. He published advertisements saying he was "forced" out of business, but offered no explanation why.[22]

Piggly Wiggly opened its first self-service Portland store in 1921. It was incorporated by D. H. Tripp, H.W. Kirkbride and Martha Schleusner as Piggly Wiggly Portland Co.[23] Clarence Saunders, the Tennessean who had patented the Piggly Wiggly floor plan four years earlier, had been forced out of company ownership as a consequence of national stock market maneuvering and short-selling. His corporate successors changed the marketing strategy to selling Piggly Wiggly franchises to local investors, and hundreds of Piggly Wiggly outlets quickly surfaced across the nation. "The stores are operated on the cafeteria principle and the interior arrangement is laid out in aisles," the *Oregonian* noted in a brief item. "Upon entering, the customer is given a basket to take care of purchases while passing along. All goods are in sight with prices marked. Upon completion of the selection, the customer passes to the checker and cashier, who computes the bill and places the purchases in a handy carry-all bag."[24] Portland's first Piggly Wiggly rented space inside the Liberty Market at Southwest Fifth and Yamhill, and the landlord was the Pioneer Market Co. operated by Fred and Henry Meyer .

That self-service was still an unusual experience in Portland grocery stores in 1921 was evident in Piggly Wiggly's first advertisement announcing its opening. The ad took a tentative approach, urging shoppers to come in, look around and experience the new format with no obligation to buy. There was an unstated suggestion that shoppers compare prices against those of other grocers. "The operating cost of Piggly Wiggly stores is the lowest of any heretofore known method of retail distribution," the ad said. "The benefit of this saving in operation cost is given our customers in lower prices." The advertisement suggested that customers may have felt they were targets of subtle or explicit sales pitches in stores where clerks selected items at the buyers' requests. At Piggly Wiggly, "you will not be asked to buy, nor will you be criticized for not buying. You can look and be at home in our store; go through its four separate aisles as a tour of inspection. If you see something you want to buy of your own free will and accord, without argument, persuasion, intimidation or suggestion from anyone...we will be glad to have you as a customer."[25] The advertisement offered no specific items other than a general mention of staples, fresh fruits and vegetables. Although it seemed risky at the time, shoppers came to like the freedom of making their own choices. "We know now that the average consumer, given a carrier and left to wander around the supermarket without any interference, will sell herself more merchandise than the best salesman behind the counter," a trade journal concluded in 1941.[26]

The convenience of self-service buying caught the attention of Portland shoppers – and the attention of Fred and Henry Meyer. By 1924, when Piggly Wiggly Portland Co. was dissolved, it had grown to five stores in Portland. The successor firm, Oregon Piggly Wiggly Co., was created that year with Fred G. Meyer as president and Henry Meyer as vice president and secretary.[27] Expansion was clearly on their minds: on a state form asking for the nature and general plan of the business to be followed, they listed, "Retail Chain Grocery Concern, operating Standard Piggly Wiggly Stores in Oregon."

Robert A. Hudson was not a founding director of Oregon Piggly Wiggly, but his wholesale grocery supply company was its largest supplier. The break between Fred Meyer and his brother, Henry, and Hudson was now at hand. By 1926, Henry Meyer had replaced Fred Meyer as president of Oregon Piggly Wiggly and had sided with Hudson in whatever the dispute was between Hudson and Fred Meyer. Fred Meyer no longer played a managerial role in Oregon Piggly Wiggly, but he remained a significant stockholder and the landlord at the Fifth and Yamhill site. It must have galled him to watch the fast growth of the Piggly Wiggly chain, which in just a few years grew to 30 stores. Meyer began offering his shares for sale in June, 1927, with advertisements lauding the growth of Piggly Wiggly and the opportunity to invest with a "successful wholesale grocer," Robert A. Hudson. In nine years, the national number of Piggly Wiggly stores had grown to approximately 2,000. The stock in Oregon Piggly Wiggly returned an annual dividend of 7.35 percent, the advertisements noted.[28] Subsequent ads removed any reference to Hudson and merely said Fred G. Meyer, located at 620 Pacific Building, was selling Piggly Wiggly shares from his own stock.

Fred Meyer filed a legal complaint in 1927 alleging that Oregon Piggly Wiggly had refused to open its financial records to him as a shareholder as required by the corporate bylaws. [29] He contended he needed the information to help him sell his $47,000 worth of Piggly Wiggly stock. Defendants included Henry Meyer and Hudson. An answer filed by attorney George S. Shepherd, also an officer in Oregon Piggly Wiggly, contended that Meyer had a "sinister design and ulterior motive" in wanting access to Piggly Wiggly records, since Meyer was a competing retailer and a Piggly Wiggly landlord. The answer to to Meyer's complaint also accused Fred Meyer of seeking trade secrets "for the purpose of aiding and abetting competitors." The matter went to trial before Multnomah County Circuit Judge Jacob Kanzler in December 1927. The burden was on the defendants to explain why they would not open their books. The chief witness was Henry Meyer.

Henry Meyer noted that Fred Meyer had raised the Piggly Wiggly rent from $300 to $360 per month, a figure that Henry Meyer felt was unjustified. "Some two years ago, when my relations with Fred Meyer were more friendly than they are at the present time, we discussed that location and he told me – I am a stockholder in the Pioneer Market Co., too, which holds a lease on there – that $250, he would be glad to get it for that location," Henry Meyer testified. He added that Piggly Wiggly decided to pay the higher rent because it would be difficult to move the office and the store fixtures. As for his decision not to show his brother the financial records after 1925, Meyer testified: "It was my opinion and also the opinion of the directors of the company that the information had not been used properly, that is, it had been used against the interests of the company." The bitterness extended down to the practical matter of access in and out of the Piggly Wiggly location. The store did not have its own door to the street; customers entered and exited through the interior of the larger market building. Henry Meyer accused his brother of setting up temporary tables for the delicatessen and coffee shop "practically blocking the aisles so that it is impossible for anyone to get in and out of the grocery store." Fred Meyer did not testify at the hearing.

Judge Kanzler ruled that Fred Meyer was entitled to the records specified in the company bylaws. Oregon Piggly Wiggly filed an appeal with the Oregon Supreme Court, but Shephard, the Piggly Wiggly attorney, missed a deadline for his appellate brief and the trial court ruling was affirmed.[30] Piggly Wiggly soon left the contentious location, and Fred Meyer expanded into the space with other tenants and his own operations. In February, 1927, Eva Meyer, Fred Meyer and Blanche Wollett filed supplementary articles of incorporation for Mybros Inc. The new corporate name became Fred Meyer Inc. Eva Meyer had replaced Henry Meyer as the third member of the board of directors. [31]

Hudson and Henry Meyer worked closely together in the Piggly Wiggly chain and in Hudson's food processing and wholesale company, Hudson House Inc., until Henry Meyer's retirement in 1966. He died of cancer the following year at age 71. Fred Meyer never spoke about the Piggly Wiggly break-up in detail. Oran Robertson, who went to work for Fred Meyer in 1945 and ultimately succeeded Meyer as chairman of Fred Meyer Inc., knew Meyer as well as anyone. This is all he remembered: "There were some family disagreements on that, so he closed it up and walked away from it and left Bob Hudson and his brother Harry (Henry) to run it. From that day forward, he never spoke to his brother the rest of his life."[32] The Piggly Wiggly chain grew to 30 stores in the Portland area. Hudson renamed them 3 Boys Markets in 1967, shortly after Henry Meyer's retirement. Hudson's empire ran aground in 1972, however, when the 85-year old entrepreneur, who had started his business in 1907, saw his debts outpace his revenue. Retail losses swamped profits in Hudson's food processing and wholesale operations. By the early 1970s, the domination of the Portland region's food market by big players such as Fred Meyer Inc., Safeway and Albertson's proved too much for the much smaller 3 Boys stores.

"I have always been a lone operator, and to be quite frank with you, I think that's where I made my mistakes," Hudson said at a news conference in 1972 after he had been stalling creditors. [33] Hudson's hands-on attitude long after the customary retirement age was a trait he shared with his erstwhile partner, Fred Meyer, although the Meyer empire continued to thrive in Meyer's old age. Unlike Hudson, Meyer surrounded himself with smart, hard-working managers who kept the Fred Meyer brand moving forward, sometimes against Meyer's own wishes, as the aging entrepreneur entered his 70s, 80s and 90s. All of Hudson's stores, warehouses and food-processing plants, by contrast, were sold off to pay creditors. When Hudson died in 1974 at age 87, he was remembered more as Oregon's "Mr. Golf" for promoting high-level amateur and professional golf matches in Portland than for his long career in food processing and retail grocery operations. His obituary appeared on the front page of the morning paper's sports section.[34]

The quick success of the Piggly Wiggly chain likely fueled Meyer's ambitions to expand his own retail operations. In 1925, William Constantine returned to Portland after spending nearly two years in Los Angeles and resurrected his tie with Meyer and Mybros Meats. Constantine announced that he and Meyer planned to open a chain of meat markets throughout Portland, with the Yamhill location being their first.[35] The brief announcement marked the first time that Fred Meyer revealed any plans for expanding a retail operation. In 1927, the Mybros Meats officially changed the company name to Constantine's Inc., but the company never grew under the Constantine's name.

A more significant development had occurred in December, 1924, when Fred and Henry Meyer, using the Mybros name, expanded into tobacco products. A two-line classified ad suggested "smokes" as a Christmas gift for men at MYBROS CUT-RATE TOBACCO SHOP at Fifth and Yamhill.[36] It was the first instance of Meyer using advertising to promote a retail business. In the decades ahead, he would become one of Portland's biggest retail advertisers. The tobacco shop was a success. As a result of his interest in the efficiency and time-motion studies of the era, Meyer determined that selling whole cartons of cigarettes took no more time or effort for the sales clerk than selling individual cigarette packages. He focused on carton sales, offering 10-pack cartons of Camels, Chesterfields and Lucky Strikes for $1.19 per carton.[37] In the Great Depression that lay ahead, Meyer's tobacco sales would become a vital element in allowing him to meet his growing payrolls.

After disassociating himself from Henry Meyer, the small classified ads starting in 1927 referred to the "Fred Meyer Cut-Rate Tobacco Shop, 5th and Yamhill sts." Fred Meyer had found the marketing niche that would carry him for decades: low prices. His Christmas-season ad in 1927, printed in the newspaper's smallest type in the classified advertising section, claimed 25 percent reductions on cigars, cigarettes and tobaccos. "Holiday packings of all major brands at cut prices," it read. "Shop here first."[38]

Of course, Meyer was not personally standing in a market stall selling tobacco products. His primary business was still leasing space to others. By late 1925, Fred and Eva Meyer had moved their office from the hurly-burly of the open markets on Yamhill Street to Room 201 of the Broadway-Yamhill Building, the same structure that housed the Hippodrome and later the Orpheum Theater before it was torn down in 1975 to make way for the downtown Nordstrom store that now sits on the full block. Hardly more than a year later, the Meyers moved their headquarters to the sixth floor of the Pacific Building, a grand new office building designed in an Italian-renaissance palazzo style by architect A.E. Doyle, whose numerous new commercial buildings were changing Portland's downtown skyline throughout the prosperous 1920s. While eminently stylish, the Pacific Building facing on Yamhill was also convenient for the Meyers: Its front door was a mere half-block from the Liberty Market across Fifth Avenue.

While Meyer was disentangling himself from the Piggly Wiggly business in 1928, his thoughts were already moving on to his next major project. Eva Meyer once said that her husband's hobbies were real estate first and business second.[39] He combined the two in his first real estate development and a ground-breaking retail business late in 1928 at what he called the Alderway Building, a four-story structure that still stands on a quarter-block at the northwest corner of Southwest Alder Street and Broadway. Meyer signed a 99-year lease on the property, with the understanding that he would tear down the old Pantages Theater that had been built in 1912 as a vaudeville house and that since 1926 had been running talking movies under the Music Box name.[40] In its place he would erect a modern retail and office building.

Meyer's motivation was to open a self-service drug store. To his way of thinking, if a person could go into a grocery store and select a bottle of ketchup, why not go into a drug store and take a bottle of mouthwash off the shelf and carry it to the check-out stand? [41] "It used to make me mad in those days to go into a drug store and try to buy a bottle of cough medicine," Meyer once said. "They would always try to sell you something else. No matter what you asked for, they would try to sell you something else." [42] Acting on the precepts advocated by Max Heindel and Harrington Emerson, Meyer sought the best counsel he could find. The Portland Retail Druggists Association apparently told him the association would not allow a licensed pharmacist to work in a self-service store. As a result, Meyer couldn't properly call his enterprise a "drug store." Others he consulted with didn't think customers would respond favorably to a drug store by any name without a druggist or prescriptions. Meyer listened to all the opinions– and decided to push ahead, anyway.

He hired the Portland architectural firm of Claussen & Claussen, headed by brothers H. Fred Claussen and William E. Claussen, Chicago natives who had established a practice in Portland in 1908. It is possible Meyer met them because they designed an apartment building at 2087 Northwest Overton Street where Fred and Eva Meyer resided for about five years starting in 1928. Regardless, it was a reputable firm that had designed numerous buildings large and small, including the Heathman and Roosevelt hotels, the 12-story Buyers Building at Southwest Third Avenue and Alder Street, and Laurelhurst School. At four stories, the Alderway Building added nothing significant to the downtown skyline, but the *Oregonian* listed it along with four taller buildings as most notable achievements of the construction year. Meyer's building cost $200,000. "The building ...utilized the old steel frame of the theater building, found, upon beginning of operations, to be as strong as the year it was built," the newspaper said. "This was a departure in general building practices that drew wide comment and publicity in building

Fred Meyer's self-service toiletries and remedies store took a portion of the ground floor at the Alderway Building. The small laundry entrance was at the left. (Oregonian)

circles all over the country."43 Meyer had another reason to be pleased: the building was finished in time for the holiday season, just as he had urged.

Fred and Eva Meyer moved their office from the Pacific Building to the second floor of their new Alderway Building and leased portions of its commercial frontages on Alder and Broadway to a women's dress shop and to a cosmetics and hair-products retailer. The early leases were handled by David B. Simpson, who became a principal in the major Portland commercial realty firm of Norris Beggs & Simspon. Simpson and Fred Meyer developed close personal and business relations that lasted until Simpson's death in 1976. Simpson spent his business and personal life circulating in the highest echelons of the Portland business and social communities. He served as president of the Portland Chamber of Commerce and as a member of the City Planning Commission, where he played a key role in post-World War II planning of Portland's freeway system. Simpson's involvement in Portland's early land-use planning circles and his commercial real estate expertise assisted Meyer in acquiring sites for new stores in the decades ahead. Simpson's early schooling in military academies and his tenure as an Army captain provided the kind of no-nonsense bearing that Meyer preferred.

As for his new store in the Alderway Building, Meyer carefully avoided "drugs" or "pharmacy" in the title. He called it, "Fred Meyer Toiletries and Remedies." Unlike most Portland drug stores at the time, Meyer's store offered no ice cream counter or soda fountain. Not having a pharmacist was not Meyer's only hurdle at the outset. He had difficulty acquiring over-the-counter supplies from reluctant wholesalers. "So I bought out a couple drug stores to get some stock. To get rid of it all I had to install more self-service drug stations," he told a newspaper reporter 20 years later. [44] Meyer was not above stretching the truth about his hardships when he was speaking for public consumption. However, there would be future occasions when he would have difficulty convincing suppliers to sell to him, whether the product was bread or Levi-Strauss & Co. denim jeans. Some manufacturers believed the reputations of their products were demeaned if they were offered for sale in discount stores. Meyer, ever competitive, arrived at a strategy for such occasions. His account of acquiring inventory outside of the customary supply chain, a practice known as "bootlegging" in the industry, likely was true when he opened for business in the Alderway Building. It is a story he recounted several times in later years.

Fred Meyer Toiletries and Remedies was a hit from the start. "I started a drug store where you could walk up and take what you wanted. No one would give you an argument," Meyer said later. "As soon as they found out about the store where they didn't have to fight the clerk for the thing they wanted, people flocked in."45 Glen Day, a 1929 high school graduate who started working for Meyer in the early 1930s, recalled the public's reaction. "Oh, surprise. Certainly much faster sales and more sales, because we were able to lower the price of products. We no longer had some gal standing at a glass case showing the customer different shades of lipstick or powder or face creams or whatever was going on."[46] The only employee visible during most of the day was the cashier. Fred Meyer's first major retailing innovation was the nation's first self-service drug store. Given its immediate success, Meyer had no further trouble acquiring inventory for the store through the customary wholesale channels.

Meyer also offered a tiny storefront in the Alderway Building for taking in dirty clothes to be laundered or dry-cleaned. He negotiated a bulk rate with the Multnomah Hotel for laundry service and with the Laurelhurst Cleaners for dry-cleaning. Glen Day said the small laundry space measured fewer than 100 square feet. "But the volume of business we poured through there was astronomical. We had doctors and lawyers and a lot of businessmen downtown bring their laundry in to us. We gave them pretty fast service... the quality of it was good and the price was right. So those were the major ingredients."[47] The tiny laundry operation also provided an unexpected break-through for future business. Always keeping an eye out for bargains, Meyer acquired a supply of men's socks and underwear from another retailer's surplus inventory. He offered them for sale in the tiny laundry, and customers dropping off or picking up laundry snapped them up quickly. The sales convinced Meyer to make men's wear a permanent department when he expanded later at other locations. True to his belief in efficiency, Meyer wasted no space in his new Alderway Building. A stand sold cigars and cigarettes in the lobby.

During the late 1920s, Meyer expanded his reach on Yamhill Street, where the canvas-topped stalls of the "public" market on the sidewalks continued drawing large numbers of shoppers to the buildings that faced on to Yamhill. Meyer gradually expanded grocery sales under the Fred Meyer name as vacancies arose in the market buildings whose leases he controlled. "I wanted to build up businesses and then lease them or sell them," he said later. "I was lazy enough to want to lease out my properties and let the other fellow run them. But it didn't work. The others were always getting into trouble and I would have to take over the business to make it pay out."[48]

One of Meyer's strategies was breaking down bulk staples, such as flour, sugar, salt and coffee, into smaller packages that were easier for daily shoppers on the busy street to purchase and carry. He hired young, inexperienced workers to create the smaller packages at night for sale the next day. One of them was his stepson, Earle A. Chiles. It was the same strategy employed by the pioneering Lutey store in Butte, Montana, a decade earlier. National producers had not yet caught on to the changing trends in food retailing. As late as 1925, the American Sugar Refining company was urging wholesalers to buy and promote its small packages instead of bulk sugar. "Now, if the grocer must scoop his sugar, weigh it, wrap it, tie it...lose some by spillage–then we acknowledge that the margin of profit is not worth the trouble," the company said in a sales brochure. But with its packaged sugars, "you eliminate all the handling costs, all expense, all losses. On that basis, 200 percent profit is practically clear."[49] Within a decade, grocery producers accepted the importance of colorful packaging and consumer-oriented product sizes as essential elements in attracting the eyes of self-service shoppers. But that development was yet to come.

Meyer called these outlets his "package" stores in buildings that bore the names of Vista Market and Central Market on Fourth and Yamhill and the Mybros Market – later "Fred Meyer"–at Fifth Avenue. Meyer was not alone selling from these locations; as the decade neared its end in the old Liberty Market facing on both Fifth Avenue and Yamhill Street, other tenants included the Liberty Fish Market, a delicatessen run by John S. Hoggan, Meyer's early-day coffee-company partner, and the long-running Mayo & Hasson Bros. Fruit Co.

One of Meyer's tenants in 1929 at Fifth and Yamhill was an optometrist, Everett J. Chatfield. He was the brother of Eva Chatfield Meyer and Mary Boyle, and had moved to Portland with his family from Baker City after Eva Meyer's divorce from Ira Chiles. Fred Meyer believed that his brother-in-law did not work as hard as he should have, but Meyer couldn't complain because Dr. Chatfield was a tenant, not an employee, and thus was free to work at his own pace as long as he paid

The Alderway Building as it survives in the 21st Century is Fred Meyer's remaining legacy in downtown Portland. (Author photo)

his rent. Even if his work ethic did not match Meyer's, Dr. Chatfield in the next decade went on to set up optometry shops in a half dozen Fred Meyer locations before his retirement.

As the busy decade neared its end, Yamhill Street was booming and Fred Meyer's new Alderway Building with its self-service drug store was a success. Less than a year after Alderway opened, however, the stock market crashed on Wall Street. Dramatic consequences registered immediately across the country. The next chapter of Fred Meyer Inc. would unfold in the worst economic recession in United States history.

---

[1] Dawson, Carol, and Johnson, Carol, *House of Plenty: The Rise, Fall and Revival of Luby's Cafeterias,* University of Texas Press, 2006, p. 23.

[2] Chirgwin, Ray, oral history interview, Oregon Historical Society, sound recording 1301, 7-24-1989.

[3] U.S. Patent Office, No. 1,242,872, issued Oct. 9, 1917.

[4] U.S. Patent Office, No. 91,780, issued 5-27-1913.

[5] Lutey, Kent, *Lutey Brothers Marketeria, America's First Self-Service Grocers,* Montana: The Magazine of Western History, Spring 1978, pps. 50 to 57.

[6] Killoran, Rollin, OHS sound recording 1308, Sept. 22, 1988.

[7] *Oregonian,* 8-2-17, p.10.

[8] *Oregonian,* 6-22-1918, P. 8.

[9] *Oregonian,* 12-28-1918, p.7.

[10] Killoran, Rollin, *op. cit.,* Sept. 22, 1988.

[11] *Ibid.*

[12] Robertson,Oran B., OHS sound recording 1312, Oct. 25, 1989

[13] *Nothing Really Changes,* Forbes, Jan. 23, 1978, p. 68.

[14] *Oregon Journal,* Sept. 4, 1978, p. 4.

[15] Oregon State Archives, corporation index, 6-5-1920.

[16] Baker, Gary, OHS sound recording 1301, May 9, 1989.

[17] Chirgwin, *op.cit.,*July 24, 1989.

[18] Oregon Corporation Department, file no. 26429, Nov. 14, 1923.

[19] Oregon Corporation Department, file no. 26422, Nov. 10, 1923.

[20] *Oregonian,* Jan. 15, 1918, p. 4.

[21] *The History of Fred Meyer Inc.,* no listed author, date or publisher, located in Multnomah County Library.

[22] *Oregonian,* May 18, 1923, p.21.

[23] Oregon Corporation Department, file no. 24043, May 20, 1921.

[24] *Ibid.,* Oct. 31, 1921, p. 16.

[25] *Ibid.,* Nov. 5, 1921, p. 12.

[26] Zimmerman, M.M., *The Supermarket and the Changing Retail Structure,* Journal of Marketing, April, 1941, pps. 402-409.

[27] Oregon Corporation Department, file no. 26814, May, 22, 1924.
[28] *Ibid.,* June 5, 1927, p. 27.
[29] *Fred G. Meyer v. Henry Meyer, et al.,* Oregon Supreme Court , file no. 6174, 1928.
[30] *Ibid.*
[31] Oregon Corporation Department, supplementary articles of incorporation, file no. 26422, Feb. 15, 1927.
[32] Robertson, Oran, OHS 1312, Oct. 25, 1989.
[33] *Oregonian,* Aug. 31, 1972, p. C9.
[34] *Ibid.,* Sept. 6, 1974, C1.
[35] *Oregonian,* Sept. 6, 1925, p. 2.
[36] *Oregonian,* Dec. 16, 1924, p. 22.
[37] *Ibid,* May 23, 1926, p. 12.
[38] *Oregonian,* Dec. 5, 1927, p. 15.,
[39] Chirgwin, *op cit.*
[40] Lacher, Gary, and Stone, Steve, *Theatres of Portland,* Arcadia Publishing, 2009, p. 31.
[41] Killoran, *op cit.*
[42] Richards, Leverett G., *Introducing the Man Nobody Knows,* The *Oregonian* Magazine, Nov. 11, 1949, p. 6-7.
[43] *Oregonian,* Jan. 1, 1929, p. B1.
[44] Richards, *op cit.*
[45] *Ibid.*
[46] Day, Glen, OHS sound recording 1306, June 16, 1989.
[47] *Ibid.*
[48] Richards, *op cit.*
[49] Boorstin, Daniel J., *The Americans: The Democratic Experience,* Random House, New York, 1973, pps 440-41.

CHAPTER FOUR

MY-TE-FINE Goes to Hollywood

Finger-pointing about the causes of the Great Depression started immediately after Black Thursday, followed by Black Tuesday, in October, 1929. While many possible factors were blamed, including the rise of chain grocery stores, no one ventured to guess that the recession would last for a decade or longer. Fred Meyer, however, thrived during that grim decade, despite a setback that would have frightened many entrepreneurs. Meyer added new stores, created his signature retailing innovation, hired men and women who would be vital to his future success, and fought successfully in the courts for low consumer prices and women's employment opportunities. It helped, of course, that his primary products were essential items for daily life and that he built his reputation on low prices. It was in the 1930s that he moved his advertisements from classified ads in tiny print in the back of the newspaper to larger "display" advertisements published on the same pages as the daily news. He adopted the slogan, "Fred Meyer for Thrifty Buyers," which appeared at the bottom of each advertisement. His message of thrift and low prices won the favor of Depression-era customers. The decade also saw the company introduce its "MY-TE-FINE" in-house brand, which was applied to items ranging from razor blades to bacon, candy bars to canned goods. By the middle of the decade, Fred and Eva Meyer ranked among the highest-paid business executives in Portland.

"My folks used to buy their groceries at Fred Meyer and thought he was the greatest because of his sales tactics of making people feel that there were getting the best deal in down," said Ray Chirgwin, an early Fred Meyer employee. "And in lots of instances they were." Meyer often offered a "loss leader" product that he sold at no profit or even at a small loss to draw customers to his stores. Then he made his profits from other products that consumers bought as they completed their personal shopping lists. "And the public took to it," Chirgwin said. "He was a Depression merchant. He knew how to woo the public. That's where he was a genius." Meyer's loss-leader strategy stunned competitors. "Well, the other merchants it just panicked them, because they couldn't understand how somebody could give a jar of Best Foods mayonnaise for the price he had on it. But the customers all came in and bought everything else, and he more than made up, don't you see. But he did it without giving too much away in those days. That's all he needed, was one or two good giveaways." [1]

Chirgwin was a recent high school graduate with aspirations of going to college when the Depression hit. Instead of college, he landed a job at Fred Meyer. Because of his past experience working at a 20th Century market, Chirgwin started at $18 per week instead of Fred Meyer's customary starting pay of $15. Early in his tenure and before he had met Fred Meyer personally, Chirgwin was stocking shelves one night at the Fifth and Yamhill store. A man in a suit came up behind him. "What are you doing?" the stranger asked. Chirgwin was puzzled by the question since the man obviously could see that Chirgwin was stocking shelves, but Chirgwin figured it was no time to be sassy. "I'm putting cans on the shelf, sir," he replied.

"And how are you putting them on the shelf?" the man asked. Still puzzled, Chirgwin replied, "With my two hands."

The man asked, "How many cases do you put up every day on the shelf?"

"Gee, I don't really know."

"Well, estimate it," the stranger said. Chirgwin paused a moment and gave the man a number. "He immediately told me how many tons of extra weight I had lifted in a certain period that wasn't necessary if I'd put that case on a stool. I wouldn't have had to bend down. Well, that's good, constructive criticism, but the delivery was rather rough. I never forgot it."

The man walked away. Chirgwin turned to a co-worker and asked who the man was. "That was Mr. Meyer," the employee said.[2] Meyer liked hiring young employees and training them in his methods. Chirgwin wasn't the only employee to experience an unusual introduction to his ultimate boss, who throughout his career was always known as Mr. Meyer.

Having finally devoted himself in his early 40s to building a retail chain, Meyer turned his penchant for commercial real estate into a search for new sites. With the help of David Simpson, the commercial real estate broker, Meyer in January 1931 selected the southwest corner of Third Avenue and Morrison Street, a location that earlier had housed the Brownsville Woolen Mills store. After interior repairs, the second Meyer location devoted to toiletries opened two months later.[3] The small Morrison Street outlet was never a big contributor to Fred Meyer's business. But Meyer's next venture broke the mold, both for Fred Meyer Inc. and for retailing in the Pacific Northwest.

People and cars still packed the Yamhill Street markets between Second and Fifth Avenues. As early as 1918, Police Chief Nelson F. Johnson advocated a one-way street plan and street car loops to help ease downtown congestion, notably on Yamhill. "I tried to drive through Yamhill Street the other day, and we had to give up and back out," Johnson noted.[4] The City Council declined to adopt his recommendations in 1918, or again when a similar plan was offered four years later. Police periodically stepped up enforcement on Yamhill by ticketing double-parkers who stopped to make purchases. Meyer, who had once thought of opening meat markets with William Constantine in Portland neighborhoods, believed it was time to expand beyond downtown. He studied vehicle traffic counts kept by the city, and also collected double-parking tickets on Yamhill and paid the $1 fines. He kept track of the addresses, and noticed that many of the shoppers were coming from the fast-growing so-called "suburban" neighborhoods of Laurelhurst, Irvington and Rose City Park.[5]

An elegant 1,491-seat theater, the largest located out of downtown, completed in 1926 at Northeast 41st Avenue and Sandy Boulevard, gave that Northeast Portland district an informal new identity: Hollywood.[6] It was across the street from this landmark theater that Fred Meyer elected to create his first shopping center, eventually comprising groceries, fresh foods, toiletries, clothing, candy, tobacco and other items all under one roof. It was the first of what came to be known as one-stop shopping centers, which proved to be the great legacy of Fred Meyer Inc. Food was the magnet that drew shoppers, but profit margins were higher on the non-food items customers added during the same shopping trip. Yet the one-stop concept was never a single idea that leapt from Meyer's fertile brain, but was rather a matter of business evolution. Fred Meyer had wanted to diversify, but his wife, Eva, did not want to expand geographically. "So he started adding products," said Cyril Green, who would serve as company president four decades later. "Now, that's how he told it."[7]

Working with Simpson, his commercial realtor, Meyer signed a 10-year lease in May, 1931, for an 18,000-square-foot site along the north side of Sandy Boulevard between Northeast 41st and 42nd Avenues, a stone's throw from the dramatic Hollywood Theater across the street. The 10,000-square-foot building leased by Meyer had been erected in 1914 as the home of the Boulevard Garage, an auto servicing and sales business. Meyer used the remaining 8,000 square feet of flat ground for parking and an automobile service station. "The property is located on one of the city's most important arterial streets and in a business district that is growing by leaps and bounds," the *Oregonian* noted.[8] While Meyer was attracted by the large volume of auto traffic on Sandy, his new market also sat at the intersection of the Sandy Boulevard and Beaumont streetcar lines. Streetcar patronage was trending downward by 1931, yet the electric-powered street railways still carried hundreds of thousands of passengers each year and Sandy was one of the busiest routes. Meyer wanted $30,000 worth of renovations completed in time for a June 15 opening. He missed that target by a mere 12 days.

Fred Meyer's Hollywood Public Market, as it was called, was the first of two Fred Meyer stores at that location. The 1931 version was reminiscent of the early Yamhill Street markets in that large portals between the building's structural columns could be opened onto Sandy Boulevard during good weather, creating an attractive street scene with fresh produce abutting the sidewalk. At night and in poor weather, glass doors sealed the interior. A large billboard perched on the roof with a giant human finger pointing to the parking lot. Meyer thought arrows could be confusing; fingers were inescapably clear.[9] Meyer's hopes for the new store were immediately rewarded. The June 27th opening attracted what may have been the largest throng yet for an East Side business premier. "All of the many shops in the building were crowded from morning until night," the next morning's paper noted.[10] Departments at the outset included toiletries and remedies, flowers, groceries, meat, fruit and vegetables, a delicatessen and coffee and teas. Laundry service and men's and women's apparel would be added in the next few years. Van de Kamp Dutch Holland Bakers, a large Los Angeles bakery chain expanding into Portland and Seattle at the time, held a lease abutting Meyer's Hollywood market at the corner of 41st Avenue. It erected one of its signature two-story shingled ersatz windmills. The windmill soon would be incorporated into the market, as well. With the addition of clothing, drugs, automotive and other goods to the full-line grocery store, the original Hollywood location was the first of what later came to be known as one-stop shopping centers.

The original Hollywood store was a series of older buildings connected together, including the Van de Kamp windmill on the corner. (OHS Neg. 005932)

Even near the end of his long life, Fred Meyer made no claim to being first with the one-stop idea, and acknowledged that the concept never struck him as a specific idea. Portland historian E. Kimbark MacColl interviewed Meyer in February 1978, close to Meyer's 92nd birthday. In his summary of the interview, MacColl wrote of Meyer, "Admitted that 1931 was a key year in his business growth. No overall plan or scheme. Just the workings of the economic system – let it unfold."[11] Yet modesty and happenstance aside, Meyer likely was the first in the United States to pair full-line grocery sales with general merchandise. A hometown newspaper and two business historians gave that distinction to Frederik Meijer, a Grand Rapids, Michigan, retailer who eventually expanded one-stop shopping centers into five Midwest states. But Meijer's first Thrifty Acres store, while much larger than anything Fred Meyer had yet built, didn't combine grocery and general merchandise until 1962.[12] Meijer himself never claimed that he was the originator of the one-stop concept. By the late 1930s, Fred Meyer had already combined groceries with men's and women's clothes, drugs, toiletries, flowers, sporting goods and automobile accessories. Though Meijer might not have been well-versed in Fred Meyer Inc. history, the two patriarchs had met and discussed their retail businesses on more than one occasion. Their friendship was strong enough that Meijer placed in his Grand Rapids office a photograph of the two men smiling. Decades later, a retailer from rural Arkansas who experimented with several retail formats over the years, drew heavily on the Fred Meyer Inc. examples in building the Walmart Super Centers that eventually became America's biggest retail company.

Unbeknownst to Meyer as he built the original Hollywood store, an entrepreneur on the other side of the country had come up with a similar idea for selling groceries. Michael E. Cullen in August 1930 opened the first King Kullen Grocery Company store in New York City's borough of Queens. In a plant sent to his boss, a Cincinnati grocery-chain operator named Bernard Kroger, Cullen had proposed a concept for a big store with self-service, high volume sales, low product margins and aggressive advertising campaigns. But Kroger apparently never received the missive, and Cullen set out on his own. Like Meyer, Cullen remodeled a vacant automobile garage into a self-service grocery store that was slightly smaller than Meyer's, but considered huge in its day. Research several decades later led the Food Marketing Institute, an industry research and lobbying organization, to bestow the title of America's first supermarket on Cullen's store, although Fred Meyer and other entrepreneurs had similar ideas close in time. Cullen's strategy, as he once expressed it, was virtually identical to Meyer's: "The one thought always uppermost in mind—How can I undersell the other fellow? How can I beat the other fellow? How can I make my company more money? The answer is very simple: — by keeping my overhead down, and only by keeping this overhead down can I beat the other fellow." [13] Meyer in the next few years played a pioneering role in adding soft goods and variety items to his grocery supermarket to create what became called a one-stop shopping center.

Soon after the Hollywood opening, Meyer's step-son, Earle A. Chiles, returned to Portland from Boston. Chiles had started working for his stepfather as a teenager in the market stalls on Yamhill Street. Now he brought home a master's degree in business administration from Harvard University and a wife, Virginia Hughes Chiles, whom he had met while attending Harvard. The new Mrs. Chiles was formally educated as well, having graduated from Boston University and attended the Massachusetts Institute of Technology. To the self-schooled Meyer, college degrees if anything were strikes against Earle A. and Virginia Chiles. Their personal relations outside of work were marginally cordial until Eva Meyer's death in 1960. After that, Fred Meyer largely eliminated any social activity with the Chileses. Earle A. Chiles became company president in 1955 and held the title until 1968, but he was not a forceful figure in management.

"Earle was an entirely different type of individual" than his stepfather, said Herbert Retzlaff, who worked closely with both Meyer and Chiles for 30 years as the company's chief financial officer. "And he (Chiles) didn't like confrontations. He shied away from a good fight. Meyer being just the opposite , a very domineering sort of fellow that stood out in a crowd and dominated the people around him. And Fred Meyer was very good to Earle, because he was very fond of Mrs. Meyer. But the working relationship was, well, let's say one-sided."[14] Oran Robertson, who joined the company in 1945 and ultimately succeeded Fred Meyer as board chairman, said Chiles drew so much criticism from Meyer in executive meetings that Chiles eventually quit making suggestions.[15] Dale Warman, a high-ranking executive who worked with Chiles late in Chiles' career, described Chiles as "really a great gentleman.

He was like his mother. And that's probably why he always had such a hard time with Mr. Meyer. Mr. Meyer was always very hard on him."

One of Fred Meyer's favorite sayings, Ray Chirgwin recalled, was, "'The trouble with you people is you never think. You never use your head.'" Meyer couldn't tolerate answers from anyone if he felt they were not factual or well-reasoned. He was heard to call his employees dummies. "And I remember him telling Mrs. Meyer just exactly that. 'If you had a brain, how could you make such a statement?' And a tear would run down her cheeks. He used to call Earle a dummy all the time."[16]

When he returned to Portland from Boston, Chiles took charge of hiring for Fred Meyer Inc. Given the scarcity of jobs in Portland's Depression economy, there was never a shortage of applicants. One was Rollin Killoran, who had grown up as the son of a small-town grocer in rural Idaho whose father had gone broke in the face of a new cash-and-carry competitor. Killoran started college at the University of Oregon with hopes of becoming a lawyer but hard times forced him to quit school. He was working for food and coffee – no pay – at a small Portland grocery when he heard about an opening at Fred Meyer. Chiles needed someone to work relief hours at four new laundry and dry-cleaning locations. Chiles apparently thought the 25-cent-per-hour job was beneath Killoran's abilities. "Please, I'm hungry," pleaded Killoran, who was newly married. "Give me a shot at it." Killoran at the time had no desire to spend his career in the grocery business, but anything was better than starvation. Hired in 1932, Killoran travelled around the city by streetcar to cover lunch hours or substitute shifts in the small laundry outlets.

Thus Killoran found himself working late one cold winter night at the Hollywood laundry counter. He closed the two swinging doors to Sandy Boulevard to keep out the cold. "And a guy came in and propped the doors open. "And I said, 'You know, it's awfully cold in here.'"

The man said, "Do you know what these doors are?"

"Yes, I know what they are."

"What are they?"

"Well, they are to keep the cold out and the heat in, if there is any," Killoran answered.

"No, that isn't true," the man replied. "They are an invitation to come in when they are open, and when they are closed they are an invitation to go away." Killoran stood silent. The man started to leave, then turned and added, "I'm Fred Meyer."[17] Meyer probably didn't remember his introduction to Killoran, who would become one of Meyer's close associates over many of the next 46 years. Killoran, of course, never forgot it.

Killoran wasn't alone working late night shifts. As a convenience to shoppers, and with an understanding that nothing could be sold when the doors were locked, Meyer kept his stores open until 11:30 p.m. That caught the attention of the State Welfare Commission, which threatened to prosecute him for violating a state administrative rule preventing women working in Portland retail establishments, other than hotel cigar stands or confectionery stores, later than 6 p.m. Rather than wait to defend himself in court, Meyer took the offensive and filed suit contending that the state commission had exceeded powers granted to it by the state's enabling legislation.

Meyer hired Portland attorney Daniel J. Malarkey to represent him. Malarkey was recognized as one of the best and most aggressive attorneys in the city, and thus met Meyer's dictum of seeking good counsel. As a former state legislator for ten tears between 1902 and 1914, Malarkey had been a major figure in passing legislation that established Oregon's first minimum wage law for women and the state's compensation system for injured employees. The State Welfare Commission he was challenging on Fred Meyer's behalf was a successor to the Industrial Welfare Commission that Malarkey had helped create. Malarkey became a trusted adviser to Fred Meyer personally, and he served as one of five directors of the privately-held Fred Meyer Inc.

from 1938 until his death in 1940.

The details of Meyer's employment practices in this case were never litigated in detail. Attorneys for the state contended that Meyer's legal complaint failed to state a cause of action. Multnomah County Circuit Judge Louis P. Hewitt disagreed and eventually ruled in Meyer's favor. When the state appealed to the Oregon Supreme Court, Malarkey argued that the enabling legislation was designed to protect women and children from conditions that would have "pernicious effect on their health or morals," but did not say which hours were to be worked. His brief said Meyer employees were allowed at least nine hours between shifts, never worked more than six days in a calendar week and never more than nine hours in one day or more than 48 hours in any week. However, women's shifts ended at 8 or 8:30 p.m.

Ruling in Meyer's favor, the unanimous appellate court said, "...(I)t seems clear that the legislation intended to empower the commission to fix the maximum number of hours of labor which could be performed in one day or in one week and not the particular hours of the day during which work could be done."[18]

Meyer's next foray into the courts did not fare as well. In July, 1933, he filed suit against several Portland bakeries, alleging they conspired not to sell him bread products.[19] Circuit Judge Hall Lusk ruled there was insufficient evidence to prove a conspiracy, but said the case could continue on the issue of whether wholesale bakeries could require Meyer to sell their products at specified prices.[20] The records of that case are not available, but Meyer in the next few months satisfied his bread needs by buying the Van de Kamp baking plant on East Broadway along with its windmill-shaped retail store adjacent to his Hollywood market. Meyer spent $30,000 remodeling the windmill to make it a component of the Hollywood market and adding a bakery department at the Fifth and Yamhill store downtown.[21] In one of his largest newspaper ads yet, nearly two full columns, Meyer trumpeted the Van de Kamp purchase and vowed to retain the Van de Kamp employees, recipes and quality. He also pledged to reduce prices. One-pound loaves of white, whole wheat, raisin, rye and potato bread, which had been selling for 9 to 12 cents per loaf, were now all 8 cents each.[22] The bakery lawsuit and the Van de Kamp purchase were evidence of Meyer's persistence. As Killoran, who was slowly working his way up the ranks from his laundry job, later said, "He was a dominant individual (who) would never give up. He just kept going and trying another door, come in this door and get kicked out of there, go in another door until finally some way, somehow, it worked out."[23]

The year 1933 was a busy year for other reasons. Working with Simpson, the commercial real estate broker, Meyer in July leased the five-story Brown Building on Southwest Sixth Avenue between Washington and Alder Streets. (The name was changed to Exchange Building many years later. It still stands at 514 S.W. Sixth Avenue.) Meyer an-

After financial trouble at the Alderway Building, Meyer moved his office to the nearby Brown Building and opened this 6th Avenue store. (Oregonian)

nounced plans for a new store on the ground floor and moved his offices from the Alderway Building one block away. Meyer told the press that he needed more office space, partly because of new legislation limiting working hours to 40 per week. As his retailing empire expanded, it increased the need for more clerks to handle invoices and billing.[24] That was far from being the full explanation, however. Because of the Depression and his inability to land enough tenants, Meyer was not able to keep up payments on his 99-year lease of the Alderway Building. Turning it back to the owners cost him $500,000 on the deal. Yet he seldom ever mentioned it, just as he almost never mentioned the breakdown in relations with his two brothers living in Portland. "Such things used to bother me a lot," he said in 1953, referring to the Alderway setback, "but I've learned since to just let them happen and take them in stride."[25] Meyer carried that attitude the rest of his life: Put losses behind, don't dwell upon failure, keep looking ahead. The Alderway episode substantially dulled Meyer's interest in real estate investments, except for developing his own stores. Instead, he turned his full attention to being a retail merchant. The Sixth Avenue Fred Meyer opened in November, offering groceries, fruit, toiletries and "women's accessories," such as handbags, hosiery and lingerie.[26]

The addition of women's clothes and accessories marked the arrival into Meyer's business of Mary A. Boyle, Eva Meyer's sister. Boyle had previous retail experience in Portland in women's wear. She spent the rest of her lengthy career working for Fred Meyer and proved to be a valued business associate and close friend. She often traveled with Fred and Eva Meyer on trips and socialized with them regularly in Portland. Women's wear proved to be a major component of the company's future success because profit margins on clothes exceeded margins on groceries. Since most grocery customers were women, there was a natural synergy with the new department. Boyle survived Fred Meyer, who remembered her with a $25,000 bequest in his will, the same amount he left for his stepson, Earle A. Chiles.[27]

Total company employment had grown close to 200 in 1933. Meyer paid employees in cash, and there were paydays when Meyer knew he would be short. His strategy to raise money quickly was to run a sale on cigarettes, since he had a two-week grace-period in which to pay the cigarette supplier. In 1933, when individual packages sold for 15 cents, Meyer advertised cartons of 10 for $1. "Our stocks are freshest because our sales are largest!" was not an idle boast.[28] During a period of record unemployment, Meyer allowed workers willing to take their chances on any part-time work to sit on the mezzanine at the Hollywood Market. Sometimes there was a need for men to help park cars or load groceries. Those who picked up a few scattered hours would be paid the same day with coins. Meyer liked the idea of sending workers home with a feeling of money jangling in their pockets. In an extremely painful economic time, he wanted his workers to feel a degree of success.[29]

Fred and Eva Meyer left Portland for a full month early in 1933, motoring across the country and back. Like most Meyer "vacations," he spent much of his time on the road inspecting other chain stores and getting to know top owners and managers. Meyer willingly traded ideas with non-competing companies outside of the Pacific Northwest, but there were no friendly relations with direct competitors. "Almost every merchant in town was against Fred Meyer," Killoran recalled. "He sold for prices – they had been robbing people – and he cut the prices, and as a result everyone hated him except the customer."[30] Two of Meyer's better commercial friends were the Alpha-Beta Stores and Vons, which operated numerous stores in Southern California. Alpha-Beta had started early in the self-service era as a concept, not a commercial name. Its founders stocked grocery items on their shelves in alphabetical order to help customers find what they were looking for. Like Fred Meyer stores, both the Alpha-Beta and Vons chains eventually branched into non-food items. Meyer often sent employees to study operations in chains outside of Portland, and he frequently accepted visitors from those chains in return. Fred and Eva Meyer went as far as New York on their 1933 jaunt, where Fred Meyer likely visited his younger sisters Sophie and Marie, the only siblings from his nuclear family with whom he maintained relationships.

ORNING OREGONIAN, THURSDAY, FEBRUARY 2, 1933

UPTURN TO FOLLOW DROP, SAYS MEYER

Portland Merchant Home After Extensive Trip.

MANY SECTORS VISITED

Interest in Business Conditions Paramount in Every Part of Country, He Finds.

Deflation of inflated values must run its course before there possibly can be any noticeable upturn in business conditions, and when the bottom is reached money will appear as though it had hopped out of the ground, according to Fred G. Meyer, president of Fred Meyer, Inc., holding company for the Meyer's markets, upon his return to Portland yesterday from a month's tour of the country.

"Business in Portland is as good as any place," Mr. Meyer said. "Those cities that specialized in the production of luxuries are the hardest hit. People here are more conservative and less inclined to speculate. Speculation in all lines with the resultant inflation of values brought on the present economic crisis. We are now going through the slow, but sane, process of readjustment. No one can tell when or where it will end."

Business Data in Demand.

Mr. Meyer, accompanied by Mrs. Meyer, swung south through California, then east through the southern states, north to New York and back to Portland. He was able to make

—Fisk studio photo.

MR. AND MRS. FRED G. MEYER

Who found on a tour of the country that business men were too busy readjusting their affairs to weep over the memory of prosperity as it existed in [illegible].

Eva Meyer seldom appeared in the press. This news report shows the two entrepreneurs in their mid-40s. Fred Meyer had not yet switched to the bow ties for which he became noted. **(Oregonian)**

Meyer discussed his trip with a newspaper reporter after his return. "He was able to make many deductions from observations, and he learned much concerning business conditions from conversation with merchants in the various cities he visited," the anonymous journalist reported. For his part, Meyer blamed the Depression on speculators and inflated values that arose from speculation. "We are now going through the slow, but sane, process of adjustment," he said. "No one knows where or when it will end." [31] Studio portraits of Fred and Eva Meyer accompanied the article; he had not yet adopted the bow-ties that would become virtually a trademark.

The tumultuous year of 1933 was the last for the vibrant, municipally-operated public market on Yamhill Street. Since 1927, city officials had been trying to figure ways to relieve the human and automobile traffic on the congested street. Their answer, ultimately, was a massive, 620-foot-long reinforced concrete building of four stories and rooftop parking for automobiles. The new Portland Public Market, which opened for business in mid-December, 1933, was located between the Willamette River and Front Avenue between the Hawthorne and Morrison Bridges. From its announcement in 1927 until its grand opening, plans for locating and financing the huge building sparked endless controversy including lawsuits and allegations of bribery.[32] One key question was whether shoppers would cross busy Front Avenue to get to the new market, even with its two-floors of parking. The project likely prompted discussions between Fred Meyer, who opposed it, and his personal lawyer, the successful Daniel J. Malarkey, who represented the private developers who built it. Days after the new building opened, Fred Meyer Inc. was one 27 Yamhill Street retailers, including some like Mayo & Hasson Fruit Co. who had been there nearly 20 years, who published an advertisement titled, "NOTICE TO THE PUBLIC: We Are Not Moving."[33]

The new market building was wonderful in many ways. Prominent Portland architect Ellis Lawrence designed it in a muscular Art Moderne style with two square spires poking from its roof. The structure was built in a mere five months, with two sets of workers toiling 16 hours per day. The contractor noted that if the structure stood vertically instead of horizontally, it would rise 50 stories.[34] Inside, the main floor held room for as many as 200 food vendors. A mezzanine offered personal services such barbers, beauticians, a dentist and an optician. An elevator carried passengers and purchases to the upper two floors of parking. In all, it was the largest public market in the United States.

Crowds flocked to the new building at the outset, but the success was short-lived. As some had predicted, Front Avenue proved to be a barrier for shoppers downtown. And as Fred Meyer was proving with his successful Hollywood Market, many Portlanders were willing to do their shopping away from the downtown core. Development that was once planned to accompany the new market never materialized. The big concrete building didn't attract the excitement of the open storefronts and canvas covered stalls of the old Yamhill Street scene. "While the Portland Public Market may have attracted the curious, it never attracted the loyal customer," an historian concluded later. [35] The market closed in 1942. The U.S. Navy rented it the following year for the remainder of World War II. The *Oregon Journal* newspaper bought the building in 1946 for its newsroom and printing plant; the rooftop also became the landing site of the Journal's pioneering newsroom helicopter until it crashed on a Portland hillside late in 1947.[36] The *Journal* moved out in 1961. In1964 the City of Portland acquired the building and eventually demolished it to make way for Tom McCall Waterfront Park.

Fred Meyer's ability to recognize talent and evaluate personalities quickly paid him a major dividend in the early 1930s. A traveling saleswoman for Lever Brothers was making a pitch about cosmetics to a Fred Meyer buyer when the patriarch happened to hear a portion of her presentation. Impressed by her slightly unusual accent and speaking ability, Meyer hired Anola "Peter" Mudie to work as a consumer representative. In 1933, Meyer started buying a 15-minute slot on KOIN radio for "Fred Meyer Consumer News," presented by Peter Mudie, six days per week – for most of the next 31 years. Her distinctive nickname came from a goose that had tormented her as a child outside the family home in Ferndale, Washington. Mudie spent four hours a day preparing the shows, which might include interviews with farmers or food processors, reports on her tests of new kitchen equipment, updates on seasonal produce and interesting recipes. Of course, she mentioned the latest specials at Fred Meyer stores.

"She was better known than Fred Meyer," recalled Jack Crocker, who rose through the ranks to company president in 1968. If her program had been merely a long infomercial, listeners eventually would have changed stations. But that wasn't Mudie's approach. "She never felt she was just out there selling merchandise," Crocker said. "She was out there trying to help the customer with what to buy, when to buy it. For example, if corn on the cob had just come in from the field, she would tell them so. She might tell them not to buy something, too. She was totally independent. There was no obligation to anyone in the company."[37] Mudie wrote and spoke clearly, values dear to Fred Meyer. "She could give you the flavor of something over the air until you could taste it," said Dale Warman, who was working his way up from a part-time college student to vice president and later marketing director. "And she had credibility, like she was God in the consumer's mind."[38]

Mudie struggled for years with glaucoma and other eye difficulties that severely restricted her eyesight after her first thirteen years on the air. She would write inch-tall letters on legal pads as she prepared her scripts. After she quit broadcasting in 1964, Mudie continued working for Fred Meyer one day a week in the company test kitchen for another 20 years, to within a year of her death at age 90. "Fred Meyer accepted her word if she questioned the quality of anything being sold," said Helen Mason, who had worked with Mudie as a sales promotion assistant. "Hers was the final word. He considered her to be a central part of his success." [39]

By 1934, Meyer likely already had plans to expand his successful Hollywood store. In October that year, working with broker David Simpson, he bought the full block on which it sat for $75,000.[40] As he would several times again, Meyer put the store property in the name of a separate corporation that leased the land back to Fred Meyer Inc. The underlying real estate company – there eventually would be as many as nine – secured loans for the land purchases with long-term leases from Fred Meyer Inc., the "operating" company. This system allowed Meyer to keep long-term debt off the books of Fred Meyer Inc. when he sought financing for inventory or new construction.[41] It also was a tool Meyer used to create wealth for his stepson, Earle A. Chiles, who was given minority stock in all the real estate companies. But after Fred Meyer's death, the strategy led to lengthy and costly litigation over the value of the real estate companies when Fred Meyer Inc. was ultimately sold and whether those companies had been paid reasonable rents over the decades. The prolonged litigation would mark the final break between the company and the widow of Earle A. Chiles, Virginia Hughes Chiles, and their son, Earle Meyer Chiles.

As the Great Depression limped into its fifth year with no end in sight, Fred Meyer Inc. was one of the few Portland companies expanding in the face of hard times. A 17-year old high school junior named Gretchen C. Davis landed a job in the bakery department of the Fifth and Yamhill store after being turned down by all the city's larger department stores. Seven decades later, she still remembered the elements of her training. "We were taught how to address a customer, suggest additional merchandise, box a cake, the correct bag for a one-pound loaf of bread, and that the customer was always right." There was one special rule about personal appearances for women in the bakery department, as well. "We were warned not to wear red nail polish, as Mr. Meyer did not like to see a red finger stuck in a coconut cake."[42] No detail was too small for Fred Meyer.

Meyer had new stores in mind and more food-production facilities in the offing, but he found himself back in court in 1935 accused of selling ice cream at too low a price. Early on, weak prices for agricultural products had been deemed a major cause of the Depression. Congress and most states, including Oregon, responded with agricultural adjustment acts intended to stabilize prices to farmers. The Oregon attorney general sued Fred Meyer Inc. for selling ice cream at 29 cents per quart, in violation of a 40-cent minimum price set in a marketing agreement established by an ice cream area committee set up under the state law. The penalty was a $500 fine for each day of violation. The dispute had first arisen soon after the Feb. 1, 1934, introduction of the state-imposed minimum price, when Meyer was selling ice cream for 25 cents per quart.

In talks with the county district attorney, Meyer's lawyer, George W. Mead, a partner of Dan Malarkey, contended that the state price primarily benefited retailers and manufacturers. Of the 15-cent difference between Meyer's price and the state price, Mead said only three-quarters of a cent went to the farmer. He contended that the 40-cent price was unfair to consumers because it allowed too much profit to the manufacturer and retailer. Nevertheless, Mead agreed that Fred Meyer would sell temporarily at the 40-cent price while considering its options.[43] The state filed suit against Meyer in 1935 after Meyer had reverted to a 29 cent price.[44]

Two of Dan Malarkey's law partners, Mead and Robert Sabin Jr., convinced a Multnomah County Circuit judge to dismiss the case against Meyer. They argued that the membership of the ice cream committee was never adequately defined, and that the committee exceeded its powers. The lawyers contended that, at 29 cents per quart, farmers were receiving adequate support and the public was benefitting from the lower price.[45] Based on the federal model, the state committee needed to include a "substantial majority" of an industry, measured in dollars or units of output, to approve an agreement and submit it to the governor for approval. The Oregon Supreme Court, in a 5-to-1 vote agreed, ruling that the law gave "coercive and unrestrained powers to an indefinite and indeterminate group of persons." The court said the state law failed to fix any standards by which an adequately-defined committee might operate. "This leaves wholly to persons outside the legislature the power to determine whether there shall be a law at all, and if there is to be a law, what the terms of that law shall be."[46] It wasn't a difficult victory for the Meyer legal team, since courts in some other states had reached the same conclusion.

Fred Meyer, meanwhile, was pressing ahead with expansion plans, keeping an eye out for bargains created by companies that couldn't survive the hard times and creating his own private label. In the middle of the decade, he held a contest in which he asked employees to suggest a name for a private label that would be applied to products sold only in Fred Meyer stores. Chain stores such as Fred Meyer could negotiate with food processing companies to produce items bearing the retailer's own brand. If the chain could place high volume orders, these private label products could be sold at prices below national brands. Margaret Spencer, who worked with Mary Boyle in the women's clothing department, came up with the winning entry: MY-TE-FINE. Given that Margaret Spencer was married to Walt Spencer, the head of Meyer's grocery department, it is possible she was aware that her winning entry was surprisingly close to another trade name that had been use since 1918: My-T-Fine Pudding. Regardless, MY-TE-FINE was a label that Fred Meyer Inc. used for more than 50 years. At first, it was used on a wide variety of products, including bacon, razor blades, house paint, and candy bars, as well as on canned fruits and vegetables. Over time, it became limited to canned foods. The company took its brand seriously, and tested all products in its own test kitchen before deciding which ones met the company's quality standards. Ever the merchandiser, Meyer used the slogan whenever he could in public. Customers who asked Meyer the obligatory, "How are you?" at store openings, invariably got "MY-TE-FINE" as their answer.

The year that Fred Meyer turned 50, 1936, was a busy one at Fred Meyer Inc., which added three stores and a new candy-making and baking plant. In January, 1936, Meyer opened a small outlet at Southwest Fourth Avenue and Morrison Street in the ground floor of the Rosenblatt Building. It offered a mere 1,800 square feet on the ground floor, plus a mezzanine seating up to 54 at a fountain-lunch operated by an independent firm. The shop offered remedies, prescriptions, tobacco and candy. [47] Just two months later, he added his first Hawthorne Boulevard store at 3610 Southeast Hawthorne, in a somewhat Mediterranean-looking brick building with decorative red roof tile accents. The building had been a neighborhood grocery before falling vacant. With fewer than 9,000 square feet, it was just a fraction of what Meyer would build later at Southeast 39th and Hawthorne. The first Hawthorne building, which survived into the first decades of the 21st Century as a popular restaurant, opened with groceries, a delicatessen and a fresh fruit section managed by Corno's Fruit Co. [48]

The first Hawthorne store at Southeast 36th Avenue was a mere fraction of the size of the store with rooftop parking that followed several years later on the north side of the street. (OHS Neg. 005936)

In September, Meyer bought the manufacturing equipment of the Vogan Candy Co., which had fallen into the hands of creditors after nearly 20 years of operations. Eva Meyer already was running a smaller candy kitchen in the Brown Building downtown, and Meyer merged that with the new equipment at a separate location at Southeast 11th Avenue and Hawthorne Boulevard, leaving his wife in charge. When a manager noted years later that the company made little if any money from its Fifth Avenue private-label candies, Fred Meyer replied, "But Mrs. Meyer likes candy and she likes the candy kitchen." [49] The candy kitchen remained.

Meyer's final addition, late in 1936, was a somewhat larger existing building that made a much bigger public splash when it opened. Working again with broker Simpson, Meyer leased a building at the southeast corner of Northeast Martin Luther King Boulevard (Union Avenue at the time) and Killingsworth Street. It had housed the Marquardt Bros. Drug Store and Wm. E. Fleming Dry Goods before being remodeled into what Meyer called his Walnut Park store because of its proximity to the Walnut Park Theater. Like the first Hawthorne store, Walnut Park eventually would be replaced with a much larger version. The first Walnut Park store comprised 11,000 square feet. For its grand opening in November, 1936, Meyer erected two large circus tents on an adjacent empty lot. Over the course of six days, eight hours per day, visitors under the tents were treated to music, vaudeville performances, meat-cutting demonstrations, cooking classes with Peter Mudie, and appearances by radio celebrities. The first day drew a crowd estimated at 20,000.[50] Meyer's grandest store opening yet was a harbinger of celebrations to come. "He used to tell me, 'Ray, people like crowds. Whatever it takes to get a crowd, get it,'" recalled Chirgwin, who had worked his way into Meyer's managerial ranks. [51] For several years, Walnut Park was the most successful store in the Meyer chain, even when it was surpassed in size by others. Factors contributing to its success were its proximity to Vancouver, Washington, and Washington state's decision in 1935 to institute a sales tax; Many Washington state residents were willing to drive into Portland to avoid the tax on goods they purchased.

Soon after it opened, the Walnut Park store was decorated for the Christmas season, 1936. Meyer liked big signs. (OHS Neg. 005937)

With the addition of his stores at Sixth Avenue and on Morrison Street, Fred Meyer now flanked the big downtown Meier & Frank department store on three sides. Meyer's tiny outlets added up to hardly a tenth of the square footage in the landmark downtown department store, but the big store and its feisty upstart waged intense competition. Although Meier & Frank did not carry a full line of groceries to match the Fred Meyer store at Fifth and Yamhill, it offered many food items, a delicatessen, cosmetics and remedies, as did Fred Meyer. As Fred Meyer slowly expanded into housewares and men's and women's clothes and even into large appliances, the sources of competitive conflict mounted.

"So our real competition was Meier & Frank," recalled Killoran, who in the late 1930s was breaking in as Fred Meyer's advertising manager. "They tried to match everything we did price-wise and vice versa. We'd run an item that was particularly hot—by hot I mean the price was low, maybe our cost or below–to get traffic in the stores. They'd send their employees over and buy as many of them as they could and we do the same thing to them. It was a real hot and heavy competitive situation."[52] Killoran recalled one incident when Meyer obtained a substantial quantity of men's Arrow shirts at a large discount from a Midwestern retailer that was quitting business. Arrow's primary customer in Portland was Meier & Frank, and both the big Portland department store and the Arrow Shirt Co. were irritated to see Fred Meyer selling "bootlegged" merchandise that he could not acquire through customary channels. Killoran said Arrow sent employees to Portland to join those from Meier & Frank in buying Fred Meyer's Arrow shirts, one at a time. "It took them days to buy, but our customers got a lot of them in the meantime."[53]

Large-volume buyers such as Meier & Frank wangled for advantages in negotiating with suppliers. In time, Fred Meyer's wholesale buyers became masters of the art as the Fred Meyer chain grew in retailing influence. But Fred Meyer was the underdog to Meier & Frank in the Depression. "They tried to keep us from getting merchandise," Killoran said. "They'd tell whoever the manufacturer was that if they sold to Fred Meyer, they'd get kicked out of the Meier & Frank store. That was pretty important. Even though they had only one store their volume was very, very large compared to ours or anyone else's. So we had our troubles."[54]

Fred and Eva Meyer were doing well for themselves, however. The continuing Depression had focused public and official attention on salaries for top executives as disclosed in some high-profile lawsuits. In 1934, the U.S. Senate instructed Treasury Secretary Henry Morgenthau to conduct a survey of salaries paid to executives of publicly-held corporations and private businesses engaged in interstate commerce.[55] When Morgenthau in 1936 issued results from Oregon, the list showed Fred Meyer at $37,500 and Eva Meyer at $22,500. The only higher-salaried person on the list was H.A. Green, president of Doernbecher Manufacturing Co., at $41,187. Other notables included: T.H. Banfield, president of the Iron Fireman Manufacturing Co., $30,000; Franklin T.

Griffith, president of Portland General Electric Co., $21,392; P.T. Jackson, publisher of the *Oregon Journal* newspaper, then the city's largest, $28,730; and J.C. Ainsworth, chairman of U.S. National Bank of Portland, $17,340.[56] Given that few women in the era held high-paying jobs, it is likely that Fred and Eva Meyer were the highest-paid working couple in Oregon. Their combined income of $60,000 would have the buying power of $1,042,000 in 2013, according to a U.S. Department of Labor inflation calculator.[57]

Fred Meyer had a vacancy to fill in September 1937. His advertising manager, Mel Smith, quit for health reasons. Killoran had been attending night classes in business and advertising at the recommendation of Earle A. Chiles. Meyer invited Killoran to join him one weekend at Fred and Eva Meyer's personal retreat located on 8.5 acres above the Salmon River, just across the Arrah Wanna Bridge near Wemme. The wooded site became known as Eva's Eden because she liked it so much and used it to indulge her interest in gardening and flowers. A full-time gardener was kept on staff. The Meyers established a pattern of leaving Portland at noon on Saturdays for Eva's Eden and returning at noon on Mondays. The acreage included a few small cabins and a shingled main house with gables, fireplace and knotty pine paneling. The main house resembled a country hunting lodge more than a mountain cabin. The Meyers eventually added a swimming pool, and used Eva's Eden for staff meetings and company picnics. It was there that Meyer offered, and Killoran accepted, the job as advertising manager.

Fred Meyer ran its advertisements in Portland newspapers on Tuesdays and Fridays. After Killoran's first week on the job, Fred Meyer invited him to attend his first managers' meeting. Meyer assured him it would be a low-key affair. Killoran was surprised, then, when Meyer launched into what Killoran remembered as a five-hour criticism of his first ads. "He could be kind of vicious and rough sometimes," Killoran said. "You know, 'Nobody but a damn fool would make that kind of remark,' sort of thing." By the time the meeting ended, Killoran was soaked in perspiration. On his way out, Meyer told him, "There is nothing personal in this." Fred Meyer wanted things done his way. Killoran's initiation to the executive meetings left him with no doubt about who ran Fred Meyer Inc.

"From then on, for at least a year, every ad we ran he criticized," Killoran said. When Meyer failed to object to an advertisement, Killoran took it as a compliment.[58] Advertising was essential to successful operations. Meier & Frank, Safeway, Piggly Wiggly, and the Portland Public Market, among others, all ran large, regular ads to entice grocery shoppers. Meyer preferred the afternoon *Oregon Journal* as his primary advertising vehicle. It was a logical choice, since in the 1930s the afternoon paper boasted a larger circulation than the morning *Oregonian,* where Meyer ran smaller ads. Killoran said Meyer once mentioned another reason for disliking the *Oregonian*: it had run an article that Meyer didn't like about one of his stores. It might have been a small item published in 1934 in which the newspaper reported Meyer paying a $10 fine in *Portland Municipal Court* after an inspector found that a refrigerator temperature exceeded a 50 degree limit for storing grade-A milk.[59] He also might not have liked articles the same year when state inspectors found his ice cream fell short of state regulations on butterfat.[60] While his lawyers fought the butterfat matter in court, Meyer showed his disdain for the fuss. He renamed the product "Hocus Pocus Sub-Standard Ice Cream," and kept selling it. Later, he gave it the more felicitous name, "Hocus Pocus Frozen Dessert." The company carried Hocus Pocus for some 25 years. Regardless, Meyer took great pride in his advertisements and the prices they listed. As a future Fred Meyer Inc. president once recalled, "He said during the Depression when he walked along Yamhill Street, if they weren't saying , 'There goes Fred Meyer, that son of a bitch,' he knew he wasn't running hot enough ads."[61]

Meyer's next expansion plan led to a rare defeat. Working under the corporate name of Moreland Co., he had gradually acquired a narrow strip of approximately 10 acres extending 2,200 feet along Southeast McLoughlin Boulevard between Southeast Reedway Street and Bybee Boulevard. In 1938, he sought a zone change from a residential designation to commercial/light industrial. Meyer proposed a $560,000 development that would include a one-story shopping center, buffered from the residential Westmoreland neighborhood by 80 new houses. The store would include a tea room at the southern edge, facing into Crystal Springs Creek. Meyer already had contributed to a city-approved project that added a south-bound connection from the heavily-traveled McLoughlin Boulevard for traffic heading westbound on Bybee Boulevard; Meyer paid $10,000 for materials and the city received $33,900 in labor costs from the federal Works Progress Administration.[62]

Notable among the neighborhood residents who opposed Meyer's plan were E.C. Sammons, a young businessman on his way to becoming president of U.S. National Bank, and Estes Snedecor, a well-respected U.S. Bankruptcy Court judge. Residents feared commercial intrusion into their single-family home neighborhoods on both sides of McLoughlin. Other opposition came from R.H. Baldock, the state's highway engineer, who worried that additional access points on and off McLoughlin would slow traffic on that heavily-used arterial. A three-member committee of the City Planning Commission suggested a compromise that was acceptable to Meyer, but the full commission rejected the compromise on a 5-to-3 vote.[63] The commission's decision was affirmed later by the Portland City Council. Meyer, who never gave up easily, made additional attempts to rezone the land in 1950 and again in 1960, without success. He tangled with the same opponents both times and made a rare public demonstration of the Meyer temper his executives often saw in their closed meetings. Fred Meyer didn't like losing.

That Meyer was firmly in charge of the company and didn't want to be told what to do also became apparent in a bizarre episode late in the 1930s known only to three people. They were Ray Chirgwin, who had become food manager at the Sixth Avenue store, Chirgwin's boss, Bud Sturgess, and Meyer. Inventory was received into the Sixth Avenue store via an elevator under the public sidewalk in front of the store. It was covered by a metal door upon which pedestrians walked when the elevator was not in use. Trucks delivering food and other merchandise parked at night on Sixth Avenue and unloaded goods into the elevator. Because the trucks ran their diesel motors while they were stopped for unloading, fumes and particulates from the exhaust drifted into the elevator, down the shaft and into the basement where employees priced the items and prepared them for stocking shelves on the floors above. Chirgwin said the fumes made the basement unpleasant for the nighttime workers, and drifted into the sales floor above, which was not vented.

Chirgwin sent memos to Meyer suggesting that a ventilation system be added. Knowing that Meyer always wanted facts and details, Chirgwin consulted with engineers, found a potential solution and had identified costs. After he did not hear back from Meyer, he sent another memo, this one signed by all department heads who worked in the Brown Building. The memo with the signatures angered Meyer enough that he called in Sturgess and instructed him to fire Chirgwin. Sturgess suggested that the three of them meet. Meyer set the meeting for 8 p.m. the same day.

Meyer arrived a few minutes late, by Chirgwin's account, pointed his finger angrily at Chirgwin and said repeatedly, "What's your name? What's your name?" Chirgwin knew he didn't have to answer the question because Meyer knew full well who he was.

"Is your name Fred Meyer?" Meyer finally asked.

"No."

"I'm Fred Meyer. When I get a letter with more than one name on it, it's a petition. And nobody is going to petition Fred Meyer in his own business." According to Chirgwin's account– which is the only description of the episode– Meyer spoke angrily and mostly without interruption for six hours. Chirgwin said Sturgess left after two hours, having heard enough. At some point, Chirgwin's eyes fell on a lead paperweight on Meyer's desk with a base of about four square inches with a metal spindle protruding from the center. "I looked at that, and I thought of striking him with it," Chirgwin recalled years later. "He doesn't know how close (he came)...there would have been no Fred Meyer." Into the sixth hour, Meyer finally started slowing down. Chirgwin recalled him saying something about a man who had given up sex for business, but by then Chirgwin had quit paying attention. "And so at two o'clock, now he mellowed. I mean, he ran out of vindictiveness. He just couldn't think of anything more, I guess." The two men walked in the direction of Meyer's downtown apartment at 1410 S.W. Broadway, because Chirgwin's car happened to be parked nearby. [64] Chirgwin did not lose his job, but the ventilation was never installed.

Understandably, the incident made Chirgwin question Meyer's mental stability. There was some talk later that Meyer had suffered heart problems. "But for a period there in the late thirties he walked with a cane and he was high-strung and he was nervous," Chirgwin said. "And most of his employees stayed out of his way, and didn't go out of the way to make conversation with Mr. Meyer because normally you got lectured if you did." In a codicil to his will, signed in June, 1978, Meyer gave $15,000 to the State of Oregon for exclusive use of Dammasch State Hospital. The state mental hospital was named posthumously in 1955 for Portland physician and former state legislator F. H. Dammasch, who had lobbied successfully for its creation. Dr. Dammasch was one of several doctors who treated Meyer over the years, and close Meyer associates remembered Meyer referring to Dammasch as being his favorite of the many doctors he saw in his long life. Whether the doctor-patient relationship between Meyer and Dr. Dammasch involved mental counseling or therapy is not known. It is also possible that Meyer recognized his own problem and worked through it without help. Part of his Rosicrucian beliefs, in simplest terms, suggested that the mind could prevail over health problems. "If you had a cold and your nose was dripping and running, that was fantasy to him," Killoran said of Meyer. "You didn't really have a cold. You just thought you did. That particular factor gave him an unusual drive."[65]

With the Westmoreland setback recently behind him, Meyer announced his biggest project yet in February 1939. In a deal negotiated by David Simpson, Meyer purchased a failed Packard automobile dealership on West Burnside between Northwest 20th Avenue and 20th Place. The total floor space would cover 50,000 square feet, more than the equivalent of an entire city block, and several times the size of his pioneering "suburban" site at Hollywood. Another 20,000 square feet would be devoted to parking. The west end of the building would include a service station and automobile accessories department. The sloping site posed a challenge for the Claussen & Claussen architecture firm to convert the structure into a single shopping venue, since the former car dealership offered three entrances at differing elevations along Burnside. Meyer decided to call it the Stadium store given its proximity to Multnomah Stadium, the big private ballpark owned and operated by the Multnomah Athletic Club.

In 1939, the long-running Great Depression was entering its tenth year. For public consumption, Meyer said he decided to move ahead with the Stadium project in response to the inaugural speech of Oregon's new governor, Charles Sprague, who urged businesses to press ahead rather than wait for the economic climate to improve.[66] Privately, the decision was based more on Meyer's analysis of traffic patterns and his desire to reach clientele in the affluent West Hills neighborhoods. He added more upscale items in the grocery and delicatessen sections with wealthier patrons in mind.[67]

Meyer hoped to have the new store finished by June, but construction didn't begin until mid-September and wasn't completed until early December. During the renovation, Meyer fell through a rotten board in a ramp and suffered a leg injury serious enough to make him use a cane. One of the innovations at the Stadium store was the presence of air conditioning, a first in the Fred Meyer chain. Meyer walked through the store with his food manager, Chirgwin, inspecting the 20 various departments under one roof. Innovations included a version of a self-service produce department Meyer had seen in a Philadelphia market and stalls for up to 30 non-Meyer vendors.[68] Meyer had turned 53 when the Stadium store was finished. He would live to see it dramatically expanded and remodeled at least twice. Yet for 1939, the new store was remarkable, and Meyer was pleased with what he saw. "Ray, what do you think of all of this?" Meyer said. "Isn't this something?"

Chirgwin replied, "It's a nice market, Mr. Meyer, and at least it has fresh air." The words were out of Chirgwin's mouth before he realized he didn't want to remind Meyer about the ventilation squabble and Meyer's long harangue at Sixth Avenue. But no outburst ensued. "And then he just turned and shook his head and walked away," Chirgwin recalled. "That was it.""[69]

The grand opening was less elaborate than the Walnut Park extravaganza. There were balloons and clowns for the kids, and appearances by local political dignitaries. Mayor Joseph K. Carson scissored a big ribbon, flanked by a beaming Eva Meyer and a fedora-topped Fred Meyer. Crowds were heavy throughout the day, even without the circus tents and special attractions offered at Walnut Park. "We've never had a bigger or more successful opening," Fred Meyer said late in the day. The new store added about 150 jobs, bringing total company employment to nearly 1,000.[70]

The Stadium store was still in its early weeks when Chirgwin got a call at home late at night from an assistant. "Ray, we're closing down the store," the assistant said. "We're walking out, the whole gang." Chirgwin ordered him not to close. The assistant said, "Well, Mr. Meyer came in here raving, and he had this cane, and he went down the aisle and he pulled all the cans off the top shelf, let them fall on the floor. And then he called us all dummies." What irritated Meyer was the fact that the cans were stacked higher than many female customers could reach easily. Knocking them off was his way of instructing how he wanted the shelves stocked. The Stadium incident became a well-known tale at Fred Meyer Inc. "Our existence with Fred Meyer was all the same," Chirgwin said years later. "We did our best we could do and took our chewings. And the pattern fell to everybody that worked for him. There isn't anybody who worked for him that can say that he was a gentle old man."[71]

New West Side Store Building to Rise

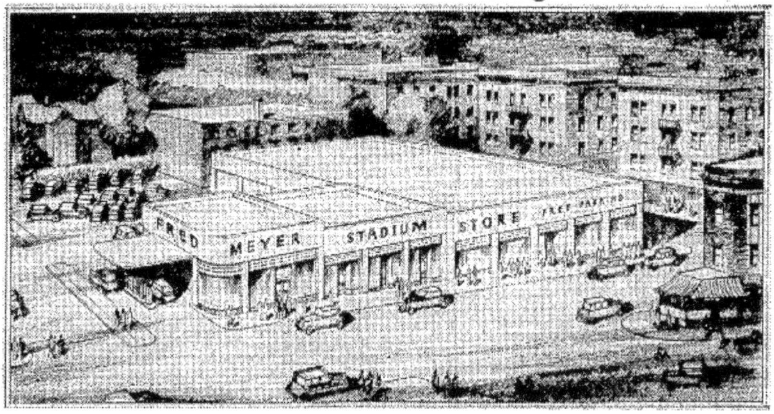

Designed by Claussen & Claussen, local architects, this modern store building will be erected at Northwest Twentieth avenue and Burnside street for Fred Meyer, who has purchased the site from Fred E. Taylor through David B. Simpson of Norris, Beggs & Simpson.

The original Stadium store was cobbled together in 1939 from existing buildings. Fred Meyer already was thinking about erecting his own new buildings, but World War II intervened. (Oregonian)

The final year of the decade brought a new employee to the higher ranks of the Fred Meyer fold who would play a key role for more than 30 years. Herbert Retzlaff was the son of a German military engineering officer who had retired before World War I. Retzlaff had once hoped to become an architect, but he transferred his professional interests to earning a business degree in Munich during the high-inflation years after the First World War. Retzlaff had looked for jobs in Italy and South Africa when a friend of his family said she knew the general manager of Portland Gas & Coke Co., Hilmar Pabst. Retzlaff arrived in Portland in 1924 at age 21. For the next 15 years he worked for Portland Gas & Coke on two different occasions, moved to San Francisco, returned to Portland, worked for a steamship company and became a certified public accountant. As a CPA, he worked on some temporary projects at Fred Meyer Inc., and then found himself recruited by Leonard Roberts, Fred Meyer's controller, who was planning to leave town. Retzlaff thought working for an aggressive company like Fred Meyer would be more interesting than spending the rest of his life looking at an endless array of corporate financial records. Retzlaff joined Fred Meyer Inc. full-time in 1939.

Retzlaff's job put him in daily contact with Fred Meyer. It was a relationship that proved both challenging and stimulating for Retzlaff. "Eventually we became very close and, in fact, I was his right hand man. I had to be because he had taken courses in accounting and somebody said he knew just enough accounting to be dangerous. He had his own ideas of what you could do and how you could juggle the figures but it wasn't always kosher." Meyer and Retzlaff had their differences over the years, and once Retzlaff banged his hand on the table and announced that he was quitting when Meyer insisted on a tax strategy that Retzlaff contended was illegal. But when Retzlaff showed up the next day, it was as if nothing had happened. "He was sitting at his desk and I walked right by to my desk. He saw me. I saw him and none of us ever said another word about that incident."[72]

During his decades with the company, Retzlaff was impressed continually by Meyer's knowledge, his ability to learn and his memory. "He had an extremely good memory and he was extremely well -read. He read constantly. He went to night school. He took accounting courses, business administration courses. He took courses, I guess, in food preparation and he retained what he learned or read. He liked Shakespeare and Goethe." One of Meyer's favorite quotations was from

Goethe: "Are you in earnest? Seize this very minute; What you can do, or dream you can do, begin it; Boldness has genius, power and magic in it." Goethe may have best captured Meyer's personal approach to running Fred Meyer Inc.

---

[1] Chirgwin , Ray, OHS sound recording 1303, July 24, 1989.
[2] *Ibid.*
[3] *Oregonian,* Jan. 18, 1931, p. 2.
[4] *Ibid,* Jan. 8, 1918, p. 11.
[5] Robertson, Oran, OHS sound recording 1312, Oct. 25, 1989.
[6] Lacher, Gary, and Stone, Steve, *Theatres of Portland,* Arcadia Publishing, 2009, p. 109.
[7] Green, Cyril, OHS sound recording 1307, Feb. 27, 1989.
[8] *Oregonian,* May 3, 1931, p. 23.
[9] *Ibid,* Sept. 5, 1978, p. B5.
[10] *Ibid,* June 28, 1931, p. 2.
[11] MacColl , E. Kimbark, one-page typed notes of interview with Fred Meyer, Feb. 22, 1978, found in E. Kimbark MacColl Papers 1891-2006, Box 14, Portland State University Library Special Collections.
[12] See *Grand Rapids Press,* Nov. 25, 2011, and Vance, Sandra S., and Scott, Roy V., *Wal-Mart: A History of Sam Walton's Retail Phenomenon,* Twayne Publishers, 1994, p. 124.
[13] McFadyen, Tevere, *The Rise of the Supermarket,* American Heritage Magazine, vol. 236, issue 6, 1985.
[14] Retzlaff, Herbert, oral history interview, Oregon Historical Society, sound recording 1311, Feb. 22, 1989.
[15] Robertso , *op cit.* Dec. 20, 1988.
[16] Chirgwin, *op cit.*
[17] Killoran , Rollin, OHS sound recording 1308, Sept. 22, 1988.
[18] *Meyer Inc. v. Keasey,* 145 Or 266 (1933), 274.
[19] *Fred Meyer Inc. v. Continental Baking, et al.,* Multnomah County Circuit Court no. 110523, 1933. While this lawsuit is listed in the plaintiff-defendant index for 1933, the microfilm roll containing the case file was reported "missing" in May, 2013.
[20] *Oregonian,* Aug. 3, 1933, p. 4.
[21] *Oregonian,* Feb. 11, 1934, p 3.
[22] *Ibid*, Feb. 18, 1934, p. 11.
[23] Killoran , *op.cit,* Nov. 3, 1988.
[24] *Ibid,* July 30, 1933, p.2.
[25] Newkirk, Lamar, interview with Fred Meyer for Time Magazine, Sept. 9, 1953, found in OHS Fred Meyer Collection 199, OSD 2/6.
[26] *Ibid,* Nov. 4, 1933, p. 4.
[27] *Ibid,*Sept. 7, 1978, p. 1.
[28] *Ibid,* Feb. 12, 1933.

---

[29] Robertson, *op cit.* Feb. 2, 1989.
[30] Killoran, *op cit.*
[31] *Oregonian,* Feb. 2, 1933, p. 12.
[32] MacColl , Kimbark E., *The Growth of a City,* Georgian Press, 1979, pps. 488-99.
[33] *Oregonian,* Dec. 23, 1933, p. 4.
[34] *Ibid.,* Dec. 15, 1933, p.20.
[35] Eigo, George, A Market for the City: The History of Public Markets in Portland, Oregon Historical Society, 2002, p. 21.

[36] Jackson, C.S. and Stein, Joe, *The Newsroom Dragonfly,* Oregon Journal, 1947.
[37] Crocker, Jack, OHS sound recording 1304, June 13, 1989.
[38] Warman, Dale, OHS sound recording 1315, April 27, 1989.
[39] *Oregonian,* March 9, 1985, p. C4.
[40] *Ibid,* Oct, 21, 1934, p. 20.
[41] Retzlaff, *op cit.*
[42] This recollection was received by Fred Meyer Inc. in 2007 in response to a public request for memories about the company. It is in the Fred Meyer Collection 199, box 35, folder 11, OHS.
[43] *Oregonian,* Feb. 16, 1934, p. 10.
[44] *Ibid,* June 12, 1935, p. 5.
[45] *Ibid,* June 29, 1935, p. 12.
[46] *Van Winkle v. Fred Meyer Inc.*, 151 Or 455 (1935).
[47] *Oregonian,* Jan. 19, 1936, p. 17.
[48] *Ibid,* March 1, 1936, p. 8.
[49] Crocker, *op cit.*
[50] *Ibid,* Nov. 19, 1936.
[51] Chirgwin, *op cit.*
[52] Killoran, *op cit.*
[53] *Ibid.*
[54] *Ibid.*
[55] Mullane, Joy Sabino, *Perfect Storms: Congressional Regulation of Executive Compensation*, 57 Villanova Law Review 589, 2012.
[56] *Oregonian,* March 31, 1936, p. 2.
[57] U.S. Department of Labor, Bureau of Labor Statistics, accessed at www.bls.gov/data/**inflation_calculator**.htm
[58] Killoran , *op cit.*
[59] *Oregonian,* April 13, 1934, p. 11.
[60] *Ibid,* Aug. 8, 1934.
[61] Green, Cyril K., OHS sound recording 1307, March 15, 1989.
[62] *Oregonian,* Dec. 14, 1939, p. 1.
[63] *Ibid,* July 16, 1938, p. 12.
[64] Chirgwin , *op cit.*
[65] Killoran , *op cit.*
[66] *Oregonian,* Feb. 5, 1939, sec. 2, p. 1.
[67] Chirgwin , *op cit.*

[68] *Oregonian,* Dec. 3, 1939, p. 16.
[69] Chirgwin , *op cit.*.
[70] *Oregonian,* Dec. 10, 1939, p. 18.
[71] Chirgwin , *op cit.*
[72] Retzlaff , *op cit.,* Feb. 15, 1989.

CHAPTER FIVE

Fast Lane to the Rooftop

If there was any doubt in Fred Meyer's mind about the risks, in 1939, of opening his largest store to date at the Stadium location, the store's sales answered them. He was confident about his decisions when he made them because he had weighed all the facts he could muster. "We gamble it's going to be a success because everything is a gamble," he once said. "If you wanted to walk across this street, you're going to gamble that you get to the other side. But you look both ways first, don't you?"[1] As the new decade opened, Meyer, now approaching his middle 50s, was on the cusp of perfecting the one-stop shopping formula. World War II slowed his growth but not his planning.

Fred and Eva Meyer took a two-week driving trip early in 1940 to Florida, then up the East Coast before circling back to Portland. Of course, they spent much of the trip looking at other retailers for business ideas. In Florida the Meyers hit an unusual February freeze that seriously damaged the state's famous citrus fruits. "We went to Florida for the winter – and we got it," Fred Meyer joked.[2] He also wired back to his office instructing his buyers to stock up on oranges and lemons while they could. "So we made money on the boss's trip," said Glen Day, who had advanced from his early days at the Alderway laundry to serve as Fred Meyer's personal assistant.[3]

The early months of the new decade brought some key personnel changes. In 1939, Rollin Killoran, the advertising manager, told Fred Meyer that he deserved a raise. Meyer did not agree. Killoran replied that Meyer was failing to account for the final principle of Harrington Emerson's book, *The Twelve Principles of Efficiency* – adequate reward for performance. Killoran said he would leave when Meyer found a replacement. Meyer nodded. And then he quietly did nothing about finding a new advertising manager. Nearly two years later, Killoran stopped waiting and quit. Killoran would become one of the few Meyer intimates to leave and come back later.

In the meantime, Ray Chirgwin, who had risen from stock boy to a food management position, decided to quit, too. He had suffered ulcers in the late 1930s but refused his doctor's recommendation to change jobs because jobs were scarce. He had become disenchanted with Meyer's abrasive behavior, including a time when Meyer once asked, "How much do you make? Now break your salary down to a second. How many seconds have we been standing here talking? That's what it's costing me."[4] In 1940, Chirgwin took over a small food wholesale business with a single truck. He wanted to see if he could use the techniques for motivating employees he had seen at Fred Meyer Inc. without resorting to Meyer's personal abrasiveness. When Ray's Food Service Inc. was sold in 1998, the company had 500 employees, customers in five states and annual sales of $80 million.[5]

Fred Meyer, meanwhile, announced plans in May 1940 to quadruple the size of his drug store at Southwest Fourth Avenue and Morrison Street.[6] He added a beauty parlor and a lunch room on the balcony and women's shoes in the basement. Six months later, with newspapers filled with news of massive German air attacks against London and several other major English cities, Meyer expanded on the carcass of a failed automobile dealership on five acres at Southeast 82nd Avenue and Foster Road and opened a Southeast center in November 1940. "It was a location that to many observers seemed hopeless," an *Oregon Journal* article noted later. [7] It lacked the presence of nearby affluent neighborhoods that bordered Meyer's Hollywood and Stadium stores. Meyer did not heavily promote the Southeast grand opening, but he did raise a large tent for a few days for demonstrations, music and appearances by two lion cubs that were on loan from Wenatchee, Washington.[8] Eva Meyer helped give away a pony. [9] The Foster Road store would grow larger in the future, like many other Meyer locations. In the late 1960s, it would play a key role in a subsequent burst of the Fred Meyer Inc. evolution.

As early as 1936, Meyer was thinking of erecting new buildings instead of remodeling older structures to implement his one-stop shopping ideas. The Claussen & Claussen architecture firm drew plans that year for a new Hollywood store that featured roof-top parking, an idea that Meyer had borrowed from the Portland Public Market downtown. The new Hollywood store wouldn't be built for another 13 years, but it looked surprisingly like the 1936 drawing.[10] By early 1941, Meyer concluded that his first self-service remedies store in the Alderway Building was too small for efficient operations, and he unceremoniously closed it after nearly 12 years.[11] Meyer's inability to build during World War II did not prevent him from expanding, however. In 1943, he took over a grocery building and bakery operated by E. Ray Wilson at Southeast Stark and 80th Avenue and called it his Montavilla store. It existed until 1961, when it was replaced by a new, larger one-stop shopping center on Northeast Glisan Street. Meyer in 1943 also leased from the Housing Authority of Portland a new building at North Willis and Chautauqua Boulevards, intended to serve the war housing projects in North Portland. The Columbia store survived until 1957, when it was replaced by a new, larger shopping center on North Lombard Street.

The war years provided continuing challenges for staffing the Meyer enterprise, which now needed more than 1,000 employees for its seven-day-per-week operations. Meyer advertised continually in the help-wanted ads, often looking for women to fill jobs once held by men who had been absorbed by the military. One such request was for "butcherettes," a word coined by Meyer for women interested in work-

Plans for a new Hollywood store in 1936 showed Meyer's first interest in roof-top parking, an idea likely inspired by the Portland Public Market. When ultimately erected, the building showed slight differences from this plan. **(Oregonian)**

ing in his retail meat departments.[12] His ads stressed possibilities of working in stores close to the worker's home, a definite advantage during an era of gasoline rationing. Meyer's ads also tersely spelled out opportunities for advancement from entry-level jobs, a long-standing Meyer policy that had served him well. "Here's how it works," one ad explained. "You start as a sales or stock clerk; progress according to your ability to section head, manager, supervisor or merchandiser."[13] One title was noticeably missing from that list: store manager. In his continual quest to improve efficiency and cut costs, Fred Meyer had decided by the late 1930s that he didn't need store managers.

The reason was that a Fred Meyer Inc. store manager in a multi-department store couldn't know all the operational details and inventory in a store with 20 or more departments. So when a buyer from the main office visited a store to gather information about what was selling or not selling, the store manager knew less than the department head running that department. "Theoretically you'd have every buyer, because they were supervisors, talking to the store manager," said Cyril Green, who started as a stock boy and eventually rose to company president. "But functionally, they didn't do that. They went down and talked to the people who were handling their merchandise." As a result, "I think they found the job redundant and they got rid of it."[14] Meyer operated the rest of his life without store managers. Instead, he had a "chairman" for each store who resolved conflicts with department managers and dealt with store-wide issues such as parking or security. But the title carried little weight – and little extra pay. The highest title listed in the Meyer hierarchy was "merchandiser." A merchandiser in charge of a certain category, such as produce or women's clothing or sporting goods, supervised department heads of those departments in Fred Meyer stores. Merchandisers and buyers worked in the Fred Meyer headquarters, and reported in periodic meetings to Meyer himself.

The rationing of staples such as sugar and shortening during the war years provided a continuing challenge for the Meyer bakeries. Glen Day had advanced from working as Fred Meyer's personal assistant to supervising a "mishmash" of services that ranged from bakeries to wine to the automobile service centers.[15] Then in his early 30s, Day was one of the company success stories whose promotions were based on reliability and accomplishment. After 1943, Day was overseeing bakeries at

Southeast Eleventh and Hawthorne and at the newly-acquired building at Montavilla. He bought turkey red wheat from Eastern Montana and ground it into flour. His bakers came up with the idea of using honey instead of sugar as a sweetener. The company called it Vita-Bee Bread, and its popularity made it a continuing success on store shelves. Day bought honey in 55-gallon drums and remembered bees circling the drums delivered to the loading dock.[16] The company also had a quota of 100-pound bags of sugar it received to sell to consumers; it hired teenagers to divide the sacks into two-pound packages that returned a better overall price.[17]

In 1944, the Portland Soroptimist Club, an association devoted to advancing opportunities for professional women, named Eva Meyer its woman of the year.[18] She had been a longstanding member and officer of the Portland chapter, which dated to 1929. "There were lots of rumors in those days about the fact that Mrs. Meyer ran the company," said Oran Robertson, who joined Fred Meyer Inc. the following year. The Soroptimist award may have reinforced that idea. "She did not. She was very much a part of the company, but she did not run the company, nor did she make the major decisions or give direction to the company."[19] By 1944, Eva and Fred Meyer had changed their residence, a decision that likely was largely Eva's. They moved into one of two penthouses atop the Envoy Apartments at 2336 Southwest Osage Street, then Portland's tallest and most stylish apartment buildings. The two-story penthouse had a living room with vaulted ceiling, parquet floors, plaster walls, a stairway with a wrought iron railing leading to a second floor and an exterior deck facing north,[20] where the Meyers could indulge their love of flowers and gardening to a limited extent. The building also was an easy walk to the Stadium Fred Meyer store, where Fred Meyer did most of his personal grocery shopping for the rest of his life.

During these years, the Fred Meyer corporate office was located on an upper floor at 633 Southwest Fourth Avenue. It was one large, open room, with Fred Meyer's desk surrounded by desks of Eva Meyer,

Herbert Retzlaff, Earle A. Chiles and other top officials. Fred Meyer wanted no class distinctions among employees, including himself. For morning coffee breaks, Fred and Eva Meyer usually walked around the corner to the Mannings Coffee Café on Yamhill Street. It is where they developed a lasting relationship with a young woman named Pauline Lawrence, who had come to Portland with her husband, John, and their daughter early in the war. Lawrence was born as the oldest of eleven children in Neelyville, a small town deep in southern Missouri. She married a high school classmate at 16 and had a daughter at 17. "My way of looking at it was to marry a man, have children, have a farm, have every kind of animal there was," she said late in life. [21] It didn't work out that way. Their small farm failed. John Lawrence turned to industrial work and ultimately landed at Willamette Iron & Steel in Portland in 1942. Development of the Portland shipyards put tremendous stress on Portland's wartime housing supply. The Lawrences' first home was in a single room; their only cooking device was a popcorn popper.[22]

Pauline Lawrence had learned to cook for her family before age 10. She wanted to learn professional cooking at Mannings. But Mannings' management likely saw the same traits that impressed Fred and Eva Meyer. She hired on as an assistant manager, instead. Lawrence was a young woman with high intelligence, a friendly personality, a devotion to customer service and a willingness to work hard. Her hair, clothes and makeup were always flawless. Her demeanor bespoke of professionalism. The only hint of anything less than perfect about Lawrence was her was occasional lapse in confusing singular and plural verbs when she spoke. English clearly hadn't been her favorite subject in school.

Although Lawrence was not a server at Mannings, she greeted the Meyers daily and saw that their desires were met. Fred Meyer liked milk instead of cream with his coffee and he liked his toast burned. He often would eat the pie before the meal. Eva Meyer was trying to control her weight. Of the two customers, Pauline probably liked Eva better; she recognized Eva's gentleness and business experience, and believed they'd had similar experiences growing up in small towns and working hard for a living. One morning Lawrence noticed that Fred Meyer's hat was crooked on his head. She told him so. "And I just picked it up and set it down straight." Meyer, then in his late 50s, wasn't used to being treated that way. He always was the person in charge. "Don't you mind about my hat," he shot back. "You take care of business." Lawrence, however, noted that his hat was on straight the next morning, and from then on.[23] One of Fred Meyer's best strengths was quickly assessing talent and diligence. It is no surprise that he wanted Pauline Lawrence working at Fred Meyer Inc.

The courtship was not speedy, however. Lawrence took dietetics classes at night while working at Mannings. She was with the company for 10 years when she lost a promotion to a less-qualified man. "I was very, very unhappy to be treated this way, so I left." Fred Meyer offered her a job, but she turned it down. Her husband had moved to a responsible, stable job at Gunderson Brothers, a Portland heavy manufacturing firm, and she decided to stay at home and be a housewife. Nonetheless, a Fred Meyer personnel employee called her back for a second interview. This time Fred Meyer was more explicit. "I have big plans for you," he told her. "I've watched you all these years. I have a job for you. I think you can manage anything you want to manage. If you will come to work for me I will build as many restaurants as you can manage."[24] Most Fred Meyer stores had coffee counters. They were intended to be places where shoppers could refresh themselves, stay in the store longer, and resume shopping to spend more money. It was Eva Meyer's idea to upgrade them to more extensive restaurants. Pauline Lawrence joined Fred Meyer Inc. in 1952. "I could see myself then, the head of a chain of restaurants," she recalled much later. "Right from the beginning, because he'd promised it, and I knew he'd stick to his promise. And he fulfilled everything he said he would."[25] From then on, Lawrence was one of Meyer's busiest executives and closest friends. Indeed, her face was the last he saw when his life ended in 1978.

As World War II drew to a close, Fred Meyer wanted to add an engineer to his staff to assist with what proved to be a speedy expansion of his one-stop-shopping empire in Portland. A woman in Salem saw a help-wanted advertisement and forwarded it to her husband working in Seattle. Oran B. Robertson, then an industrial engineer for Boeing Corp., read the ad thinking it offered an opportunity to work overseas. Because of structural problems with his feet, Robertson had not been eligible to serve in World War II. Instead, he had gone to Boeing where he started as a production worker building B-17s and B-29s, then advanced to an engineering job in which he helped plan and build new Boeing plants in Tacoma, Chehalis and Everett, Washington. He could have stayed at Boeing, but he felt his chances for major advancement were limited because he wasn't born into the Boeing family and, already happily married, wasn't about to marry into it, either. The idea of working overseas appealed to Robertson, but it turned out the job he was applying for was based in Portland. He showed up on a Thursday to meet with Fred Meyer, who was then a few months short of 60 years old.

Elmer Williams, Meyer's personnel director, pulled Robertson aside shortly before the interview. "Have you ever met Mr. Meyer?" he asked. Robertson had not. "Well, I want to tell you," Williams advised, "he's a pretty difficult guy." [26] Forewarned, Robertson walked into an interview that lasted the entire afternoon. As on many other occasions, Meyer quickly sized up Robertson, 27, as a young man with intelligence, ability, dedication and a strong work ethic. Like many other Meyer executives, Robertson had grown up with hardship. He was born in the small town of Turner, Oregon; his father died when Robertson was two, and his mother moved to nearby Salem. As a child in the Depression, Robertson started selling newspapers on Salem street corners at age 12, then advanced to a rural route as soon as he could drive. He also spent three years as a sign painter before taking the Boeing job in 1938. He worked during the day and took engineering courses by correspondence and at the University of Washington at night during the war, and also taught part-time at a vocational high school. He never completed an engineering degree.

At the end of the Thursday interview, Meyer asked Robertson to come back on Saturday to work on a design problem involving a proposed warehouse. Robertson agreed to return, although he didn't think he was interested in working for Fred Meyer. One reason: The job Meyer offered paid him about half what Robertson had been making at Boeing. Yet, after the Saturday stint, Robertson came back again. Meyer liked what he saw in Robertson, and Robertson was impressed by Meyer. "I truly had a great deal of respect for the man, for his intelligence and ingenuity, so I decided to stay and I did."[27] For the next 30 years, Meyer and Robertson spent most of their Saturday mornings meeting privately to review new building plans, renovations, restaurant designs and store layouts. There would be many twists in the road ahead, but ultimately Oran Robertson was the one to succeed Fred Meyer as chairman of Fred Meyer Inc.

Working through surrogates so that his identity did not become known and drive up prices, Meyer had been quietly assembling land for several new shopping centers he wanted to erect after the war ended. However, his first major project was not a store but a complex of three warehouses he decided to build on the south side of Sullivan's Gulch in Northeast Portland, just a couple short blocks north of Laurelhurst School. He acquired the industrial-zoned land at Northeast 44th Avenue and Hazelfern Place from Union Pacific Railroad and said it was centrally-located to serve his growing network of large stores. His plan, revealed late in 1945, drew strong opposition from Laurelhurst School parents and from affluent Laurelhurst neighborhood residents. They thought big freight trucks were incompatible with narrow neighborhood streets, and feared for the safety of Laurelhurst students walking to and from school. In hindsight, Meyer's site selection was puzzling. Although a route had yet to be selected for a major east-west freeway, Sullivan's Gulch had been identified years before as a logical route, and Meyer's new warehouses would lie directly in its path.

Meyer's opponents asked the Portland City Council to stop his project, and to purchase the land for a public park.[28] The residents also vowed to raise enough money to buy Meyer out. The City Council granted a 40-day period for fund-raising. Meyer already had his building permit, however, and pressed ahead with construction. When the 40 days expired, the opposing residents admitted defeat.[29] The warehouse project was already nearly half finished. After its completion, however, the warehouse was used for only a few years. The State Highway Commission agreed in 1952 to buy it for $750,000 to make way for the Banfield Freeway. One critic accused Meyer of taking more than $500,000 from taxpayers' pockets, since the construction cost had been listed as $175,000.[30] Regardless, the highway commission approved the deal. Meyer asked for and received free rent in the buildings until the end of 1953. Meyer's new warehouse on Swan Island was completed ahead of schedule in 1952 and he rented it periodically for other uses until he needed it.[31] When Portland historian E. Kimbark MacColl interviewed Meyer shortly before his death in 1978, Meyer professed not to know his warehouse would be in the freeway's path.[32] His memory might have been hazy at age 92, but his commercial realty agent and good friend, David Simpson, had been a key member of a Portland-area planning committee that identified Sullivan's Gulch as a probable highway path in 1943, and Meyer's retail success was built in large part on his understanding of the city's transportation routes. The state tried to recapture some of the $750,000 sale price by selling salvage building materials. A portion of the Laurelhurst warehouse remains in place on the south side of Interstate-84, divided into offices and work spaces for small businesses.

The American economy boomed after World War II. Soldiers coming home and pent-up demand dating back to the Great Depression led to buying sprees for homes and cars. Fred Meyer took full advantage. Except for a couple small locations in downtown Portland, he was done with remodeling old buildings. From now on, he'd design and build his own big stores and use them to implement new retailing ideas he had developed on his own or seen elsewhere. In the decade between 1949 and 1959, Meyer opened nine big new shopping centers, almost all on Portland's municipal edges where they were easily accessible to the region's growing multitude of suburban, automobile-oriented residents.

The first two buildings constructed specifically to Meyer's specifications were at Northeast 70th Avenue and Sandy Boulevard, called the Rose City store, and a completely rebuilt structure on the site of the original Hollywood store. Both featured simple glass and concrete facades and both included rooftop parking. Escalators, still a novelty, carried shoppers from the sales floors to parking above. Rose City opened in February 1949 to crowds so dense that police twice blocked the doors so people could leave before more were allowed in.[33] One of the attractions was a chilled meat counter that offered individually wrapped cuts of fresh meat; butchers were hidden from view in a back room.[34] Those attending the opening ceremony included Mayor Dorothy McCullough Lee and approximately 100 small business owners from along Sandy Boulevard. A pattern that would be repeated often was already clear: While homeowners might not want the intrusion of a big store in their neighborhoods, nearby businesses loved Fred Meyer. They fed on the traffic his one-stop shopping centers attracted.

Visitors who ventured to the rear of the Rose City store were puzzled by a lone house, surrounded on three sides by the concrete walls of Meyer's new building. The homeowner, the only one to figure out that land around him was being assembled by Fred Meyer, held out for a higher price. The strategy didn't work. When the owner finally offered to sell as construction began, Fred Meyer told him it would be too expensive to change the building plans.[35] If nothing else, no homeowner was going to be bragging about outsmarting Fred Meyer. Another oddity about the Rose City building was not apparent to the naked eye. One of Oran Robertson's few mistakes as an engineer was hidden from view. He hadn't realized until late in the design that the neighborhood was not connected to the Portland sewer system. The consequence: "A septic tank the size of a swimming pool."[36]

Excitement over the Rose City store didn't end with the week-long opening celebration. "People were coming from all over the United states, even from Europe, to see that store because it was the first store than had been built with roof parking like that," recalled Dale Warman, then a 20-year old Warner Pacific College student who started working part-time at Rose City, first carrying out bags of groceries and then advancing to cashier. Like other Meyer employees, Warman had learned about hard work as a youngster. His father had lost the family farm in rural Colorado during the Depression, and the young Warman delivered newspapers, pumped gas, and worked as a janitor at the local bank. In Portland, he took a part-time job selling women's shoes at Meier & Frank, but he knew about the buzz being created by Fred Meyer. So he leaped at the chance to work in the new store. "I hadn't been there many weeks 'til I determined that, man, this business is exciting....I mean, a lot more upbeat. Selling shoes to ladies isn't the most exciting thing... We really felt we were with a company that was doing the unusual things, which we were."[37]

Only 10 months after the Rose City opening, the company celebrated completion of its new Hollywood store at Northeast 41st Avenue and Sandy Boulevard. Never willing to cut off sales, Fred Meyer directed his staff to keep the old Hollywood store open as much as possible while the new one was being erected on the same site. The basement grocery department remained in operation the whole time while construction went on overhead. Groceries then moved up to the first floor when it was ready. When finished, the new store with rooftop parking and large Fred Meyer sign looked much like the 1936 plan by Claussen & Claussen architects, although that firm was no longer in business. The new structure fully enclosed the former parking lot and automobile service station that were features of the pioneering 1931 Hollywood store.

The five-day grand opening followed what had become a standard Fred Meyer script: carnival rides, free samples, food demonstrations, movies for children at the Hollywood Theater, music, vaudeville acts and a doggy parade. It also included a gimmicky promotion, never to be repeated, in which the company advertised a "healthy two-month old baby" as a raffle prize. "Prize includes a year's supply of food and complete layette," an advertisement read. [38] Civic and church groups complained. The Boys and Girls Aid Society threatened a lawsuit. The head of the Portland 20-30 Club, a leadership organization for young adults,

Portland Mayor Dorothy McCullough Lee, wearing a lei, and Eva Meyer opened the second Hollywood store. The girl on the right was less thrilled. (OHS Meyer Collection, box 12.)

declared, "If the baby is human, as the ads imply, then a new low has been reached, when a human life is classed as a door prize."[39] Fred Meyer let his new public relations director, Hal White, who had been an assistant to former Portland Mayor Earl Riley, field the questions. White, savoring the publicity, dropped hints suggesting the baby was not a dog, cat, pig or rabbit. In fact, Fred Meyer had run a similar promotion nine years earlier at the opening of the Foster Road store and there had been no public outcry. In that case, the "baby" was a piglet. In Hollywood, the infant turned out to be a chinchilla. Always a supporter of local businesses, Meyer had bought it at a pet shop about a mile away.[40] The "Hollywood Fair" five-day grand opening drew some 300,000 visitors, based on an estimate of free tickets given away for prize drawings.[41]

With the new Hollywood store, Meyer added about 100 employees to his payroll, bringing the total to 1,800. Rose City and Hollywood each provided more than 40,000 square feet of retail space, numbers that were huge at the time. The one-stop shopping concept continued to expand, however, and after four decades those two buildings proved to be inefficient for the newer operations. Thirteen years after Meyer's death, both stores were closed by Fred Meyer Inc. in 1991. Rose City was leveled to make way for a new Safeway grocery store. Hollywood, after a period of vacancy, was remodeled slightly to become a Rite-Aid drug store. The basement was closed as a retail space, but the rooftop parking remained. The big rooftop sign also survived, bearing a different name.

Fred Meyer's foresight about regional trends and his patience in waiting for them to materialize were rewarded in 1950 with the completion of his Burlingame store near Portland's southwest boundary. In 1934, the Portland Planning Commission, whose president was Meyer's commercial broker, David Simpson, "recognized that somewhere in the vicinity of the junction of Barbur Boulevard and Terwilliger Boulevard there should be a business center."[42] The Portland City Council subsequently agreed and changed the zoning from residential to allow for a large-scale commercial development. Meyer announced his plans late in 1948, and started removing 60,000 cubic yards of hillside. Soon thereafter, however, the city bought a portion of the site at Terwilliger and Barbur to build the traffic circle that still exists at that intersection. As a result, Meyer moved his proposed building a short distance to the west and carved out an even larger gash from the hillside to create a flat site at Southwest Tenth Avenue and Barbur Boulevard. Dozens of nearby residents asked the City Council, without success, to stop the project by switching the zoning back to residential lots. The new building featured an innovative design by consulting engineer Leslie Poole in which the ceiling was suspended from five large reinforced-concrete trusses, making the sales floor pillar-free.[43] It was a construction style that Meyer never repeated because a faster, cheaper method lay just ahead.

The five-day grand opening at Burlingame was the most elaborate Fred Meyer event yet. The company rented the largest circus tent it could find on the West Coast and added a Ferris wheel and carnival rides. During several daily auctions, customers who had accumulated "Fred Meyer bucks," coupons based on a percentage of prior Fred Meyer purchases, bid enthusiastically on $50,000 worth of merchandise and small appliances, mostly provided for free by suppliers who wanted the publicity. "He was the greatest operator in the world for promoting something on somebody else's merchandise," a former employee said of his former boss.[44] Fred Meyer bakeries turned out 10,000 free scones and jam each day. The 42,000 square feet of sales floor were composed of green concrete. A dock for motorists picking up groceries held 12 cars at once.[45] Crowds were estimated at 70,000 to 75,000 on each of the first two days.[46] The sixteen Fred Meyer stores were now handling a million transactions per week.[47]

Meyer's penchant for standardization went so far as to include a script for employees answering the telephone in the Burlingame meat department. The thought of taking calls was daunting to a young meat cutter who didn't have a phone in his own home, and who wasn't confident about using it. If a call came in, he was instructed to read from the script placed near the phone. The phone rang one evening on the night shift and the meat cutter did exactly as he had been told. "Good morning, good afternoon or good evening, whatever the case may be," he read aloud. "This is (your name) of Fred Meyer's. How may I help you?" Laughter erupted on the other end of the line. The caller was Fred Meyer. The script was removed the next day.[48]

With his foot still heavy on the expansion accelerator, Meyer and his development team were back before the City Council late in 1950 seeking zone changes for two more new stores. The first proposal, at Southeast 39th Avenue and Hawthorne Boulevard, won council approval despite some neighborhood objections about loss of housing for a parking lot.[49] The second proposal, a reincarnation of his 1938 plan for a store in Westmoreland, failed a second time, and gave the public a brief look at Meyer's temper. The battle pitted Meyer once again against E.C. Sammons, an Eastmoreland resident who had risen to president of U.S. National Bank. At a Planning Commission meeting, Sammons suggested that Meyer donate the property to the city as a park. If not, Sammons said he would start a fund drive to buy the land from Meyer for a park. Meyer testily refused. "Mr. Sammons' generosity in giving away someone else's property loses its generosity when it is noted that the property is virtually in his own front yard and that he now enjoys some 212 well-kept acres of park and playground in his immediate neighborhood and should be well satisfied. The taxpayers have been very generous."[50] Sammons repeated the offer when the land-use case arrived at a packed City Hall chamber the following month. "It's not for sale," Meyer repeated. The City Council rejected Meyer's request on a 4-0 vote. Sammons tried to shake Meyer's hand afterward as a conciliatory gesture, but Meyer refused. "I won't sell it," Meyer told news reporters after the vote. "They haven't got enough money to buy it."[51] Fred

Meyer was not accustomed to not getting his way. He would try yet again at Westmoreland 10 years later.

At the request of Hawthorne Boosters, a neighborhood business group, Meyer agreed to call his big new store at Southeast 39th Avenue "Hawthorne" instead of "Sunnyside." It opened in September, 1951, with the usual five-day Fred Meyer fanfare. His publicist estimated the first-day crowd at 100,000, a number that was not otherwise verified.[52] Hawthorne, too, had a green concrete floor and was the third and last Meyer store to offer roof-top parking. About half of those spaces remained into the next century after several intervening renovations, including the addition of a partial upper story. However, roof-top parking had reached its peak. As the company turned to Portland's suburbs for its further growth, bare land was cheaper to buy for parking lots and a new, cheaper construction method wouldn't support the weight of cars on the roof. The first example of the new system was not a store, but a warehouse on Swan Island that replaced the Laurelhurst facility Meyer had built in the path of the Banfield freeway.

In 1950, Howard Andersen was a young University of Washington-trained engineer whose employer had sent him to California to learn about a new construction technique. It was called tilt-up construction, in which concrete walls were poured flat on the ground and then lifted by crane into vertical placement after the concrete had dried. Andersen's employer wasn't interested in trying it, so Andersen went into business for himself. His first major project was the Fred Meyer warehouse on Swan Island. "Well, I built the project so fast that they weren't ready for it," he recalled years later. "They rented it out to the home people, they rented it to the car people for car shows, they rented it out to the U.S. Post Office for Christmas mail before they ever moved in."[53] The project was the first of its kind in the Pacific Northwest. "So about half way through the project, Mr. Meyer and (Oran) Robertson showed up and they said, 'Could you build a store for us?' And I said sure. And they said, 'How fast can you build it?' I said, how fast do you want it? And they said, 'As fast as we can get it built.'" The 51,000 square-foot store at Interstate Avenue and North Lombard Street was the largest yet in the Fred Meyer domain. Andersen's construction company, Andersen-Westfall, finished it in 57 days, working double shifts. It opened in November 1953.[54]

Meyer and Andersen became good friends, and Andersen built every new Fred Meyer store in the remaining 25 years of Meyer's life. But Andersen had to show that Meyer's penchant for being boss did not extend to Andersen's construction workers. Andersen got a call from a superintendent on the Interstate project in 1953, complaining that Meyer was trying to tell the subcontractors what to do. Andersen told Meyer that if he had any complaints, he should talk first to Oran Robertson about them. According to Andersen's account, he then told Meyer to leave the job site "or I'll split you right down the middle with a two-by-four." From then on, Meyer did his inspecting on weekends. Years later on another project, Meyer noticed that some wooden forms had been constructed with four nails, while others had eight. He wrote Andersen a memo stating he wasn't worried about the nails, but about the labor costs. "Would you look into it?" Meyer asked. The request became a company joke among Andersen's employees. [55]

As big as his new stores were, Fred Meyer wasn't yet ready to abandon his early small shops on Yamhill Street. Dale Warman was food manager at Fourth and Yamhill in the early 1950s when a fire sprinkler rupture flooded much of the storeroom. Warman was dealing with the problem when the company patriarch walked in. "He encouraged me to move some of the really dead stock that was off in another area to make sure it got wet." Warman complied, but it bothered him ethically. "I guess he figured he was paying enough for insurance, and he wanted to get even somehow." It reminded Warman of an incident as an adolescent when he was working as a janitor in a bank in a small Colorado town and found cash on the floor one night. He turned it into the bank president the next day. The money on the floor was no accident, but rather a test of Warman's honesty. The bank president said Warman passed the test. Warman realized that perhaps he had passed Fred Meyer's test, too.[56]

Although he'd been with the company only a few years, Warman was promoted to food manager at the new Interstate store. Crowds were larger than expected; shelves were substantially stripped of merchandise almost every day, requiring new inventory to be brought in overnight from other stores. Fred Meyer cut a huge cake and then waded into the crowd. "He'd stay around and walk the aisles and meet people," Warman said. "He was a great peddler. He really was."[57]

In addition to the excitement of the new stores, Fred and Eva Meyer were on the move again personally. Construction was finished in 1951 on a dramatic new 13-story apartment building at 1000 Southwest Vista Avenue, called the Vista St. Clair. Unlike the Envoy Apartments, which architecturally was a transitional building between traditional historical styles and modernism, the Vista St. Clair fell resolutely into the modern category. Its sleek white exterior was completely shorn of architectural ornament; like a sister building downtown, the Ione Plaza, the Vista St. Clair was a pure expression of geometry, concrete and glass. Fred and Eva Meyer rented a penthouse apartment with stunning views and an outdoor deck. Their new home was still within walking distance of the Stadium store. It would be the last residence that the couple, now heading into their late 60s, would share.

While the number and size of Fred Meyer stores were growing at a fast pace in the 1950s, Meyer also was accumulating and training personnel who would be top executives in his remaining years. Pauline Lawrence came aboard in 1952 to upgrade Fred Meyer lunch and coffee counters. It was no small task. "In those days, we ran some of the worst coffee shop restaurants that man could possibly create," recalled Oran Robertson, who quickly came to admire Lawrence's knowledge and dedication.[58] Lawrence's father, who was the dominant parent in her childhood, died the same year she came to work for Fred Meyer. It occurred to Lawrence that her father shared some of the same traits as her new employer: persistence, a strong work ethic and an optimistic a belief that people could achieve almost anything they wanted. "There wasn't a negative thought in his mind, and I didn't want negative thoughts, either." Meyer might have sensed that Lawrence would not tolerate abrasive behavior toward her, or maybe she was so close to perfect he never felt the need to criticize. Years later, it occurred to Lawrence and others that while she recognized Meyer as something of a father figure, he probably saw her as the daughter he never had.[59]

Jack Crocker, who had started as a grocery bagger in high school, returned to the company after serving in the military and graduating from the University of Oregon in accounting. He was hired to help Herb Retzlaff manage the accounting staff, but Meyer had bigger plans for him. Crocker remembered his first meeting with Meyer; Crocker was 25, Meyer was 63. "You see that chair you're sitting on?" Meyer asked. "When you saw that chair, what did you think about?"

"I thought about sitting down," Crocker answered.

"That chair is a condition, and a condition controls the operation," Meyer said. "Remember that all your life, that the conditions around you control the operation."[60] Meyer wanted to standardize every operation he could, so employees could learn to work efficiently and follow standardized instructions. Besides working with Retzlaff on accounting, Crocker became the in-house efficiency expert, studying ways to improve routine procedures such as ringing up sales, bagging groceries and improving employee schedules. One study led to resizing paper grocery sacks. Crocker wrote detailed manuals illustrated with photographs to show to managers and employees.

Crocker had been on the job for about a year when he watched Meyer drive his wife to tears in a management meeting. Crocker challenged Meyer about it afterward, suggesting that Meyer should never treat his wife that way. Crocker felt odd, being a man of 26 chewing out a man of 64. "He listened to me and said, 'OK,'" Crocker recalled. But at the next weekly meeting, it was Crocker's turn for criticism. "I've never been the target of anything like I was that day," he said. "Oh God, he gave it to me. He really just let me have it every possible way he could."[61] A few years later, Crocker went on long automobile trips with Fred and Eva Meyer looking at stores in the Southwest. Meyer's treatment of his wife on those trips was completely different. "When we were in Phoenix and Palm Springs he just treated her like a queen. And she was very fond of him, too." Crocker and others had trouble reconciling Meyer's behavior toward Eva. The only conclusion they reached was that business was the most important element in his life, and he got so wrapped up in it that he lost sight of his closest personal relationship.[62] For 11 years, Crocker's desk sat between those of Fred and Eva Meyer at the corporate office on Fourth Avenue. Crocker and his wife were among the few guests invited to dinner at the Meyers' Vista St. Clair penthouse. Crocker in 1968 would become president of Fred Meyer Inc., if rather briefly, before his relations with Meyer suddenly deteriorated.

In 1954, Fred Meyer Inc. built its first store in the Gateway district near Northeast Halsey Street and 102nd Avenue. The store itself was a replica of the Interstate building opened the year before, but Gateway included a 23,000-square foot companion building, connected by a covered walk-way, that was leased to more than a dozen other independent businesses. The two buildings shared a spacious parking lot for 1,200 cars.63 The Banfield freeway was not yet finished, but an exit for eastbound traffic onto Halsey was assured. In the next three years, the Gateway center added new buildings for Olds & King, the first downtown Portland department store to open a suburban location, W.T. Grant and F.W. Woolworth. As a grouping of store linked with walkways, Gateway was Portland's first regional shopping mall, designed to attract motorists from several miles around. However, it was overshadowed just a few years later by the opening of Lloyd Center with its larger number of shops, fancier "magnet" department stores such as Meier & Frank and J.C. Penney. The Lloyd Center also offered more parking and a more impressive architectural design.

Fred Meyer's management team in 1955 included Earle A. Chiles, front center, as president, flanked by Dorothy Norton, assistant treasurer, and Herbert Retzlaff, first vice president. Vice presidents going up the stairs were Rollin Killoran, Balfour Gibson, Glen Day, Arthur Merrick, Oran Robertson and Alvin Jones. **(OHS Retzlaff folder)**

Early in 1955, Fred and Eva Meyer planned a trip to Europe, accompanied by Eva's sister, Mary Boyle. They would be gone three months and visit eight countries. At the time, the two Meyers and Earle A. Chiles were the only shareholders in privately-held Fred Meyer Inc. Chiles held the title of general manager. Fred Meyer decided it was time to solidify the company's managerial structure, perhaps preparing the company in case of some dreadful event during the trip. The Meyers and Boyle had already departed when Chiles convened a dinner meeting late in April, 1955, at the University Club, where he opened a letter from Fred Meyer announcing the changes. [64] Chiles was the new president, replacing Fred Meyer who henceforth would be board chairman. Herbert Retzlaff became first vice president, adding that title to his job as controller. Six other new vice presidents, all seasoned company veterans, and their areas of supervision were: Glen Day, warehousing and bakery; Balfour Gibson, personnel; Alvin P. Jones, grocery and produce; Arthur Merrick, apparel; Oran Robertson, engineering; and Rollin Killoran, drug and variety. Killoran had left Fred Meyer Inc. in 1941, but returned 11 years later after working with other companies in Oregon and California. The only female face in the crowd was that of Dorothy Norton, Meyer's personal secretary for 20 years, who was promoted to assistant treasurer. The new titles didn't mean much; after Fred Meyer returned from Europe, he was still the company kingpin.

During stops in France, Italy, Spain, Germany, England, Holland, Switzerland, Denmark and England, Fred Meyer spent most of his time looking at retail stores. He found little of interest. "There appears to be little effort on the part of merchants to introduce self-service and the other changes that have been so effective in cutting costs and raising living standards in America over the last 40 years," he reported. "In none of the hundreds of towns and cities we visited did we find anything resembling our modern American markets with self-service. Mostly the stores even when they are part of large chains are little different from our corner grocery store of 20 years or more ago." Cities didn't seem interested in building parking lots; store managers seemed indifferent to change.[65] Fred and Eva Meyer returned to Europe two years later as part of an American delegation attending an international trade fair in Holland, but once again he saw nothing that impressed him about Dutch retailing.[66]

Eva Meyer, Mary Boyle, center, and Fred Meyer headed to Europe in 1955 after Meyer solidified his management structure. (OHS Meyer file 734B)

Pauline Lawrence started her Fred Meyer career at the bakery and ice cream plant at Southeast Eleventh Avenue and Madison Street. Her first instructions from Meyer were to improve ice cream production, sales and margins. After that, she began developing recipes for baked beans and other items to be sold at deli counters, and then entrees and desserts at coffee shops and cafeterias. In 1954, she heard about a new cooking device invented by the Raytheon Corp. in Boston that could cook items much faster than conventional ovens. The discovery had started in 1946 when a Raytheon engineer working with a low-density magnetron – a device developed during World War II for radar–discovered that it melted a chocolate bar in his coat pocket. When the engineer aimed the magnetron at kernels of popcorn, the kernels suddenly burst and flew about the lab.[67]

After several years of product development, Raytheon called its first microwave oven a Radarange. Fred Meyer, who was always interested in technology that would improve efficiency, sent Lawrence to Boston to learn about it. The first ovens weighed 750 pounds and stood almost as tall as a refrigerator. Lawrence spent two weeks testing the oven with chicken, turkey, prime rib, beef and pizza to see what it could do. Pizza was a failure, but Lawrence liked the other possibilities. Lawrence wanted to buy, but Raytheon said it wouldn't sell because it had no way to service the machines so far away. Lawrence called in a Fred Meyer electrician, Bill Oyala. After Oyala demonstrated to Raytheon's satisfaction that he could dismantle the machine completely and successfully reassemble it, Raytheon sold Fred Meyer Inc. the first microwave ovens west of the Mississippi River. Each one cost $2,500. "Mr. Meyer was a great one on new ideas...and he used to say, 'There will be a time when every housewife will have a microwave oven and we want to be ready for it,'" Lawrence said. [68]

If Pauline Lawrence was the surrogate of a daughter for Fred Meyer, Meyer in 1957 met the man who became the surrogate of a son. Gerry Pratt, then 30, was a new reporter at the *Oregonian* newspaper who soon became its business editor. Pratt came from the kind of underprivileged background that Meyer respected. The son of a single mother with many children, Pratt grew up on rural Vancouver, Island, British Columbia, in a home where there seldom was enough money to cover basic needs. Pratt dropped out of school as a young teenager to take whatever manual labor jobs he could find. Eventually, he had a chance to work for a newspaper, and found that he had a knack for writing, regardless of his lack of formal schooling. After working for Canadian newspapers, Pratt landed a tryout at the *Oregonian* in 1955. His sprightly style, eye for detail and fresh use of life-like sounding quotes quickly lifted him out of the sports department into general news and thence to the business department.

Pratt's first apparent exposure to Fred Meyer shows the exuberant signs of a reporter enthralled by the interviewee. His opening sentences: "Don't believe everything you hear about Fred Meyer. Only the fabulous stories are true." [69] Over the following years, Meyer apparently became smitten by Pratt as well. Pratt became *Oregonian* business editor in 1960 and the next year started his frequent business column, "Making the Dollar." In an era when the morning newspaper had finally surpassed the *Oregon Journal* as Portland's largest newspaper, the *Oregonian* seemed to pride itself in dour blandness. Pratt's column was exactly the opposite. It was lively, creative and one of the most-read features in the paper. Pratt wrote about Meyer dozens of times during his tenure as business editor. The two often ate dinner together and sometimes traveled together. Pratt left the newspaper in 1972– to go to work for Fred Meyer Inc. Meyer eventually gave Pratt a chance to prove himself as a businessman, a decision that didn't lead where either of them had hoped.

The final year of what many called the Fabulous Fifties – a fabulous decade, indeed for Fred Meyer Inc. – proved to be one of the most dynamic and challenging for the company. It opened two new stores, at Southeast 122nd Avenue and Division Street on Portland's east side, and at Raleigh Hills in the nascent era of Washington County's vibrant suburban growth. The two identically-designed stores added 120,000 square feet to the company's growing retail space and another 300 employees, lifting the company-wide total to 2,000. Washington County planners objected to a 52-foot sign Meyer planned to erect at Raleigh Hills, contending that the zoning allowed only 45 feet. Meyer filed a lawsuit against the county, arguing that he already had permission for 52 feet. Never willing to let bureaucrats have the upper hand, Meyer continued erecting the taller sign and said he would shorten it later if he lost in court.[70] The Raleigh Hills site had been used previously as a dairy farm, and residents urged Fred Meyer to keep a large red barn that had become a local landmark. Herbert Retzlaff, Meyer's controller and first vice president, said keeping the barn would allow it to be depreciated for tax purposes. While Meyer's development team tried to think of ways they could use the barn, it blew down in the huge Columbus Day windstorm of 1961, a loss recognized under tax law as an act of God. "So we had a tax write-off for the barn," Retzlaff said. [71]

In September, 1959, Meyer used the occasion of an employee banquet to outline a $30 million expansion plan over the next 10 years, revamping existing stores and adding new ones. Aside from a new building in Oak Grove planned for 1960, Meyer did not divulge how many or where the new shopping centers would be, but said they would be bumped up to 80,000 square feet each – the equivalent of two downtown Portland city blocks. Expansions were planned for Walnut Park and Burlingame, as well as at the warehouse on Swan Island.[72] Eva Meyer likely was not enthralled by the plan. "She did not want the company to get large," said Oran Robertson years later. "She knew everybody in the stores and knew all the managers on a first-name basis. And she liked a small company. And we all did, as far as that goes."[73] Dale Warman offered a similar assessment after knowing Eva Meyer for 10 years. "She always felt like he (Fred Meyer) was killing himself, you know...She didn't want the company to grow because she could just see that he was going to become more and more involved. I don't remember all the details, but supposedly he had to renegotiate with her every time they added a store."[74] Fred Meyer usually got his way.

Two weeks before the decade ended, Fred Meyer Inc. announced the acquisition of four drug and variety stores in Seattle that bore the Marketime name. Terms of the sale were not disclosed, but the transaction was described as a part of Meyer's recently-announced 10-

Only a few weeks before her death, Eva Meyer and Fred Meyer opened the Division Street center. Anola "Peter" Mudie is slightly visible behind Eva Meyer. (OHS Meyer Collection, Box 14.)

year expansion plan. The deal was signed by Fred Meyer and by John H. Davis, the Marketime president who had been a co-founder of the drug company established in 1946. As a result of the sale, Davis soon joined the Fred Meyer Inc. board of directors. Davis had built his wealth in Seattle much the same way Meyer had in Portland, through knowledge of local real estate. He was a former partner in the Haskins & Sells accounting firm and had served on the board of directors of the Seattle Trust & Savings Bank. Unlike Meyer, Davis had a strong outside interest in raising and riding horses. The fact that he could be blunt and outspoken would become remarkably evident in years ahead.

There was a nagging bump, however, in that busy final year of the 1950s: the Federal Trade Commission, an independent regulatory commission created in 1914 to enforce various federal laws, accused Fred Meyer of violating an amendment to the Clayton Antitrust Act of 1936. The Clayton Act had been passed when Congress realized that small independent retailers had no chance to compete with large chains that had superior buying power. By the late 1950s, Fred Meyer Inc. had become one of those large chains, with sales in 1957 of more than $40 million.

The FTC's complaint against Fred Meyer stemmed from a promotional campaign the company had used since 1936 involving coupon books. Each book usually had about 70 pages, each page featuring an item that the store sold for a reduced price. Fred Meyer charged suppliers of products featured in the coupon books $350 for each page of advertising. Some suppliers further underwrote the campaign by giving the company price reductions on its purchases of featured items. Customers paid a dime for each book and surrendered the appropriate coupon when making a purchase. In 1956, the first year the FTC investigated the coupon system, Fred Meyer sold some 140,000 coupon books and redeemed approximately 900,000 coupons. The problem, the FTC contended, was that the companies whose products were included in the coupon books effectively had paid Fred Meyer's printing costs. Moreover, some of the deals offered in the books included prices that seemingly could not be matched by any competitor. The FTC initiated litigation that would last for more than a decade over whether Fred Meyer had unlawfully induced some of its suppliers to engage in discriminatory pricing in violation of the Clayton Act.

Meyer, however, offered no apology for his aggressive business tactics. "It has always been the policy of our company to make available to the public merchandise at the lowest possible price and, accordingly, we have purchased and distributed merchandise at the lowest prices possible, consistent with good merchandising practices."[75] Over the next 16 years of negotiation and litigation, Meyer fought the trade commission case as hard as he could, including a trip to the United States Supreme Court. Ironically, an expert witness called to explain intricacies of wholesale purchasing and selling was Fred Meyer's own younger brother, Henry Meyer, an executive with the Hudson House food wholesale firm. The two brothers had not spoken to one another for 30 years since their litigation involving the Piggly Wiggly chain in 1928. Herb Retzlaff crossed paths with Henry Meyer a few times over the years and saw him during the trade commission proceedings. He said Henry asked several questions about his older brother, and Retzlaff decided to tell Fred Meyer about the conversation. "He had mellowed by then," Retzlaff said of Fred Meyer, "and he said, 'Oh, did he, did he?'" when Retzlaff said Henry had asked about him. "Well that is nice to know something," Fred Meyer said.[76] Yet if the two brothers ever spoke to one another again, none of Meyer's top executives heard of it.

As the decade drew to a close, Fred Meyer was four weeks away from the worst day of his life. The shock of it would cast a pall over his personal life and dramatically change road map for the future development of Fred Meyer Inc.

---

[1] Chirgwin , Ray, oral history interview, Oregon Historical Society, sound recording 1303, July 24, 1989.
[2] *Oregonian,* March 15, 1940, p. 13.
[3] Day , Glen, oral history interview, Oregon Historical Society, sound recording 1306, June 27, 1989.
[4] Chirgwin, *op. cit.*
[5] *Oregonian,* March 17, 1998.
[6] *Ibid,* May 26, 1940, p. 8.
[7] *Oregon Journal,* Aug. 7, 1950, p. 6F.
[8] *Oregonian,* Nov. 27, 1940, p. 13.
[9] *Ibid,* Dec. 1, 1940, p. 30.
[10] *Ibid,* July 19. 1936, p. 16.
[11] *Ibid,* April 6, 1941, p. B2.
[12] *Ibid,* Nov. 6, 1943, p. 12.
[13] *Ibid,* May 14, 1943, p. 15.
[14] Green, Cyril, oral history interview, OHS, sound recording 1307, Feb. 27, 1989.
[15] Day, *op. cit.*

[16] *Ibid.*
[17] Crocker, Jack, OHS sound recording 1304, June 1, 1989.
[18] *Oregonian,* July 2, 1944, p.5.
[19] Robertson, Oran B., OHS sound recording 1312, Dec. 20, 1988.
[20] *Envoy Apartment Building,* U.S. Department of Interior, National Park Service, National Register of Historic Places Registration Form, Jan. 15, 1988.
[21] Lawrence, Pauline, oral history interview, OHS, sound recording 1309, Oct. 25, 1988.
[22] *Ibid.*
[23] *Ibid.*
[24] *Ibid.*
[25] *Ibid.*
[26] Robertson, *op. cit.,* Dec. 8, 1988.
[27] *Ibid.*
[28] *Oregonian,* Jan. 4, 1946, p. 14.
[29] *Ibid* Feb. 16, 1946, p. 11.
[30] *Ibid,* May 28, 1950, p. 10.
[31] Andersen, Howard A., oral history interview, OHS, sound recording 1300, Aug. 9, 1989.
[32] MacColl , E. Kimbark, *The Growth of a City: Power and Politics in Portland, Oregon, 1915 to 1950,* Georgian Press, 1979, p. 633.
[33] *Oregonian,* Feb. 15, 1949, p. B4.
[34] *Ibid.*
[35] Retzlaff, Herbert, oral history interview, OHS, sound recording 1311, Feb. 15, 1989.
[36] Robertson, *op. cit.* Feb. 2, 1989.
[37] Warman, Dale, OHS sound recording 1315, April 20, 1989.
[38] *Ibid,,* Nov. 29, 1949, p. 10.
[39] *Ibid.,* Dec. 1, 1949, p. 14.
[40] *Ibid.,* Dec. 2, 1949, p.27.
[41] *Oregonian,* Dec. 4, 1949, p. 4.
[42] Minutes of the Portland Planning Commission, Volume II, Report of the Zoning Committee, Sept. 30, 1936, p. 3, Portland Archives & Records Center.
[43] *Ibid,* April 2, 1950, p. C2.
[44] Chirgwin, *op cit.*
[45] *Oregon Journal,* Aug. 7, 1950, p. F1.
[46] *Oregonian,* Aug. 10, 1950, p. 13.
[47] *Oregon Journal,* op. cit.
[48] Recollection of Barry Wagler, reciting an incident involving his father. Received by Fred Meyer Inc. in 2006 in response to a solicitation of memories about the company. Fred Meyer Collection 199, Box 35, folder 10, OHS.
[49] *Oregonian,* Dec. 20, 1950.
[50] *Ibid,* Dec. 10, 1950, p. 10.
[51] *Ibid,* Jan. 10, 1951, p. 1.

[52] *Ibid,* Sept. 13, 1951, p. C6.
[53] Andersen, *op cit.*
[54] *Oregonian,* Nov. 17, 1953, special section, p. 3.
[55] Andersen, *op cit.*
[56] Warman, *op cit.*
[57] *Ibid.*
[58] Robertson, *op cit.* March 28, 1989.
[59] Lawrence, *op cit.*
[60] Crocker, *op cit.*
[61] *Ibid.*
[62] Crocker , *op. cit.,* Aug. 2, 1989
[63] *Oregonian,* April 11, 1954, p. B11.
[64] *Ibid,* April 22, 1955, p. 13
[65] *Ibid.,* June 24, 1955, p. 13.
[66] *Ibid.,* May 2, 1957, p. 5.
[67] Southwest Museum of Engineering, Communications and Computation, *Microwave Oven,* www.smcc.org/microwave_oven.htm, accessed June, 2013.
[68] Lawrence, *op. cit.* Nov. 17, 1988.
[69] *Oregonian,* Oct. 10, 1957, p. B6.
[70] *Ibid.,* Nov. 4, 1959, p. 10.
[71] Retzlaff, *op. cit.*
[72] *Oregonian,* Sept. 25, 1959, p. 1.
[73] Robertson, *op. cit,* Feb. 2, 1989.
[74] Warman, *op cit.* April 27, 1989.
[75] *Oregonian,* May 22, 1959, p. 31.
[76] Retzlaf , *op. cit.,* Feb. 22, 1989.

CHAPTER SIX

Starting Again at 74

Fred and Eva Meyer planned a trip to Hawaii early in 1960. They had been to the islands at least six times before, as brief escapes from Portland's dreary winters. Before their departure, however, Eva Meyer checked into Good Samaritan Hospital for gall bladder surgery. The operation was, at that time, more invasive than techniques that would become standard decades later. Yet gall bladder surgery was quite common in 1960 and not considered life-threatening. Eva Meyer's operation went well, but something terrible happened afterward. The cause of her death was not explained in detail in company circles. One unverified account suggested that she rose from her bed sooner than advised to wash her hair,[1] and may have suffered a blood clot in her brain. Her death at age 72 was front-page news.[2]

Fred Meyer was in a meeting at the Fourth Avenue corporate office when his secretary received the call from the hospital on January 27. The secretary, not wishing to be the deliverer of the terrible news, called on Herbert Retzlaff, the first vice president and controller. "Unfortunately, I was the one who had to tell him," Retzlaff said. He went upstairs to the meeting and called out Mary Boyle, Eva Meyer's sister.

Mary Boyle brought Fred Meyer out of the meeting. "He came out and I had to tell him," Retzlaff said. "Sounds kind of profane but he said, 'God damn it!' He didn't swear a lot but he said, 'God damn it,' and ran off. I couldn't hold him and he went over to the garage," took his car and raced to the hospital. [3] Meyer was known as an erratic driver under the best conditions, and Retzlaff feared for Meyer's safety.

Mrs. Fred Meyer, Official Of Big Chain Store, Dies

Mrs. Eva Chatfield Meyer, 72, wife of Portland chain store merchant Fred Meyer, died in Good Samaritan hospital Wednesday.

She was hospitalized the first of the year and underwent major surgery a week ago. Members of the family said she had apparently been recovering, until a sudden worsening of her condition Wednesday morning. She died at 11 a.m.

She was born in Muskegon, Mich., and moved to Portland in 1911. She was married to Fred Meyer in Seattle 41 years ago. She had been secretary-treasurer of the Fred Meyer firm since it was established. The organization now includes 36 stores and about 10 bakeries and other processing plants.

In 1949 Mrs. Meyer was named "Woman of the Year" by the Portland Women's Forum, and she was "Soroptomist of the Year" in 1943.

Surviving her besides her widower is her son, Earl A. Chiles, who is president and general manager of the firm.

Also surviving is her brother, Dr. E. J. Chatfield, and sister, Mrs. Mary Boyle, both of Portland, and one grandson.

Funeral will be private at 11 a.m. Monday.

The family suggests that a memorial may be in the form of a contribution to the Soroptomist Birthday fund for the White Shield Home.

MRS. FRED MEYER

Eva Meyer's death rated coverage on the *Oregonian's* front page. **(Oregonian)**

The effect of Eva Meyer's death on her husband and the company was profound. The most succinct account came from Fred Meyer himself, ten years later. "Well, Mrs. Meyer and I enjoyed life a great deal together, but after that there wasn't anything but work."[4] On another occasion, he said, "Eva had more sense than I did. We had more fun. She knew how to enjoy life. She knew the good things in life."[5] Pauline Lawrence, who had been promoted to the executive committee by 1960, said Fred Meyer kept to himself and saw few other people for three months after Eva's death. She thought he did not know how to have fun on his own. She remember him saying, "I didn't realize how much she meant to me and how much she did for me, and I feel sorry for the things that I maybe didn't do for Eva. She wanted to travel and I wanted to take care of business. I finally gave in and went—we traveled. I was never happy doing that. I was happier with the business, but Eva wasn't and I'm sorry for that."[6] Jean Webb, Meyer's secretary, said her boss had trouble adjusting. "He didn't know what to do with himself," she said. "I'd see him at his desk just kind of staring into space, and then he would settle down and do his work."[7]

Three days after her death, the *Oregon Journal* published an editorial lauding Eva Meyer for her role in the company and for causes she believed in, such as the White Shield Home for unwed mothers, the Soroptimist Club, city parks and the Arthritis and Rheumatism Foundation. Without being privy to the company's private decision-making process, the newspaper likely overstated her importance in calling her "one of Oregon's outstanding business executives." Yet the editorial was completely accurate when it added, "And she always had time to maintain close contacts with Fred Meyer employees, from the time there were only five of them until there were 2,400." Given her concern for employee welfare demonstrated in many ways, the newspaper said, "Mrs. Meyer thus earned the title of 'Mother of Fred Meyer Inc.'"[8]

Dale Warman had been with the company for ten years when Eva Meyer died. He had first gotten to know her when he worked at the Yamhill store just around the corner from the company headquarters. If Fred Meyer saw something in the store or in its display windows that he didn't like, Warman heard about it promptly. Eva Meyer often was with her husband on those occasions. "Mrs. Meyer was the leavening to the loaf, I guess you would say, in this company," Warman said. "She was the personality who kept the employees happy. And she would follow behind Fred and smooth our wounds, so to speak." He remembered her saying things like, "You know, this business is growing fast, he gets upset, but you know, he doesn't mean that. You know, tomorrow he won't even remember what he said to you. Just keep doing a good job." She knew all the department managers and assistant managers in the chain that had grown to 16 large stores by the time she died. "And she was always very conscious of the employees. She was the personnel department, so to speak, even though she didn't run it." Warman added, "I wish she could have lived a lot longer, because I think she would have helped Mr. Meyer be a more level-personality guy. The further I got up in management, the more I wished she was around."[9]

Fred and Eva Meyer had been married a little over 40 years. His 74th birthday was approaching when she died. He occasionally joked later about hoping "to marry a rich widow with a bad cough," but he never seriously looked for another spouse. One executive set him up with two dates, but nothing came of them.[10] Women sent him unsolicited love letters, but he laughed and threw them away. "It was too late for blondes," he said years later.[11] Fred Meyer was already involved in a long-term relationship that would last until death did them part: Fred Meyer Inc. "You rot if you retire," he said at age 91.[12]

Other changes in Fred Meyer's personal life soon followed Eva's death. His weekly dinners with Earle and Virginia Chiles ended. He gave away the rugs and furnishings at the Vista St. Clair penthouse to various company employees, and moved into a small suite at the Sheraton Hotel in Northeast Portland near the new Lloyd Center. He started having dinner once a week with Pauline Lawrence, almost invariably at the Fred Meyer restaurant at the Burlingame store in the Southwest Portland neighborhood where Pauline and John Lawrence had bought a house. Sunday mornings, he ate with Mary Boyle. He also ate weekly with Gerry Pratt, who had become business editor at the *Oregonian.* He made a few weekend visits to Eva's Eden on the Salmon River near Wemme, but there was no way to recapture the happiness he had experienced there with his wife. Those trips came to an end, and he usually showed up at the office seven days a week instead. Meyer eventually sold Eva's Eden, and a subsequent purchaser turned it into a church-sponsored youth group home. "He just didn't have the heart to go on with it," Herbert Retzlaff said of Meyer's decision to sell the woodsy mountain retreat.[13] A fire that started in the kitchen destroyed the elegant main building in 1977.[14] Subsequent owners built a modern lodge on the grounds and rented it as a vacation retreat.

Whatever restraints Meyer had felt on his earlier expansion ambitions, however, were now removed. Soon after Eva's death, Meyer told Pauline Lawrence that he wanted all Fred Meyer restaurants and cafeterias to be named in her honor, although he chose to call them "Eve's," rather than Eva's. He chose a sign for the restaurants showing Eva Meyer's face in profile, and told Lawrence to build the restaurants at the quickest reasonable pace. The restaurants weren't his only flurry after Eva's death. "We went like firecrackers," said Rollin Killoran, a vice president. "We not only bought stores, we built stores. We opened stores. We went into Washington, we went into Northern Idaho, into Montana, throughout Oregon as far south as Medford. And I think a lot of our movement was generated by his (Meyer's) wanting to do things and not having his wife to spend time with him."[15] Oran Robertson concurred. After Eva Meyer's death, "He gave more time to his work because that's all he had left."[16] Warman remembered, "He always talked about the travel they did together and some of the great times that they had. But he just kind of lost all desire to do anything except the business. And that was his life anyway, even when she was around. She always felt like he was killing himself, you know." [17]

One of Meyer's boldest moves occurred only two weeks after Eva Meyer's death. The federal Securities and Exchange Commission revealed that Fred Meyer Inc. had submitted plans for its first public stock offering. It called for the sale of 400,000 shares of common stock, including 85,000 shares owned by the estate of Eva Meyer. The filing statement said the company hoped to raise $2 million to pay for building the new store at Oak Grove, rebuilding Walnut Park, remodeling two downtown stores and equipping a new central kitchen at its big Swan Island warehouse. A price for each share had not yet been determined[18] Eva Meyer's will, which already had been submitted to Multnomah County Probate Court, said most of her estate's shares were to be given to a new Meyer Foundation to promote charity, science, education and religion.[19] However, planning for the stock offering had begun in the fall of 1959 when Meyer announced a 10-year expansion plan, and before Eva Meyer's health was in jeopardy.[20] Laying the decision at the feet of estate taxes was merely another expression of Meyer's dislike for governmental intrusion, including land-use zoning and business regulations. His frustrations with such intrusions would continue to grow in the years ahead.

The public stock sale occurred in late March, 1960, with 385,000 shares being sold at $12 each. Eva Meyer's shares raised just over $1 million. The remaining 300,000 shares generated $3.6 million for Fred Meyer Inc. expansion. Fred Meyer reserved 15,000 shares for eventual distribution among employees. The prospectus revealed that the company sales hit $50 million in 1959, and that Fred Meyer Inc. had 25 percent of the Portland-area retail food market, roughly tied with Safeway. Fred Meyer ranked first in pharmaceutical sales and first in variety sales in the Portland market, according to the supporting data.[21] Personally, Meyer liked the idea that stockholders would be motivated do to all their shopping at Fred Meyer stores. But being a public company required public disclosures of previously-private financial information – and a desire by stockholders to receive dividends. "When we went public, we had stockholders and they wanted dividends and I had to go to work," he said a decade later. "To pay dividends you have to expand and make profits...Before that, we didn't work very hard."[22] That last sentence was an example of Fred Meyer's sense of humor.

The building boom of the early 1960s produced similarly-styled buildings of generally increasing size. Oak Grove opened in July, 1960, with 61,000 square feet of floor space, the equivalent of one and a half downtown Portland blocks. The new Walnut Park store in Northeast Portland followed in August, 1961, with 80,000 square feet. That project, like the second Hollywood store, was accomplished without losing a day of sales by erecting the new building as the old one was demolished in stages. The Peninsula store, located at North Lombard Street and Ida

Avenue, at 73,000 square feet, and the Hazel Dell store in North Vancouver, Washington, at 80,000 square feet, were completed late in 1962. All these stores offered approximately 65,000 different items in their various departments.

In the meantime, Fred Meyer had not given up hope for building a store in Westmoreland on the land he had owned since the mid-1930s. He made a third and final attempt to win a zone change in July, 1960. The result was the same. The City Planning Commission voted 6-to-1 against Meyer.[23] The Eastmoreland and Westmoreland residential neighborhoods that had opposed Meyer in 1938 and 1950 had even stronger reasons this time. The neighborhoods had won a U.S. District Court order in 1956 aimed at restricting noise from Southern Pacific Railroad trains that used the McLoughlin corridor tracks and the nearby Brooklyn railroad yards. That ruling was based on the residential character of the adjacent neighborhoods, and acceding to a big Fred Meyer commercial project would have jeopardized the court's order limiting the railroad operations. E.C. Sammons, the banker who had fought Meyer all along, finally prevailed. "And he did us a favor, very honestly, because had we built a store there, it would have been much too small," Oran Robertson said long afterward.[24] The newer generation of Fred Meyer stores required much larger land parcels. Instead of losing his temper as he had in 1950, Meyer traded the Westmoreland site for land immediately north of his Stadium store, allowing for expansion at that location. The Westmoreland site became the home of Westmoreland Union Manor, a retirement home for former organized labor workers.

Retail stores were not Fred Meyer's only real estate concern in 1960. The United States Post Office, as it was known then, needed a new main post office in downtown Portland. Howard Andersen, Meyer's construction contractor, and David Simpson, Meyer's friend and real estate broker, learned of the federal government's unusual plan for acquiring a new building. The Post Office asked developers to submit bids based not on construction costs, but on a monthly lease rate over 30 years. Andersen and Meyer took one-third interests in the project, while Simpson and a Portland businessman, Milo McIvor, took one-sixth interests to complete the deal. The Meyer-Andersen team won the bid, and Anderson's company finished erecting the $11 million structure at 715 Northwest Hoyt Street in June, 1962.[25] The U.S. Post Office later bought out the development team before the lease had run its course.[26]

Having built several stores for Fred Meyer Inc. and with many more in the works, Andersen had lunch with Meyer on a regular basis. There was no time for chit-chat. "I mean, there was never, never, never any pleasure," Andersen recalled. "He'd come to lunch and he'd have a sheaf of papers. He was always going over something and asking questions." Andersen remembered one incident in which he and Meyer fell into a dispute over some detail in a drawing or a lease at Meyer's corporate office. They made a $10 bet on who remembered it correctly. Jean Webb, Meyer's secretary, pulled out the documents. Andersen was right. "So he opened up his wallet real carefully, you know. And I started flapping my hands (in the air) and he says, 'What are you doing, Andy?' And I said, 'I'm killing the moths. It's been so long since that thing's been open.' So anyway, he gave me the $10."[27]

The stock offering of 1960 also funded a $750,000 central kitchen near the company's Swan Island warehouse and a test kitchen where Pauline Lawrence and a staff of four worked on new recipes after moving from the old kitchen in Southeast Portland. The big central kitchen employed 80 people, producing food that could be easily reheated at the new Eve's Restaurants or sold pre-packaged at Fred Meyer deli counters. Lawrence ultimately developed 85 recipes for entrees, cakes, pies, salads and pastries to be trucked to the various stores. One of the most popular was a Southern baked bean recipe that Lawrence had learned as a child. The central kitchen produced it daily in 500-pound lots. Taking advantage of the new microwave ovens, Lawrence said, "We tried very hard to make the food come out as if it has been cooked right there in the kitchen on the premises." [28] Lawrence and Meyer agreed that the food should be as fresh as possible without using preservatives. Eating wholesome foods with a minimum of meat or even no meat was one of the tenets of Max Heindel's recommended Rosicrucian lifestyle. "And Mr. Meyer never ate things like hamburgers. He never ate fast food stuff," Lawrence said. "I don't believe the man ever had a hot dog in his life."[29] Lawrence tested every commercial ingredient offered to her. "I never took the word of any salesman," she said. "If they did not come up to our standard, then we didn't buy his product." She took pride when she heard reports of salesmen telling other restaurateurs, "Eve's is buying this."[30]

Lawrence, who retired in 1979, a year after Meyer's death, opened 42 restaurants or cafeterias during her tenure. Trucks filled with central kitchen products eventually left Swan Island daily for destinations in Seattle, Tacoma, Salem, and Albany. Eateries at department stores often lose money but are considered a net gain to overall operations because they refuel customers for additional shopping during the same store visit. Lawrence was an exception. "I never had red figures. I made a profit every year I was there."[31] Still, profits from Eve's were much lower than earnings from other departments, and profits were a key factor in an elaborate bonus system devised by Meyer and Herbert Retzlaff to reward managers and assistant managers. Bonuses were of no small importance. In a good year, a bonus could amount to 50 to 90 percent of a manager's base pay. It was Meyer's way of letting managers know that they couldn't rest on past success: if they wanted to be well paid, they had to continue to deserve it. Oran Robertson, who ultimately succeeded Fred Meyer as company chairman, believed that Lawrence wasn't treated fairly by the bonus system, no matter how much Retzlaff and Meyer tinkered with it. He thought Meyer made it up to her eventually by putting her on the board of directors while he was alive, and by appointing her as a personal representative to his estate and as a trustee of the charitable trust he created at his death, all positions that provided recompense.[32] If Lawrence ever complained about her comparatively small bonuses, none of Meyer's top managers remembered it.

By the middle 1950s Meyer had added Lawrence to his executive committee and its weekly sessions. She also met with him one afternoon a week to discuss restaurants. After Eva Meyer's death, she usually had dinner with Meyer once a week at the Burlingame Eve's. She saw his good side and his angry side as much as anyone. "Mr. Meyer could be a very courteous man when he wanted to be. But he could turn just like that." She had a word for Meyer's angry spells: cranky. Better than many, she learned to deal with it. "If he didn't believe it, he didn't want to hear it," she said. "And so then he would get cranky, and he wouldn't listen. And I thought I knew a little bit so it was my stubbornness, I guess, that caused me to say, 'Well, okay, we can't talk today.' And that's usually the way I did it. When he got to where he was that way I was able to walk away from it and not worry about it." She added, "He was always pretty easy for me to stand up to, but he was not easy for some people ever to stand up to. Until his dying day some people could not."[33] Her dinners with Meyer were peaceful. "I learned early that he needed somebody to talk to. And he never wanted an answer from me. I was a sounding board for him. And I think this is what Mrs. Meyer was, she was the sounding board for him."[34]

Fred Meyer Inc. was moving in many directions in the early 1960s – literally, in the case of the company headquarters. In 1963, Fred Meyer said "goodbye" to Yamhill Street where he had been a daily fixture for more than 40 years, first managing market stalls for others and then edging into retail sales himself. He closed the last Fred Meyer store on Yamhill at Fourth Avenue and moved the corporate offices that had been above that store to much larger quarters at 3800 Southeast 22nd Avenue. To a journalist as skilled as Gerry Pratt, the closure of the Yamhill store easily could have been a compelling human interest story about success and reminiscence. But there was no streak of sentimentality in Meyer. If Pratt offered to write it, Meyer declined. The newspaper reported the closure with just a few sentences and with no comments from Meyer himself – the same as when Meyer closed shop at the Alderway Building.

The new Fred Meyer headquarters was an industrial building erected in the 1920s that formerly was home to the Grand Rapids Store Equipment Co. Oran Robertson planned the interior spaces and Howard Andersen did the remodeling. Robertson mapped out a small enclosed office for Meyer, but left the other executives working in a single large room, as Meyer had wanted. There were small conferences rooms available to the side when private talks were necessary. Meyer, who had delegated the details, wasn't happy with carpeting and some amenities he considered frills. "He really got mad because he thought that offices should be open, austere and nothing fancy in them," Andersen recalled. "And no partitions and everybody should be kept out in the open so he could watch everybody, no carpet on the floor or nothing like that."[35] One consequence of the move was an interruption in Meyer's luncheons with Andersen. "He just quit talking to me. He and I used to have lunch maybe twice a month or maybe even oftener. And he just quit calling me and he wouldn't have anything to do, he wouldn't even talk to me."[36]

While it took Meyer a few months to get over his rift with Andersen, his public statements, typical of Meyer, were positive and upbeat. Indeed, he made the carpeting sound like a shrewd decision. In a lengthy newspaper column by Gerry Pratt about the new corporate digs, Meyer contended that the carpet was a long-term bargain. "We made a study and found it would save us money, though the out-of-pocket costs were $48,000 more than tile. But janitor service is so costly, we found we could save $8,200 a year in service costs." Vacuuming carpet, Meyer said, was cheaper than mopping and waxing. The savings would kick in after five years.[37] Meyer had moved out of downtown because he knew there was more expansion in the works. He needed more space for his growing managerial team, and he wanted them to have free parking.[38] It proved to be another excellent real estate move. Five decades later, Fred Meyer corporate offices were still at the same location.

Living at the Sheraton Hotel, Meyer couldn't help noticing the huge popularity of the new Lloyd Center shopping mall across Multnomah Street. In 1962, he disclosed plans for 35 acres he had ac-

Fred Meyer often donated food and merchandise to the Salvation Army and the Portland Police Bureau's Sunshine Division before Christmas. From left, he is joined in 1962 by John Erickson of the Salvation Army, Earle A. Chiles, Police Chief David Johnson and Mayor Terry Schrunk, right. (Oregonian)

quired on the eastern edge of Beaverton, then a small suburb of 8,000 residents. It was exactly the kind of site he was so good at selecting, bounded on the north and south by Oregon Highways 8 and 10, and on the east by a new freeway in the planning stages that would become Highway 217. He envisioned 1.5 million square feet of retail space in a fully-enclosed mall, surrounded by parking for 2,400 cars. He planned to call Valley West, and hoped to attract 50 retailers ranging from large national chains to small local stores. Of course, it would include a Fred Meyer shopping center. It was to be the second largest shopping mall in the Portland region, behind Lloyd Center, and would draw customers from as far away as the Oregon Coast, he said.[39] In June, 1962, bulldozers started pushing around dirt after a ceremony attended by Earle A. Chiles, Washington County elected officials and local business owners who were thrilled by the possibilities.[40]

However, the bulldozers soon left and the land sat vacant. Four years later, Meyer told stockholders, "Work continues on major leases for the Valley West shopping center near Beaverton, Oregon. The date of commencement of construction will be determined by progress of lease negotiations."[41] Late in 1967, Meyer announced two major leases for the center. J.C. Penney had agreed to a 187,000 square-foot-store and Lipman Wolfe & Co., another department store of the era, had signed on for 125,000 square feet. Meyer said construction would start in 1968.[42] But 1968 came and went and the land sat vacant. What happened behind the scenes was that Meyer let himself be spooked by a slight increase in interest rates, which rose from 6 to 6.25 percent. Meyer had always been a shrewd borrower. He had gone to the East Coast many times over the years to entice lenders into backing his real estate companies, which in turn leased the properties to Fred Meyer stores. "He understood money," recalled Dale Warman, whose career was taking him near the highest levels of Fred Meyer Inc. "And he never paid more for loans... I mean he always got the best deal." Warman heard others say, "We know when the bottom of interest rates have finally hit. .That's when Mr. Meyer is in Boston or New York negotiating."[43]

Meyer proved stubborn as ever, refusing to pay more than 6 percent interest to build the Beaverton project. It is possible that his recollection of being overextended and having to surrender the Alderway Building back in the Depression was a factor in his thinking. But this time, the rates proved stubborn as well. When they did not drop to meet Meyer's expectations, he had to buy out the leases with J.C. Penney and Lipman Wolfe. The Beaverton site sat fallow for almost another decade. The Beaverton Fred Meyer, at 205,000 square feet the largest in company history, was finally finished in 1979, a year after Meyer's death. Bad luck seemed to run with the territory. Farrah Fawcett, a television and movie star, was hired to attend the grand opening for two hours. She fled to safety 60 minutes early, after she and her security guards felt threatened by the surge of a large opening-day mob pushing toward her. [44] Beaverton became one of Fred Meyer's most profitable stores, but Meyer's reticence to bow to prevailing interest rates cost him an even larger opportunity. While he waited for a better rate, another developer in 1974 opened a huge shopping mall just a few miles away– Washington Square. It became one of the most successful revenue-generating regional malls in the United States. The patriarch of the Fred Meyer chain made few real estate mistakes during his long life. The missed opportunity at Beaverton was one.

Not long after Fred Meyer Inc. started life as a publicly-held company, a new grocery competitor surfaced in Portland that threatened to beat Fred Meyer at his own game – low prices. The company was called Baza'r, and it opened its first store at Southeast 82nd Avenue and Division Street in November 1961.[45] It was a bare-bones, no-frills store with no amenities other than its prices. Fred Meyer's grocery managers toured the building anonymously, along with hundreds of other customers. They were stunned by the prices they saw. Fred Meyer stores liked to offer one or two loss-leader products to attract customers; their other prices were competitive but not necessarily low. Baza'r, it seemed, offered lower prices on virtually everything. "And so we watched them," recalled Cyril Green, who in 13 years with Fred Meyer had risen from a part-time job as a grocery-bagger in high school to chief grocery buyer. "They were doing big business out there on 82nd and Division in their store there. Later they opened one on the west side over by what's now our Beaverton store, and they were really doing big business."[46] Fred Meyer's corporate policy had always been to match any lower prices from a competitor. But that was a tedious process because the check-stand employee had to verify the competing price and then make a special entry noting that Fred Meyer had honored the lower figure. It prolonged waiting times for other customers in the checkout line. Green and Virgil Campbell decided they needed a plan for competing with Baza'r. Campbell was a highly-respected manager who had grown up in the Depression on a Nebraska farm. After working in the Portland shipyards during World War II, he noticed a sign on Yamhill Street saying that Fred Meyer was hiring. Campbell took what he thought would be a temporary job. "Temporary" turned out to be 41 years.

Like other employees, Campbell never forgot his first direct encounter with Meyer. By the early 1950s, Campbell was managing the store at Fourth Avenue and Yamhill Street. The noon hour was the busiest time at that store, and Campbell was overseeing two crowded check stands when Meyer walked by and noticed surplus fresh produce sitting in boxes on the sidewalk. Meyer told Campbell to move the produce immediately. Campbell said taking care of customers was his first priority, and he'd get to the produce after 1 p.m. Meyer repeated his order, but Campbell, an imposing man standing well over six feet tall, stood firm. "He could see I was getting angry," Campbell said. Meyer, likely realizing that he couldn't challenge Campbell's priorities, said, "Well, we're both right," and walked away. "I've seen him chew out a lot of people," Campbell said long afterward, "but that was the only time I ever had a brouhaha with Fred Meyer." [47]

Campbell greatly admired Meyer's intelligence, but not Meyer's abrasive treatment of employees. Campbell proved that a gentler management style could still produce excellent results, and he became an informal mentor to younger managers who eventually rose to high levels in the company, as did Campbell himself. Campbell had first met

Green while Green worked part-time for Fred Meyer Inc. as a high school student. Campbell admired the young man's work ethic, and convinced Green to dump his duck-tail haircut for a more professional look. Campbell had preceded Green as grocery buyer, and from 1960 to 1970 he was the grocery merchandiser, which meant he was in charge of supervising all Meyer grocery departments. Campbell and Green decided that Fred Meyer stores did not have to be totally competitive on prices with Baza'r, just close.

Green went to Baza'r on Sundays to check prices. He knew he would be ejected if they found him writing notes on a pad, so he carried a tape recorder in his clothing attached to a tiny microphone. "I just went along and recorded all the prices and that became our price-checking mechanism with them." Green and Campbell figured that two or three cents on most items didn't matter to customers. "So we made sure we were never far from them, but we left ourselves enough room to still run our loss leaders." [48] Customers who asked for price matching still got it at the check stand, but they were advised to watch Fred Meyer ads and decide for themselves if they didn't come out just as well over a period of time. Meyer was 75 years old at this point, and his chain had gotten so large he couldn't oversee all details. Campbell and Green decided they would not tell Meyer about their new pricing strategy. "We just did it," Green said. "And little by little, I mean, Mr. Meyer probably thought we were meeting all the prices. You just can't sell everything below cost and make any money." If grocery profits dwindled, so would the size of annual bonuses for managers. Green and Campbell suspected Meyer would not have approved their scheme in advance. "Mr. Meyer was a fierce competitor. He'd expect you to fight tooth and nail, and never let anyone undersell you."[49]

William Triplett Jr., Baza'r's president, noted that Fred Meyer never started a price war, but usually would respond to one. "There are a few items Fred Meyer is sensitive to, like milk or bread," Triplett said. "He simply won't let anyone undersell him and he has his own dairy and bakery."[50] Triplett's chain grew with lightning rapidity in the 1960s, eventually reaching 89 stores in a half dozen western states. But once losses started setting in, Baza'r's demise was almost as quick. The company hastily sold off stores and eventually quit business in 1978. Fred Meyer feasted on parts of the carcass, buying three former Baza'r sites in Washington and Alaska in 1975. Given some of his past zoning battles, Meyer had learned that it was faster and cheaper to buy existing stores so long as their locations fit his needs. It is possible that Meyer himself never learned about the pricing strategy adopted by Campbell and Green. "And frankly, if he did know, I guess he didn't mind as long as sales were good – and they were– and profits were better– which they were," Green said. [51] It was the first major example of managers making decisions on their own without seeking Meyer's approval. A few years later, some other executives made a dramatic change to the interior design of Fred Meyer stores without the patriarch's approval. Meyer was angry about it – until the results flowed in.

Fred Meyer Inc.'s next expansion occurred in January, 1964, when it completed the purchase of a Spokane, Washington-based wholesale firm, Roundup Grocery Co. In addition to providing wholesale goods to nearly 400 grocery stores in Eastern Washington, Eastern Oregon, Northern Idaho and Western Montana, Roundup also owned 14 Sigman IGA retail groceries in Eastern Washington and Eastern Oregon, and three B&B grocery stores in three small Northwestern Montana towns. The purchase opened up a new retail landscape for Fred Meyer in those areas, but Meyer's executives soon found a puzzling barrier to their growth. Roundup's single largest wholesale grocery customer was Albertson's, a Boise, Idaho-based chain that was strong in Central Washington and had become a major food retailer in the Portland area, as well. Albertson's accounted for roughly 30 percent of Roundup's wholesale business. "And you know, we're sitting down here competing with somebody (Albertson's) like crazy, and up there you're trying to serve him," said Jack Crocker, who had risen to vice president status at Fred Meyer. "How in the hell do you please them up in Spokane and then try to beat their tails off here in Portland?" The Roundup purchase stymied Fred Meyer's larger growth in Spokane and closed off the Central Washington market already served by Albertson's.

In retrospect, "We never should have bought it," Crocker said of Roundup. "I think we paid $3.5 million. We gave them an offer we knew they'd turn down and they accepted it and we ended up getting the damn thing."[52] Meyer said the acquisition expanded sales possibilities for its in-house food production ranging from ice cream to frozen and other prepared foods made under Pauline Lawrence's supervision at Swan Island.[53] He intended to leave Roundup's top management team in place, but soon learned that the company was in more of a shambles than he realized; its warehouse and truck transport system were outdated and barely functional. Meyer called on one of his highly-dedicated younger managers, Cyril Green, to move to Spokane and take over Roundup. It was a big step for Green, the chief grocery buyer who was just turning 33.

Green was "scared to death" when Meyer offered him the job. "I remember when I was told. I just went limp because it's a big change for me, a big responsibility. But I recovered and went at it. But it was a great experience for me; I think one of the big breaks in my career. But frankly, saying that a guy who's just been the head buyer should be the general manager of the whole company over there was quite a leap of faith, as we call it today." It was an example, however, of Meyer's train-them-young-and-promote-from-within philosophy. Despite his youngish age, Green had spent most of the previous 17 years working in the Meyer system, taking his lumps at times from the patriarch but always learning. Less than a decade earlier, he'd been a department manager at Rose City when that store was going through its first renovation. Remodeling at Fred Meyer stores always was complicated, since shutting down was never an option. Meyer walked through the store one night and noticed garbage cans placed in a temporary but publicly-visible location. "He wrote me a scathing memo about what a dumb, terrible stupid person I was to have those garbage cans sitting out for the public to see," Green recalled.[54]

Green managed the Roundup operation for four years before being called back to Portland for another internal promotion. During his time in Spokane, he doubled the size of the Roundup warehouse, revamped the truck fleet, met with each retail customer, recruited a few new customers and figured out a complex pricing system for the growing number of inventory items. "It was an opportunity to run a business, so I was the only person at Fred Meyer who really got to run a whole business," he said. "It was great for me." It also was a profitable operation that steadily added to Fred Meyer Inc.'s bottom line, and grew to 550 employees during Green's tenure. Yet in Green's opinion, like Crocker's, the Roundup acquisition didn't make the best business sense. "Roundup, I don't think in retrospect, ever really made any constructive benefit to Fred Meyer other than the direct profit we earned on the business itself," Green said.[55] Roundup put Meyer in direct competition again with Robert Hudson, the man who had somehow squeezed Meyer out of the Piggly Wiggly operation in Portland back in the 1920s. The success of Fred Meyer stores over the years along with Safeway and Albertson's had reduced Piggly Wiggly's market share to minuscule. Hudson's primary business was now as a food processor and grocery wholesaler. He, too, had moved into the central Washington wholesale business with the acquisition of Continental Food Inc., in Yakima, at the same time Meyer was acquiring Roundup. Fred Meyer Inc. finally sold Roundup in 1980, fairly soon after Meyer's death.

Soon after the Roundup purchase, Meyer struck another deal in Washington state, purchasing a chain of eight Market Basket grocery stores in the southern and eastern suburbs of Seattle. Meyer, who had just turned 79, hoped eventually to pair them with the Marketime drug chain he had acquired in 1959. Marketime had grown from four to seven stores. "In time we will put them together to form a complete

Long after most people retire, Fred Meyer in the early 1960s was in the midst of his largest corporate expansion. (Oregonian)

operation," Meyer said. He also told reporter Pratt that he was still on the lookout for other acquisitions. "We are like the eligible bachelor, we always have three or four on our list. We intend to continue to expand."[56] The eligible bachelor had problems with Market Basket, however. The relationship did not survive the rest of the decade.

Meyer in the middle 1960s also went on a shopping trip to San Francisco to look at a possible acquisition. He was joined by Virgil Campbell and his long-time real estate friend, David Simpson. Their host planned to take them to dinner one night in North Beach, but the reservation was an hour later than planned. Would Meyer be interested, the host asked, in having a drink at one of the new topless clubs that recently had taken San Francisco's entertainment world by storm? "I'd say he's flexible," Campbell answered, not knowing how Meyer would respond. The four men went to a club and got their drinks, just as half a dozen nearly naked young women began dancing. Campbell kept his eyes on Meyer. Meyer's eyes glanced all around the room, taking in the crowd, the furnishings, even the ceiling. "I think they're doing pretty well here," he concluded. "Don't have much invested."[57] Meyer decided not to buy the San Francisco stores.

During the early 1960s, Oran Robertson, who was in charge of building new stores and designing their layouts, took a retail consultant visiting from Southern California on a tour of Fred Meyer stores. The consultant noticed the simple white exteriors, green concrete floors, hand-painted signs advertising various specials, the plain white interior walls and brown wainscoting. The drab sameness of the stores represented Meyer's preoccupation with standardization and keeping costs low. Maybe these bargain-basement appearances work here, the consultant told Robertson, but they likely would fail in large California cities. Robertson realized that perhaps the time had come to rethink the appearance of Fred Meyer stores. When it came to architecture and interior design, "Mr. Meyer had no time of day for that at all."[58] Robertson and Rollin Killoran, newly promoted to marketing director, knew that convincing Meyer to approve an aesthetic upgrade was unlikely. They decided to make changes in one of the chain's smallest stores and see how customers reacted. They chose the B&B store in Kalispell, Montana, figuring that Meyer himself would not make the airplane flight to Spokane followed by a three-hour drive to the town north of

Flathead Lake to undertake any personal inspections.

The new interior design included softer, more relaxing earth tones on the walls. Hand-painted signs disappeared. Bare concrete floors were covered with carpet or vinyl tiles. Overhead lighting was softened. Robertson and Killoran got the answer they needed when sales from the remodeled store showed a definite increase. They decided to use the new interior design format for big new Fred Meyer stores to be constructed at 82nd Avenue and Foster Road in Portland, and in Tigard. Howard Andersen, of course, would build both of those large new shopping complexes. "Mr. Meyer's idea of a building was green concrete floors and exposed ceilings, and that was it, you know," Andersen recalled. "And so they started dropping ceilings, and then they started putting tile on the floors, and they started putting carpets on the floors, and then they started using colors, and a few things like that. Mr. Meyer's idea was that if you kept everything cheap, cheap, cheap, people would think they were getting the best prices at his store."[59] Robertson's philosophy was to give people a more pleasant, comfortable atmosphere as well as decent prices.

Meyer's practice was to inspect all new construction as it progressed. Robertson managed to keep Meyer away from the Foster Road store while the interior details were added. Like Killoran, Robertson knew the fate of their bold move depended on immediate results. ``We knew if it worked they couldn't fire us, because sales would go up and you can't fight that."[60] Meyer, then 80 years old, saw the interior of the 92,000 square foot store for the first time just before the grand opening. Killoran accompanied Meyer when he first set foot inside. "And he looks around, you know, kind of funny like. I thought, 'Well, here I go. Whatever is going to happen, Robertson and Killoran are going to get the shaft.'" [61] Meyer was visibly upset. But before he had a chance to vent his anger, according to Killoran's recollection, a long-time employee in the candy department, Tina Thomas, threw her arms around Meyer in a joyous hug. "You know, Mr. Meyer," she told him, "I've worked for you for 20-some years, but I've never been proud to work for Fred Meyer until this store." [62] For one of the few times in his life, Meyer was too stunned to answer. Just before the Foster grand opening, Killoran told a reporter that the new store "has been designed to be an adventure in shopping."[63] The adventure for Robertson and Killoran included the personal reaction of their boss. Meyer's irritation with the fancier stores did stem from the company's higher costs, in Robertson's view. "He felt the customer was having to pay for that, and that it wasn't right."[64]

Both Foster Road and the Tigard store, which opened in March, 1967, showed strong sales. There was concern that Foster's interior would take a beating from dusty or muddy customers who lived and worked on nearby farmland, but shoppers treated their new store with respect. Despite the encouraging early returns, Meyer expressed his displeasure to his intimates. "Mr. Meyer was not too happy with the new design," Andersen said. "But after people told him how wonderful it was and how good it was, well then he let people think it was his idea." There was tension for awhile at the corporate headquarters, however. "He was really p.o.'ed at O.B. (Robertson) and in the process he got a little bit mad at me," Andersen said.[65] There was no turning back, however. Foster Road and Tigard became the models for subsequent remodels and new Fred Meyer stores. Always wanting to put a positive spin on his public statements, Meyer summarized Foster Road in one sentence in the company's annual report: "This shopping center presents a new merchandising concept in design and interior décor, and was well received by customers."[66] The process of changing the interior design suggested a few other themes about Meyer and the growing retail chain that bore his name. Given his age and the size of his empire, there was no way that Meyer could know everything that was going on within it. Meyer's top managers proved capable of exercising sound judgment on their own, even if Meyer himself did not fully trust them. The improved design soon would play an important role in the company's ability to upgrade its inventory in an exciting new chapter of Fred Meyer Inc.

Throughout the rapid period of corporate growth in the late 1950s and mid-1960s, lawyers for Fred Meyer Inc. were still fighting with the over the anti-trust allegations it had raised in 1959 relating to various promotions that Fred Meyer ran to attract customers seeking low prices, including the coupon books the company had sold since the 1930s. The commission accused the company of using its enormous buying power to force price concessions from suppliers that the suppliers could not offer to Fred Meyer competitors, thereby driving smaller retailers out of business. Avoiding that eventuality is what had motivated William Wright Patman to advocate for the Clayton Antitrust Act in 1936: "I believe it is the opinion of everyone who has studied this subject, that the day of the independent merchant is gone unless something is done and done quickly. . . . So we have reached the crossroads; we must either turn the food and grocery business of this. . .country over to a few corporate chains, or we have got to pass laws that will give the people, who built this country in time of peace and who saved it in time of war, an opportunity to exist—not to give them any special rights, special privileges, or special benefits, but just to deny their competitors the special benefits that they are getting, that they should not be permitted to have."[67]

It took the agency four years to craft a lengthy, 63-page decision based on advertising campaigns using Fred Meyer coupon books in the years 1956 and 1957, an era when Fred Meyer Inc. operated 13 stores in the Portland area. The company's response was brief: As president, Earle A. Chiles issued a statement saying the firm assumed the order was "just another of the many attacks on the long-standing policy of Fred

Meyer stores to buy from producers in very large quantities and to pass the savings thus made along to the retail customers in our stores. The public, and not our stores, is the beneficiary."[68]

Portland attorney George W. Mead joined forces with a bevy of Washington, D.C., lawyers to appeal the FTC's ruling to the Ninth U.S. Circuit Court of Appeals. The zeal with which they fought the case is revealed in part in the court's lengthy opinion, which addressed every issue Fred Meyer had raised on appeal. One of the arguments, for example, was that two of the individual defendants named in the FTC's case against the company—Fred Meyer as chairman and Earle A. Chiles as president—were too far removed from the company's marketing decisions to support the FTC's case against them as individuals. The court disagreed. The court observed that both men had substantial stock in the company. As to Meyer himself, the court said, "We think that, despite Meyer's denials of knowledge of the operations of the business, the Commission was justified in concluding that if 'a majority of Portland's 120,000 families' were apprised of the details of these programs, we think it is a fair inference that the Chairman of the Board also knew about them." "[69]

On the merits of the appeal about the meaning of the Clayton Act, the Ninth Circuit issued a mixed ruling. It upheld the FTC's determination that four Fred Meyer suppliers had violated a provision of the Clayton Act concerning promotional fees by substantially paying for the costs of printing the popular Fred Meyer coupon books. However, it also held that two suppliers, Tri-Valley Packing Association and Idaho Canning Company, had not violated the Clayton Act by selling canned goods to Fred Meyer at prices lower than offered to two wholesalers, Hudson House and Wadhams. According to the Ninth Circuit, the wholesalers were not technically "competing" with Fred Meyer because, as a retailer, Fred Meyer stood on a different level of the grocery hierarchy than the wholesalers. However, the Ninth Circuit affirmed the trade commission's finding that money paid by four suppliers who substantially bore the cost of producing Fred Meyer's popular coupon books violated another provision of the law concerning promotional fees. [70]

The Federal Trade Commission refused to accept the Ninth Circuit's word as final about the meaning of the murky provisions of the Clayton Antitrust Act. It appealed to the United States Supreme Court. Commission lawyers argued that the Ninth Circuit's ruling left a retailer who bought goods from a wholesaler unprotected against discriminatory prices negotiated directly between a large retailer such as Fred Meyer and a manufacturer. By a 7-2 vote the Supreme Court reversed the Ninth Circuit. Chief Justice Earl Warren conceded that the Clayton Act was not clearly written and was difficult to interpret and implement. "But, on the concrete facts here presented, it is clear that the impact of Meyer's receiving discriminatory promotional allowances is felt by the disfavored retailers with whom Meyer competes in resales."[71] The Court held that the anti-trust law requires a seller to make proportionate benefits available to both direct-buying retailers and to competing retailers who buy through wholesalers.

Justice Harlan's dissent complained that the Clayton Act was "a hodgepodge of confusing, inconsistent, and frequently misdirected restrictions." Regardless, Fred Meyer Inc. had lost the case. Its name became a permanent fixture in the world of federal regulations, however. All the Justices agreed that the FTC needed to issue guidelines to clarify the law and assist sellers in complying with its requirements. In 1969, the FTC issued what have come to be known as "Fred Meyer Guides," which are intended to inform sellers on how to comply with the law when making promotional payments and services to retailers on fair terms.

Meyer himself, of course, was unhappy with the result. "We lost the suit," he said a few years later. "We were buying cheaper than some other people because we sold more of an item. The United States was founded on the idea that you had freedom of choice and (to) buy as cheap as you can."[72] Meyer's buyers felt they weren't holding a gun to anyone's head to sign deals they didn't want. "The suppliers did get a heck of a big benefit from it in that their item sold in a lot bigger quantities," noted Jack Crocker.[73]

As 1968 neared its end, Fred Meyer had two priorities on his mind. His biggest store yet, a 173,000-square-foot center, would open in suburban Lynnwood, Washington, on 15 acres half way between Seattle and Everett.[74] Meyer attended the grand opening himself. He related his story about his gold mining venture in Alaska, and how he looked up at the big mountain, down at his small shovel and decided digging for gold wasn't for him.[75] The Lynnwood store was the first property to bear the "Fred Meyer" name in Washington state, although he had purchased the Marketime, a drug and variety chain, and Market Basket grocery stores in 1959 and 1965, respectively. He had planned to merge those outlets under the Fred Meyer banner someday, but problems had arisen with Market Basket. The solution was just a few months ahead. The other matter on Meyer's mind was a change in company leadership.

Earle A. Chiles, Meyer's stepson and son of Eva Chatfield Chiles Meyer, was nearing age 65. The company had no mandatory retirement age. Chiles had been president since 1955, although members of the company's executive committee knew it was a hollow title. The person in charge was still Meyer himself, nearing the age of 83 and showing no signs of stepping back. However, some members of Meyer's inner circle had come to believe it was time for Meyer to select a real chief executive and lessen his own grip on operations. One was Herbert Retzlaff, Meyer's long-time controller. "There was a time, as Meyer grew older and he was less, well, he was still active but there were a number of us that felt that Fred Meyer wasn't as keen as he used to be. And we felt that he should be the chairman of the board but somebody else should really run the company." According to Retzlaff, Meyer agreed to that strategy. Meyer and Retzlaff also agreed that the new president should be Jack Crocker.[76]

Chiles, of course, stood in the path of Crocker's promotion. Rollin Killoran, the marketing director and one of Chiles' many good friends, had suggested that Chiles resign, knowing that Meyer wanted a change. Chiles, according to Killoran's account, declined to leave. At a meeting of the board of directors in December, 1968, Meyer asked Chiles if he wanted to continue as president, and, if so, to explain why he should remain. It was a difficult moment for Chiles. He had spent his entire career working for his stepfather, having started as a teenager before his mother and Meyer had created Fred Meyer Inc. He had earned wide respect within the company as a gentle and compassionate man. Yet he had always had trouble standing up to Meyer's forceful personality.

"What Fred Meyer wanted from Earle Chiles was good, strong decisions," said Pauline Lawrence, who had observed interactions between the two men for 20 years. "And it was very difficult for Mr. Chiles to make a good strong decision because he knew he was going to be criticized if he made it – whichever way he made it."[77] Chiles did not make a convincing case for himself at the board meeting. "Earle was a guy that gave in easily," said Killoran, who was one of the directors. "He was not a fighter. Ultimately, it was pitiful from my point of view, of course, as I was close to him. It was a very pitiful morning for me. So then they voted and they voted Jack (Crocker) as president." [78]

There was, according to Oran Robertson years later, another reason why Chiles did not make a stronger pitch to keep his position as president. Sometime before that meeting, a discrepancy had become apparent in the accounting records of the real estate companies which owned land under several of the Fred Meyer Inc. stores. Chiles was a minority shareholder in those companies and was actively involved in their management. Chiles repaid more than $300,000 to Fred Meyer Inc., according to Robertson. Meyer did not share the information with Fred Meyer Inc. directors, [79] and Robertson said he learned about it from papers discovered after Meyer's death. Neither Meyer nor Chiles would have wanted the matter disclosed publicly.

Meyer gave brief mention of Chiles' departure as president in the Fred Meyer Inc. annual report issued soon thereafter. "We would also like to note the retirement, as of Dec. 31, 1968, of Earle A. Chiles as president," Meyer wrote. "Mr. Chiles had been with the firm for 40 years, and we wish him well in his retirement."[80] Though ousted as president, Chiles retained his seat on the corporation's board of directors. He opened an office in the Executive Building, the former location of the Fred Meyer Sixth Avenue store, to engage in real estate and investment management. If there was any bitterness on Earle Chiles' part, it was never expressed publicly. It wasn't news to him that he had not lived up to Meyer's expectations. "He wanted Mr. Chiles to be perfect, you know," Pauline Lawrence said. "And that was a disappointment to Mr. Meyer because he wasn't as brilliant, as genius, as Mr. Meyer was. But I do know I've never met a man that as kind and nice to everybody as he (Chiles) was....He spoke highly of Mr. Meyer even though Mr. Meyer never seemed to– they never seemed to get together on things."[81]

As Fred Meyer neared his 83rd birthday, his selection of Crocker as president suggested that Crocker was the likely heir to succeed Meyer as chairman. Crocker brought many of the qualities that Meyer admired. A native Portlander, he had grown up in the Depression. Although his father kept a job as an auto dealership foreman during those stressful years, Crocker was not a silver-spoon child. He remembered going to Boise Elementary School with some classmates who could not afford shoes. Crocker delivered newspapers and spent two summers while attending Jefferson High School working as a grocery bagger at 40 cents per hour at the first Walnut Park Fred Meyer. He studied accounting at the University of Oregon and served a stint in the U.S. Air Force. He finished training as a navigator for bombing raids over Germany just as World War II ended. He had never seriously considered a career in the grocery business until he found his work at an accounting firm unrewarding and heard about an opportunity to work for Herb Retzlaff at Fred Meyer Inc.

Crocker's first assignment at Fred Meyer was to try improving the efficiency of the 12-person accounting staff. His changes produced the same amount of work with eight employees. Then, with Fred Meyer's encouragement, he went about improving the efficiency of several other business functions, with the benefit of time-management training classes paid for by the company. His last title before being named president was director of operations. Meyer had added Crocker to the corporation's board of directors four years earlier. Now, at age 44, Crocker was the leader of a company with more than 3,200 employees and in control of virtually all Fred Meyer operations. At least, that was how it was supposed to work in the world of corporate management and governance: the board of directors sets policies and the management, led by the president or chief executive officer, is supposed to carry them out. Fred Meyer Inc., however, was not a typical company. And Fred Meyer the patriarch was not a typical board chairman. He still showed up for work at the corporate office six or seven days a week. Was that the sign of a man ready to ease his grip on the corporate reins of a company he had been building for 45 years?

---

[1] Killoran, Rollin, oral history interview, OHS sound recording 1308, Nov. 3, 1988.

[2] *Oregonian/Oregon Journal,* Jan. 28, 1960, p. 1. Because of a strike by some newspaper mechanical employees, the Oregonian and Oregon Journal newsrooms combined forces for a time to issue a daily newspaper bearing both nameplates.

[3] Retzlaff, Herbert, oral history interview, OHS sound recording 1311, Feb. 22, 1989.
[4] Meyer, Fred, OHS sound recording 9474, Aug. 25, 1970.
[5] *Willamette Week*, March 28, 1977. p. 2.
[6] Lawrence, Pauline, oral history interview, OHS sound recording 1309, Jan. 12, 1989.
[7] Webb, Jean S., OHS sound recording 1316, July 11, 1989.
[8] Oregonian/Oregon Journal, Jan. 29, 1960, p. 18.
[9] Warman, Dale, oral history interview, OHS sound recording 1315, April 20, 1989.
[10] Crocker, Jack, oral history interview, OHS sound recording 1304, June 1, 1989.
[11] *Willamette Week,* March 28, 1977, p. 2.
[12] Ibid.
[13] Retzlaff, *op. cit.,* March 1, 1989.
[14] *Oregonian,* Oct. 10, 1977, p. 1.
[15] Killoran, *op cit.*
[16] Robertson, Oran, OHS sound recording 1312, Feb.2, 1989.
[17] Warman, *op. cit.,* April 27, 1989.
[18] *Oregonian/Oregon Journal*, Feb. 11, 1960, p. 37.
[19] *Ibid.,* Feb. 2, 1960, p. 4.
[20] Retzlaff , *op. cit.,* Feb. 22, 1989
[21] *Oregonian/Oregon Journal,* March 31, 1960, p. 1.
[22] Meyer, *op. cit."*
[23] *Oregonian,* July 20, 1960, p. 11.
[24] Robertson, *op. cit.,* Feb. 2, 1989.
[25] *Ibid.,* June 28, 1962, p. 22.
[26] Andersen, Howard, OHS sound recording 1300, Aug. 9, 1989.
[27] *Ibid.*
[28] Lawrence, *op. cit,* Nov. 17, 1988.
[29] *Ibid.,* Jan. 12, 1989.
[30] *Ibid.,* Dec. 8, 1988.
[31] *Ibid.,* Oct. 25, 1988.
[32] Robertson, *op. cit.*
[33] Lawrence, *op. cit.,* Dec. 8, 1988.
[34] Lawrence, *op. cit.,* Jan. 12, 1989.
[35] Andersen, *op. cit.*
[36] *Ibid.*
[37] *Oregonian,* Oct. 12, 1963, sec. 3, p. 4.
[38] Webb, Jean, oral history interview, OHS sound recording 1316, July 11, 1989.
[39] Fred Meyer Inc, *Annual Report, 1962,* p. 1.
[40] *Oregonian,* June 1, 1962, p. 1.
[41] Fred Meyer Inc., *Annual Report, 1966,* p. 2.
[42] *Oregonian,* Oct. 7, 1967, p. 1.
[43] Warman, *op. cit.*
[44] *Oregonian,* Nov. 15, 1976, p. C6.
[45] *Ibid.,* Nov. 15, 1961, p. 15.
[46] Green, Cyril K., OHS sound recording 1307, Feb. 27, 1989.
[47] Campbell, Virgil, interview with author, Aug. 19, 2013.

[48] *Ibid.*
[49] *Ibid.*
[50] *Willamette Week*, March 28, 1977, p. 4.

[51] Green, *op. cit.*
[52] Crocker , *op. cit.,* Aug. 2, 1989.
[53] *Oregonian,* Dec. 1, 1963, p. 1.
[54] Green, *op. cit.*
[55] *Ibid.*
[56] *Oregonian,* Feb. 28, 1965, p. F6.
[57] Campbell, Virgil, interview with author Aug. 19, 2013.
[58] Robertson, *op. cit.*
[59] Andersen, *op. cit.*
[60] *Oregonian,* April 24, 1988, p. E1.
[61] Killoran , *op. cit,*.Sept. 29, 1989.
[62] *Ibid.*
[63] *Oregonian,* Oct. 30, 1966, p. 43.
[64] Robertson, Oran, OHS sound recording 9496, Feb. 2, 1980.
[65] Andersen, *op. cit.*
[66] Fred Meyer Inc., *Annual Report 1966,* p. 1.
[67] *Federal Trade Commission v. Fred Meyer Inc., et. al., op. cit.,* footnote 14.
[68] *Oregonian,* April 18, 1963, p. 22.
[69] *Ibid.*
[70] *Fred Meyer Inc. v. Federal Trade Commission ,* 359 F2d 351 (1966).
[71] *Federal Trade Commission v. Fred Meyer Inc., et. al.,* 390 U.S.341 (1967).
[72] Meyer, Fred, OHS sound recording 9497, Aug. 25, 1970.
[73] Crocker, *op. cit.*
[74] *Oregonian,* Dec. 2, 1968, p. 18.
[75] Crocker , *op. cit*
[76] Retzlaff, *op. cit.,* March 1, 1989.
[77] Lawrence, *op. cit.,* Jan. 12, 1989.
[78] Killoran, *op. cit.,* Nov. 3, 1988.
[79] Robertson, Oran, OHS sound recording 1312, March 28, 1989.
[80] Fred Meyer Inc., *Annual Report, 1968,* p. 1.
[81] Lawrence, *op. cit.,* Nov. 17, 1988.

CHAPTER SEVEN

Palace Revolt?

Fred Meyer was just weeks away from his 83rd birthday when Jack Crocker took over as president of Fred Meyer Inc. in January, 1969. Most entrepreneurs would have been retired or seriously cutting back on their work obligations at that age. Meyer's decision to replace Earle A. Chiles with Crocker might have been a sign that Meyer was seeking stronger management below him. Crocker accepted the job with the understanding that operating authority went with it. "I had only one objective and that was to prove to him (Meyer) that his trust in me was justified. And I never betrayed that trust at any time. I told him I didn't want to be president in name only, and he said, 'That's why you're here. That's why Earle isn't president.'"[1] The operative word in that statement was "objective"; Crocker believed strongly in management by objectives. His first question about any new initiative inevitably was, what's our objective?

Almost all who had worked with Crocker applauded his promotion. "I think it was kind of like a breath of fresh air," said Dale Warman, who had been a close Crocker associate. "We thought that maybe Jack would take some of the pressure off us– the day-to-day confrontation with Mr. Meyer– because we knew Earle never did have the respect to do that. Jack really tried. And Jack would always defend Mr. Meyer. He'd try to make you understand where Mr. Meyer was coming from." If Meyer saw an employee performing a task in an unacceptable manner, Meyer's response usually involved personal criticism. It was easy, Warman thought, for the message to get lost in Meyer's delivery. "You'd leave all upset with Mr. Meyer." But when Crocker saw behavior he wished to change, Warman said Crocker's approach was more considerate: "You know, this is not the way to do it."[2]

One of Crocker's first actions was to establish his own management team of experienced Fred Meyer employees he had known and trusted for many years. The company was divided into three major categories: food, apparel and drugs and variety. Each of those departments had a manager, and above those managers Crocker put Virgil Campbell in charge of procurement, Dale Warman in charge of sales and Cyril Green in charge of operations, Crocker's former job. Rollin Killoran, now called the first vice president, was director of marketing. Herbert Retzlaff remained as secretary-treasurer-controller, and Oran Robertson headed up engineering. There was mutual respect and good feeling amongst them; if there was an exception, it involved Crocker and Robertson. The two men got off to a bumpy start soon after Crocker had been chosen as president. Crocker sent a handwritten note to Robertson: "Just a short note, Orin, to request your help in many ways in the months ahead. You will need (to) have patience with me because I know I shall make mistakes..." Robertson wrote back in bold letters, "Dear Jock," intentionally misspelling Crocker's first name. "You've already started screwing up; my patience is wearing thin. So let's start by spelling my name right, ORAN."[3] Robertson's memo may have had a humorous intent, but time proved that Robertson had less respect for Crocker than did other members of the Meyer team.

Although Crocker was president and chief executive officer, Robertson still reported directly to Fred Meyer, not to Crocker, just as Robertson had done since he started working for the company in 1945.

It was a peculiar line on a managerial chart. Why? "Probably you'd have to look to Mr. Meyer more than you do anybody else on something like that because he's the one who wanted it that way or else it wouldn't have been that way," Crocker said long afterward. [4]

Virgil Campbell, now in charge of all purchasing, had worked his way up through Fred Meyer grocery departments since 1946, earning respect as a mentor as well as for his even-handed managerial style. He had crossed paths with both Warman and Green early in their careers and had given each one pivotal boosts. Warman was a part-time checker at Rose City where Campbell was a manager. Campbell took him off the check stand and gave him more significant duties, such as running the night freight crew. One night when both men were standing in the men's room, Warman advised Campbell that he hoped to make a career at Fred Meyer if he could land a full-time job. "How would you like a promotion right now?" Campbell asked. "I'd love it," Warman replied. "Well, you're promoted," Campbell said. "I'm going to take that new store at Hawthorne. You'll go there as my assistant manager." [5]

Campbell also saw promise in the young Cy Green, who started as a part-time carry-out person and shelf stocker at the Stadium store while still a student at Roosevelt High School. After advancing to a checker, Campbell, the grocery manager, gave Green three manuals devoted to store operations. Green read them carefully, then took a test that Herb Retzlaff gave to employees seeking promotions. Green earned the highest score. "They say the hardest part of getting to the top of the ladder is getting through the crowd at the bottom, and that really gave me identity with a large number of people in the office," Green said.[6] By the middle 1950s, both Warman and Green were managers at the Interstate store, when Crocker showed up armed with a stopwatch and measuring tape to figure out how to improve check-out efficiency.

Warman was bothered by the project for the first couple weeks. "I was running the best store and had the lowest labor cost already, and I couldn't understand why he was picking on me." Crocker had the perfect answer. "I want to use the store that already is running the lowest labor cost," he said, "because if we can prove that we can save money in your operation, then the other managers will be more willing to accept what we're doing here."[7] As a result of their work, the store re-designed its checkout stands, changed the size of its paper bags and retrained its checkers. It also standardized placement of price tags on items so a checker didn't have to search for them. A new metering system showed that hourly sales by many grocery checkers roughly doubled, cutting waiting times for customers. A checker with low hourly sales was not always a sluggard, Warman found. "It would tell me he's not necessarily not working as hard, but he's not working as smart." The study proved to Green and Warman the validity of one of Fred Meyer's favorite tenets, that conditions control operations. [8]

Campbell seemed to have an eye for talent. He had gotten to know a young salesman for Carnation Co., Gary Baker, who called on Campbell as a customer. Baker had grown up in North Portland, been a baseball star at Oregon State University, and tried his hand at professional baseball for two years before deciding he would never make it to the major leagues. Baker's younger brother, Terry, had become a national star as quarterback at OSU. Gary Baker started as a management trainee for Carnation, and began selling dairy products door-to-door in Portland neighborhoods. He moved up to wholesale sales, then became a credit manager. His business experience led him to four years of law school at night. His next promotion at Carnation would take him out of Portland. Playing golf with Campbell one day, Baker revealed his dilemma about wanting to advance but not wanting to move. Campbell suggested that Baker apply at Fred Meyer Inc.

Baker interviewed with Rollin Killoran and Jack Crocker, and took some tests. He thought he was going to be a buyer in the food department under Campbell, but the job offered to him was in personnel under Balfour Gibson, who was nearing retirement. Baker spent the rest of his career at Fred Meyer managing labor relations and negotiating union contracts. He quickly found himself impressed with the talent around him when he joined Fred Meyer Inc. in 1969. "Unlike other companies that I interviewed and talked with, this company didn't have a whole lot of college graduates working for it. On the other hand, I was so impressed with how much people knew. And how smart they were, and well educated about business. It was unbelievable."[9]

Jack Crocker, left, was Fred Meyer Inc. president in 1970 when he, Herbert Retzlaff and Fred Meyer presented a 30-year pin to Albena Skubic, a buyer/merchandiser in variety. (OHS Retzlaff folder.)

Crocker's first year as president brought the sale of the six Seattle-based Market Basket grocery stores that had been acquired by Fred Meyer Inc. four years earlier. The original plan had been to combine them with the Marketime drug and variety chain and eventually rename them as Fred Meyer stores. Crocker, as operations director, had imported the Fred Meyer MY-TE-FINE label to Market Basket and had found ways to cut operational costs. But the changes came at the expense of employee morale. "We tried to move too fast," Crocker said in retrospect. "I learned my big lesson on that and I never forgot it. And that is when you make an acquisition, you better understand there's great pride in the people in that company. You don't go in and change things overnight." Market Basket employees managed to convey their hard feelings to customers. "The employees were right," Crocker added. "We, I mean I, screwed it up. And then customers quit coming in and the sales went down. Employees quit. We just finally found some local people up there to buy the stores and we got out of it."[10]

Oran Robertson, who in retrospect appeared to be Crocker's only critic in the inner management circle, said Crocker paid too much attention to retail consultants. Fred Meyer had trained his managers to pay close attention to customers' desires. "Instead of the customer telling us what to do, we were listening to some professional from Madison Avenue who didn't know a damn thing about our business go in there and try to tell us how to run our business, which was wrong, and it turned out to be wrong, and we sold them," Robertson said.[11] In the company's annual report, the matter was handled in two sentences in a report signed jointly Crocker and Meyer: "The acquisition of these stores in 1965 did not prove as profitable as expected. Although it would be easy to list many reasons for this action, the fact is they didn't fit into our plans; and we can use this capital more effectively in larger type stores."[12] Fred Meyer Inc. posted a loss on the Market Basket sale. Reflecting a corporate antipathy toward bad news, the sale was not announced to Portland-area newspapers.

Meyer the patriarch always had the ability to put bad news behind him and to look to the future. That trait had not changed with age. The sale, however, proved that the company was not invulnerable. "We thought we were pretty good you know," Crocker recalled. "We thought we could run anything, and we were pretty good. But we found that there were times when we got cooked."[13] The Market Basket sale left Fred Meyer Inc. in the Seattle area with what some called "Lynnwood and the seven dwarves," the giant new store north of Seattle and the smaller Marketime drug and variety outlets on Seattle's southern fringes. Of course, the big Puget Sound market was too large for Fred Meyer Inc. to ignore. It wouldn't be long until the company found new inroads to Seattle-area shoppers.

Regardless of his age, Meyer almost always had a mental agenda for the Tuesday morning executive meetings. He often would start, "Well what's in the news today we should be alert to?" One of the hallmarks of Meyer's leadership was a desire to be nimble in responding to unanticipated opportunities. "He always really paid attention to the news or to what's happening with the market, or anything that we can take advantage of to help the business," Warman recalled. "I can just see him sitting there at the table. And from that, things would just start going. Usually he would have something in mind, but he was just trying to pull out from us."[14]

One example occurred in 1970 when Linus Pauling, the Nobel Prize-winning scientist, published *Vitamin C and the Common Cold,* in which he claimed that large doses of the vitamin taken regularly could prevent colds. "I mean to tell you, we got on that," Warman said. "Because we had our own Sun Laboratories where we made private label vitamins. We got big ads and radio and we put displays out in all departments. I don't know how people could have gone through vitamin C so fast. I mean, it was like trying to buy nylons during the war." It took the scientific community many years to debunk Pauling's theory, but in the short-term Fred Meyer Inc. responded to its customers' desires. Another example of the company's agility occurred when Polaroid Corp. came out with a new model of instant camera. Warman and several other managers met the plane at Portland International Airport, loaded their cars with inventory and headed to stores the same night. As a result, they had the popular new cameras for sale a couple days before the region's largest department store and a chain of specialty camera shops. The angry competitors asked the salesmen how Fred Meyer got the product so soon. "That's just the way we worked so hard, to be in the market on anything and everything," Warman said. "Go out there before you had to, before it got competitive. We set the price and so people would meet our price or try to undercut us a few pennies. But usually they didn't have the merchandise yet."[15]

Jack Crocker was barely two years into his presidency of Fred Meyer Inc. when trouble surfaced in the company's board of directors. John H. Davis of Seattle, who had been a director since 1959 when Fred Meyer Inc. bought the Marketime chain, began expressing loud objections about Meyer's age and Meyer's continued dominance over the company. Given that a majority of directors at the time owed strong allegiance to Meyer, Davis believed the board was not providing the independent guidance it was supposed to. The board included Oran Robertson, Jack Crocker, Herbert Retzlaff, and Rollin Killoran, all active executives, along with Earle A. Chiles, the former president, and Paul Boley, Meyer's close friend and prominent corporate lawyer who performed legal work for Fred Meyer Inc. Besides Davis, the only truly "outside" director was Glenn Jackson, the chairman of Pacific Power & Light Co. and one of Oregon's most powerful political figures as chairman of the Oregon State Highway Commission. Jackson and Meyer had been personal friends for some time before Jackson joined the Fred Meyer board in 1970. Davis believed that most of the directors, given their economic dependence, were unwilling to stand up to Meyer in his role as chairman.

In a sense, Fred Meyer had "bought" this problem himself. He saved cash-on-hand by giving Davis stock in Fred Meyer Inc. instead of buying him out when Fred Meyer Inc. bought the Marketime chain. At this point, Davis owned more shares than anyone except Meyer himself and Earle A. Chiles. Besides being a co-founder and former chief executive of Marketime, Davis was a successful commercial real estate investor in the Seattle area and a former partner in a major accounting firm. He was a former director of the Seattle Trust & Savings Bank and later in 1971 would become a director of the Seattle Times Co., publisher of that's city's dominant daily newspaper. In short, Davis was not a corporate neophyte, even if he did sometimes go directly from a horse barn to corporate meetings wearing dusty denim jeans. "He wasn't afraid at all to speak his mind," said Herbert Retzlaff, Meyer's controller. "And he stood up to Fred Meyer."[16]

Davis announced his protest at the March, 1971 board meeting. At some point, Davis disagreed with something Meyer said. According to Rollin Killoran, Davis told Meyer he should have retired "years ago." In an earlier meeting, he'd called Meyer senile. "Here is a guy (Meyer) that's probably in his middle 80s by then and you know, you don't talk to him like that," Killoran said.[17] Davis vowed to offer his own slate of candidates at the company's annual meeting scheduled for May 4. Davis contended that he already had 40 percent of Fred Meyer shareholders ready to back his slate. "With Meyer's advancing age, problems arising from this basic circumstance have become more and more acute," Davis said. Meyer had recently turned 85.[18]

Concerned by the criticism, Jack Crocker hired an independent management consulting firm, McKinsey & Co., to evaluate Fred Meyer Inc.'s management and corporate structure. According to Crocker, he asked Meyer more than once to talk with the McKinsey people but Meyer never did.[19] The McKinsey report recommended adding additional outside board members to assure that the board was exercising independent judgment.

True to his word, John Davis showed up at the annual shareholder meeting in Portland in May, 1971, to air his criticisms of Fred Meyer personally and to ask shareholders to elect three people nominated by Davis, instead of a slate offered by management. Jack Crocker presided. Davis objected to the "domination" of the company by its founder, and accused Meyer of running "a one-man show."[20] He said other major companies had been hurt in the past when their founders held on into their eighties, notably Ford Motor Co. and Montgomery Ward. Davis also alleged that Meyer had boosted his own pay by raising rent on one store paid to a real estate company of which Meyer was the primary shareholder.

Crocker rose to Meyer's defense. He said rents from 13 shopping centers owned by Meyer's real estate companies averaged income of $1.51 per square foot, a figure that included 37 cents per foot paid by subtenants. He said those rent figures were substantially lower than national averages for major retail space. If anyone thought Meyer was feathering his own pockets, Crocker noted that Meyer owned 460,000 shares of Class B stock which received no dividends – which Meyer could convert to Class A stock at any time and receive $275,000 a year in additional income. Instead, he said, Meyer preferred to let the company use that money for future growth.

As for Meyer's age and personality, Crocker said corporate returns would reveal if Meyer's continued involvement was a liability. The recent track record, however, showed 11 years of successive increases in sales and earnings. Crocker tried to address the issue Davis had raised about whether Meyer was domineering. He may have edged into his answer with an attempt at levity. That is how it was interpreted by Robert Landauer, one of the *Oregonian's* top journalists of the era, who reported on the meeting for the newspaper's business section. Landauer wrote, "A note of humor was momentarily introduced when Crocker said that he would 'tend to agree' with the Davis charge that Meyer is domineering." Crocker then tried to put a favorable spin on it. "But I wonder if there are many founders of companies or effective leaders who have not (been domineering) in order to do a good job."[21] One such leader Crocker mentioned was Vince Lombardi, the legendary professional football coach whose strong-willed tactics had won many National Football League titles for the Green Bay Packers. After Crocker finished his defense of Meyer, shareholders resoundingly elected the nine directors nominated by management, and rejected three nominees urged by Davis, including Davis himself. Davis was finished as a director of Fred Meyer Inc. Meyer the patriarch had survived the challenge.

For Crocker and Meyer, however, the matter wasn't finished. Meyer took offense that Crocker had agreed that he was domineering. Cyril Green, the operations director under Crocker, thought Meyer overreacted. "Is Mr. Meyer dominant? Well, what do you say? You say no, he's not dominant at all – he's a pussycat? No, Jack couldn't say that. Jack believed he owed the guy an honest answer, and yet an answer which was, I think, well said. He said, 'Yes, he is dominant.' But he went on to say a lot of nice things around that. How does a person become an entrepreneur and grow something from nothing to a multi-hundred-million- dollar company without having some characteristics of will and persistence? But boy, the next time we had the management committee meeting FGM was really hot about it." Green added, "He (Meyer) didn't like the way Jack answered. In fact, he was complaining about it like the next day to people, that it was not a very nice thing for him to say. But I thought Jack's answer was well constructed. It didn't say anything bad and it tried to put a good light on the word, but yet was a truthful answer. Mr. Meyer had the greatest amount of will of anybody I knew, and once he made up his mind to do something he wasn't going to change it. He may change it later, but he won't change it today. I mean, he was a willful person."[22]

Some members of Meyer's inner circle believed that Crocker had joined with Davis in trying to push Meyer into retirement. "It wasn't going to work," Oran Robertson said years later. "I can't believe that Jack couldn't count where the votes were, the shares of ownership."[23] Robertson thought Crocker was currying board support from Earle A. Chiles and Glenn Jackson as well from Herbert Retzlaff and Rollin Killoran. The company had never established a pension system, and Robertson thought Crocker's efforts to arrange pensions for Killoran and Retzlaff were part of Crocker's attempt to gain their backing.

Robertson's opinion was not widely shared, however. Green believed that Meyer thought Crocker was cooperating with Davis in an attempt to oust Meyer. "He felt there was a conspiracy afoot to that end," Green said. "Now was there a conspiracy afoot? I don't think so."[24] Pauline Lawrence was not yet a member of the board of directors, but she was close enough to all the principals to know what was occurring. "I don't think Jack Crocker was ever trying to maneuver Mr. Meyer out," she said. "He (Crocker) didn't want to do anything except take over the things that Mr. Meyer was getting too old to handle. He wasn't trying to undercut him." She added, "He (Meyer) was never jealous of Crocker until he got a lot of feedback from someplace. And I don't know where that feedback came from, but you know how that goes in business, there's always somebody out there wanting to keep the other fellow from getting it because they wanted it."[25] Crocker was surprised and irritated years later to find that anyone thought he was trying to replace Meyer or push him into retirement.[26]

Three weeks after the May meeting, Meyer sent Crocker a memo expressing support. "For a limited number of years I have left for active work, let's work together," Meyer wrote. "Let's all work together. Good luck."[27] Within the next month, however, Meyer's attitude changed. He came to believe that there had been a plot against him. "He was not aware of it during the plotting," Robertson said years later. "It was kind of after the fact that he found out about it."[28] Robertson, who believed that Crocker had been wasteful in some business operations, may well have been the informant. In any event, Meyer revamped his management structure in a fashion that substantially reduced Crocker's role as president. He divided the company into northern and southern divisions, placing Virgil Campbell in charge of the north and having him report to the executive committee chaired by Meyer. Meyer also retained control of the company's financial and realty operations. It was clear to Crocker what Meyer wanted. "He had made up his mind he was going to come back in and run that total company, and no matter what he had to do to get there, he was going to get there."[29]

After nearly 23 years in positions of trust, Crocker suddenly could do nothing right in Meyer's eyes. "It was just the everyday operations," Robertson said. "Any decision he (Crocker) made after that, Mr. Meyer said, 'No, you're not going to do that.' Mr. Meyer, that was one thing about him, strange as it may seem. He couldn't fire people." [30] Rollin Killoran, who was nearing retirement at the time, believed that Crocker's decision to hire the McKinsey consulting firm to review management led Meyer to believe that Crocker was trying to ease Meyer out. "But that threw the old man into a tailspin and anyone who knew him, which Jack should have known, if you wanted him to get out and quit being active in the company, that was not the way to do it. The way to do it was to sit down and talk to him. And he'd blow all over the place and maybe he would go and maybe he wouldn't but at least you gave him the dignity of doing it in private. Instead of letting some person from outside get up and read it out of a book." Killoran, too, noticed that suddenly Crocker could do nothing to earn Meyer's approval. "And when he started after you, brother, you might as well leave because it's going to be rough."[31]

Crocker understood the situation. "He was suspicious of me," he recalled. "No question about it, he was suspicious, very suspicious of me trying to gain power and taking over the company....and I didn't have any motives. I wasn't in with any of them."[32] Crocker sensed tension in the management team. He held a private dinner meeting with Meyer, and influential directors Paul Boley and Glenn Jackson, in an effort to work through the problem. The attempt failed. Meyer was not forthcoming about his concerns. As with his prior grudges involving his brothers, Henry Meyer and William Grubmeyer, and with his former business associate Robert Hudson, Meyer kept his thoughts to himself. "I wasn't anxious to leave the company and we were doing a good job, things were going well and I didn't see any reason for this tremendous problem to be like it was," Crocker said. "On the other hand, once I concluded that there was nothing I could do, then I offered my resignation because I didn't want to stay. It wasn't good for the organization."[33]

Though Crocker believed that his job was in jeopardy in 1971, it didn't stop him from achieving a major marketing breakthrough that would have a lasting positive effect on Fred Meyer Inc. For years, the company had tried to reach an agreement with Levi-Strauss & Co. of San Francisco to sell its denim jeans in Fred Meyer stores. Levi-Strauss had always declined, citing two reasons. First, it did not like the idea of its market-leading jeans being sold in discount stores for discount prices for fear that it would damage the brand's reputation. Second, Portland-based Meier & Frank Co., for many years the state's largest apparel retailer, had told Levi-Strauss that it would drop the account if the pantmaker sold to Fred Meyer. Crocker and Rollin Killoran visited San Francisco in 1971 and made a new pitch to Levi-Strauss. Crocker touted the internal upgrade of Fred Meyer stores, and pledged to create a special new department that would have the feel of a specialty shop in a large mall, not just a table in an aisle. He would call it "Pant Kingdom," with Levi-Strauss products as its main attraction. Crocker also said he would not offer Levi-Strauss pants at discount prices. A Levi-Strauss executive, Gene Vaughn, still feared the potential loss of the Meier & Frank account, but decided to let Fred Meyer Inc. place an order. According to Killoran's recollection, Vaughn said Levi-Strauss would pull out if they found Fred Meyer selling at a discount. "Fair enough," said Killoran. "Let's go." Killoran and Crocker returned to Portland to finalize their first order with Levi-Strauss. It amounted to $1.5 million, the largest single order to that date for the 100-year-old San Francisco company. "That got their attention real fast," Killoran noted.[34] In November, 1971, Fred Meyer stores opened their Pant Kingdom department with a big promotional splash. In each of 20 Portland-area stores, the Pant Kingdoms offered as many as 12,000 pairs of Levi jeans, flared pants, stripes and double knits in sizes that would fit almost any person walking in, from child to adult.

Landing the highly-respected Levi-Strauss brand meant more than a break-through in apparel. "Once you had the Levi name in your store, you could get any brand name you wanted," Crocker said, including jewelry, cosmetics and perfumes. "What I was trying to do at Fred Meyer was to develop an image of the highest quality brand names, but also an image of very great values. I wanted to combine the two, although at the time we had no intention of cutting the price on Levi because it just wasn't done. You didn't have to."[35] Meier & Frank's threat to drop Levi-Strauss if the pant-maker sold to Fred Meyer proved to be hollow. After all, how could it compete with Fred Meyer in casual pants if it dropped the category's leading brand?

Yet the major breakthrough with Levi-Strauss did nothing to change the personal feelings between Meyer and Crocker in the corporate headquarters. In November, 1971, Crocker wrote to the board of directors explaining his reasons for resigning. He did not specify Meyer by name, but there was no need to. He said he felt unable to carry out the duties of president under the circumstances at hand. "This firm has been a very major part of my life for the past 23 years, and my resignation shall in no way lessen my continued loyalty," Crocker wrote. "The management team is dedicated to the firm's continued growth. Give them proper direction, and they will continue their fine performance."[36] He voiced no bitterness when he was questioned by a newspaper reporter. "He spoke warmly of the Meyer management group, and described it as extremely strong," the *Oregon Journal* reported.[37] Dale Warman, for one, was impressed by Crocker's professionalism. "Jack was the greatest defender of Mr. Meyer, even up to the last day. He had to know he was getting screwed and that Mr. Meyer was being very unfair. I mean, you never heard a bad thing from Jack Crocker. Never."[38]

Meyer himself may have had difficulty reconciling his own feelings. "He wanted me to stay in some capacity," Crocker said years later, "but basically I was forced out, although he got very upset when I resigned. But I think you'd have to say his actions forced me out."[39] Crocker left Fred Meyer Inc. on Jan. 1, 1972 with no severance, no stock and no job. Meyer and Crocker never spoke to one another again, which was typical of how Meyer dealt with personal disputes.

In retrospect, Crocker believed that Meyer was not yet ready to give up managerial control. Meyer had suffered a fall on an office stairway in 1970, and his recovery was slow. In 1971, Crocker came to believe that Meyer wanted to prove he was still physically and mentally sound. "He felt he was being separated from his leadership role, I believe," Crocker said. "You have to see with Fred Meyer, that first of all he always had been the number one man. When Earle was president, he resented Earle as president. When I became president, he resented me as president." [40] Herbert Retzlaff, who had worked side by side with Meyer for 30 years, thought Meyer had trouble accepting that he should let the president actually run operations, since Earle Chiles had been president in name only. "And Jack became president but he (Meyer) couldn't let loose ... always had to have some say so. And finally it drove Jack to desperation and he said, 'That's that, I'm, going to quit.' And he did. And he told Meyer that. And I remember right afterwards Meyer called me in and said, 'Why did Jack do that to us?' I said, 'Well, FGM, I think you kind of helped bring it about.'" Meyer said little in response. "He didn't try to blame Jack or me or anybody else," Retzlaff said. "He just realized. He was no dumbbell. He realized it....So he very much hated to see Jack go."[41]

Green, too, thought that Meyer wasn't willing to accept a president as a real chief operating officer. "I really believe he expected Jack Crocker to be just like Earle Chiles, just to fill in the job and have the name and be a subordinate and do it just like Earle. I really think he kind of expected that. He shouldn't have, but he did." Green described Crocker as a person with high principles, who felt a responsibility to shareholders to do the job he was supposed to do, and not hold the office if he couldn't.[42] Warman believed that Meyer's ego, in the end, couldn't tolerate the attention Crocker received as president in the trade press. "Mr. Meyer had a real quirk in his personality when it came to anybody else getting any publicity," Warman said. "He would chew us out if we ever did anything with the press, and he would really be upset over some statements off the cuff to the press. I remember one time he chewed us out something terrible, but he knew who leaked it to the press. He leaked it to the press himself, but he tried to make us come out looking really bad. And it wasn't until a couple years later that the truth was out."[43] In the company's annual report to stockholders, Meyer dealt summarily with Crocker's departure, stating that Crocker "asked to be relieved of his duties."[44]

With the departure of Jack Crocker early in 1972, Meyer asked the board of directors to revamp the bylaws, giving him the powers of chef executive as well as board chairman. He retained the north-south split in operations he had established the year before, leaving Virgil Campbell in charge of northern operations and putting Cyril Green in charge of the southern region. Green found humor in the titles Meyer established for Campbell and Green – principal operating officers. Large companies commonly used titles such as chief executive officer – CEO – and chief operating officer – COO. "I bet we were the only company in the world that had a POO, but we did," Green said.[45] Meyer, Green added, didn't like the word "chief" in titles. At Fred Meyer Inc., there was only one chief. And he was still in full control. The unusual titles lasted only briefly. At Meyer's recommendation, Cyril Green was elected president in March 1972. Green's work ethic rivaled Meyer's: six days a week, twelve hours per day. When an acquaintance casually asked, "How are you?" inquiry, Green's answer often was, "MY-TE-FINE."[46]

Another much more minor change reflected Meyer's persistence in cutting costs. During Crocker's tenure, the company's annual reports had turned into full-color publications filled with lots of photographs on glossy paper. Meyer came across a business press article in

1970 that described how companies were cutting back on annual report costs. Meyer clipped the article and sent it to Robertson with a note: "We have a beautiful 1969 annual report. But it cost twice last year's costs...with conditions as they are now, the most beautiful report for 1970 can be one that shows good nett (sic) gain. Let's plan for that– cut costs to attain."[47] After Crocker's departure, the annual reports for the rest of Meyer's life eschewed color photographs and reverted to cheaper paper stock.

Crocker did not remain unemployed for long. He went to work for a chain in San Bernardino, Calif., and then in August, 1972, became executive vice president of Supervalu, a Minnesota-based wholesale grocery company with a national clientele. A year later, he was promoted to chief executive officer of Supervalu. Before that appointment, a management consulting firm checking Crocker's background interviewed Meyer to discuss Crocker's credentials. Meyer's response: "He's not going to run Fred Meyer, but he could sure run Supervalu." Over the next decade, Crocker expanded Supervalu's wholesale business and started the company on a successful path as a retailer under a variety of retail names. His success at Supervalu convinced Crocker that he had not overestimated his managerial ability. "And I didn't need a Fred Meyer to help me, either," he said. "On the other hand, I also knew that without his training I never could have done it."[48] Crocker ended his career as chief executive of the Food Marketing Institute, a trade organization representing food retailers. The institute arose from a merger in 1977 of the National Association of Food Chains and the Super Market Institute, two organizations in which Earle A. Chiles had been active during his long tenure at Fred Meyer Inc.

By 1970, Meyer decided it was time to stop living at the Sheraton Hotel near Lloyd Center where he had moved after Eva Meyer's death. He wanted more room than his hotel suite afforded. "It's so small, I don't have room to fart," he told Crocker before their falling-out.[49] The final home in his long life would be on the 19th floor of a 22-

story concrete apartment building completed in 1966 as part of the South Auditorium Urban Renewal Area in downtown Portland. In the late 1950s, the Portland City Council decided that a neighborhood known as South Portland was "blighted" and eligible to be bulldozed and rebuilt with the help of federal urban renewal grants. The old neighborhood had been an ethnic stronghold for Jewish, Italian and Eastern European immigrants who started their new American lives in old wood-framed walk-up apartments and boarding houses that had been built in the late 19th and early 20th Centuries. Many of the residents who lived there would have been customers and workers at the Yamhill Street market in its heyday early in Fred Meyer's career. In place of more than 20 small Portland downtown blocks, planners staked out a series of "superblocks" in which high-rise apartments and a smattering of office buildings floated on a sea of undulating lawns and tree-shaded walkways. Most residents of the new towers entered and exited underground parking spaces by automobile. However, there was a covered driveway at the front door where guests could be picked up or dropped off. Not long after Meyer moved in, steel posts were installed to protect the canopy. Meyer drove a large Buick. "He'd stop when he hit something," said Virgil Campbell, who lived for a time in the same building.[50] Meyer's abode was a two-bedroom unit on the 19th floor of the Portland Center Apartments at 111 S.W. Harrison Street, a building that later was renamed the Harrison East Condominium Tower. His unit offered stunning views to the south and east.

It was in his high-rise apartment that Fred Meyer suffered a major stroke in the summer of 1971. The attack paralyzed the right side of his body. Portland had not yet implemented the 911 emergency telephone system. Meyer inched his way slowly to his telephone and used his left arm to call for help. After Meyer was taken to the hospital, word filtered back to company headquarters that he might never walk again or make use of his right hand. Meyer had had health problems earlier in his life, in addition to the fall at the office in 1970. According to Oran

Robertson, Meyer had a history of heart problems including heart attacks approximately in 1940 and soon after the opening of the new Hawthorne store a decade later. Meyer had recovered from those setbacks. Now he faced the biggest challenge yet for his philosophy that the mind has the ability to overcome problems of human matter.

As soon as his condition stabilized at the hospital, Meyer asked that a triangular shaped metal contrivance called a trapeze be suspended at the head of his bed. Slowly, he used his left hand to grab his right wrist and lift his right hand to the trapeze. Repeatedly, he grabbed the trapeze with his weakened hand. He gripped the metal with his fingers and pulled with his right arm. Slowly, gross motor skill returned to his right arm. He also forced himself out of bed and tried taking steps with a walker. His gradual improvement was an understandable source of pride. When Rollin Killoran showed up at the hospital as an early visitor, Meyer told him, "They tell me I won't be able to use my right arm again." As he spoke, Meyer raised is right arm without assistance and grabbed the trapeze.[51] While recuperating in the hospital, Meyer had a small table installed in his room. He received company mail every day and issued orders. "His concentration and determination.....he was going to get well," said Dale Warman. "And for Mr. Meyer, the therapy was his own therapy. He was a very positive, very determined person."[52] At 85, there was still no quit in Fred Meyer.

Meyer returned to the office three months after the stroke. He walked more slowly, but his gait was normal. When he became tired, his right leg would drag slightly. The fine motor skills in his right hand returned more slowly. He was given a choice of learning to write with his left hand or to engage in the struggle of trying to use his right hand. Again, Meyer was not willing to concede. He spent hours with a ballpoint pen cradled in his right hand, practicing his own signature on lined sheets of paper seemingly with endless tenacity. At first, his indecipherable squiggly lines roamed all over the pages. Gradually, they started conforming to the lines on the paper, and slowly became more legible. At best, it was the penmanship of an elderly person with a wobbly hand, but the writing was clearly discernible as "Fred G. Meyer."[53] In the end, Meyer achieved his goal – signing corporate documents with his own right hand.

There were other managerial changes during this period. Both Herbert Retzlaff, controller, and Rollin Killoran, marketing director, decided it was time to retire. The two men had always assumed they would survive Meyer, whom Killoran had taken to calling "the old man" out of Meyer's presence. Unlike Meyer, however, Retzlaff and Killoran had ideas about enjoying retirement. Retzlaff left the board of directors as well. Killoran kept his board position until after Meyer's death. Dale Warman decided it was time to move on, too, not for retirement but for an executive position with Allied Stores Corp., a Detroit-based retail giant operating 354 stores under different names around the United States. Warman felt he was underpaid at Fred Meyer Inc. and he was unhappy about the treatment of Crocker, whom he considered a mentor. Meyer was recuperating in the hospital after his stroke when Warman went to see him. It was a difficult conversation. "Anyway, he just got really upset and emotional about it," Warman said. It ended with Meyer saying, "Why don't you just get out of here? Don't waste my time. When are you leaving?"[54] Unlike Crocker's departure, however, the relationship between Meyer and Warman was not yet finished.

Meyer had built his retail empire mostly from within by promoting employees he trained from their twenties and sometimes even younger. But that wouldn't work in replacing Retzlaff. Meyer needed a certified public accountant, a credential not acquired by merely working one's way up through company ranks. Jerry Sadis had grown up in Seattle, the son of a Greek father and Turkish mother who had emigrated to the United States before 1920. Sadis as a youngster worked in his father's retail fruit and fish business, and went to the University of Washington. His fallback was accounting, after he decided it would take too long to become a dentist. Upon graduation, Sadis worked with a major accounting firm for almost five years, then with two private companies in Seattle after he decided that an entire career of professional auditing wasn't going to be stimulating. In 1971, a management search firm

After recovering from a fall and reasserting control over Fred Meyer Inc., the patriarch, 85 in 1971, marks the retirement of Rollin Killoran, joined by Jane Killoran. **(Oregonian)**

asked him to consider Fred Meyer Inc. He scheduled a Saturday morning interview with Cy Green.

Sadis didn't think he was going to be interested. He showed up-dressed casually, in yellow pants, a blue blazer and white shoes. He had the start of a goatee under his full head of curly hair. He didn't know until that morning that Fred Meyer had a policy of no facial hair on executives. After two hours talking with Green, Sadis was becoming interested in the opportunity. Green suggested that they stop by Meyer's office to chat with the patriarch. After knocking, they found Meyer reading at his desk. Meyer glanced briefly at the white shoes, the rest of the outfit and then the goatee. "No," Meyer said, and went back to his reading. Sadis drove back to Seattle feeling disappointed. "To be shunted off from the chairman's office without so much as a, 'Hi, how are you?' was humiliating to say the least." He doubted he had "a snowball's chance" at the job.[55] It was too bad, he thought, because it seemed like a good company.

A week later, Cy Green called Sadis again. Could he come back for a dinner with some of the Fred Meyer executives? Sadis shaved the goatee and put on a dark suit. "I knew there was probably some interest, but I didn't know what form it would take." He found himself seated at the Arlington Club with the elder statesmen of the Fred Meyer Inc. brain trust: Oran Robertson, lawyer Paul Boley, and Roy Webster, the company's outside accountant. Across the table sat the eldest of all, Fred Meyer. Sadis was 28, Meyer 85. Sadis knew that it was standard procedure for large companies to plan their futures in five-year segments. He knew Fred Meyer sales had recently topped $290 million, and he asked about the company's five-year plan. Meyer turned to Robertson. "Obie," he said, "what's a five-year plan?" Then Meyer turned to Boley. "Paul, have you seen a five-year plan?" Sadis tried to hide his surprise. "I was shocked…textbooks always tell you you have to have a five-year plan." Meyer turned back to Sadis. If he wanted a projection, Meyer said, he'd give him one: "By 1980, we'll be a billion dollars." Sadis ran the calculation silently in his head: nine years to grow five-fold. "I said to myself, 'The old man is crazy.' I never should have said that." A year short of Meyer's target – the year after his death – Fred Meyer Inc. sales hit $1 billion.[56] Sadis joined Fred Meyer Inc. in October, 1971, as assistant controller. He was picked up from a downtown hotel by a driver on his first day on the job. Meyer was riding in the back seat with a cane. He recently had overcome his stroke. "Oh yeah, I had a minor little problem," he told Sadis. They went to breakfast that morning. Meyer seemed like "just a nice old man," Sadis recalled. But that was just one side of Meyer. Soon, Sadis saw another side of Meyer in management committee meetings. "He was a tiger."[57] Sadis didn't give up on his desire for a five-year plan. "Don't spend too much time, but go ahead and do it," Meyer advised. Sadis gathered as much information as he could from many sources, then realized that Meyer probably knew it all already. "You put this away and we'll look at it in five years," Meyer said. When the time arrived for that five-year review, Sadis found that the plan "was woefully short of what we actually achieved."[58]

In the late 1960s and early 1970s, Fred Meyer Inc. experimented with several tests for screening job applicants. Someone suggested giving top managers a standard intelligence test. The test administrator issued aliases to make sure there was no bias in scoring. Fred Meyer was given the name Steve Larkin, a professional baseball pitcher who appeared in a total of two games in his major league career. When the test results came back, some of the executives found that they had scored in the superior intelligence range. The highest score of all, however, belonged to Steve Larkin. Now well into his 80s, Fred Meyer was still the smartest person in the room.

---

[1] Crocker, Jack, OHS sound recording 1304, June 1, 1989.
[2] Warman, Dale, OHS sound recording 1315, April 27, 1989.
[3] Memos can be found in OHS Fred Meyer Collection 199, Box 9, folder 7.
[4] Crocker, *op. cit.*
[5] Warman, *op. cit.,* April 20, 1989.
[6] Green, Cyril K., OHS sound recording 1307, Feb. 27, 1989.
[7] Warman, *op cit.*
[8]*Ibid.*
[9] Baker, Gary, OHS sound recording 1301, May 9, 1989.
[10] Crocker, *op. cit.*
[11] Robertson, Oran, OHS sound recording 1312, March 28, 1989.
[12] Fred Meyer Inc., *Annual Report, 1969,* p. 1.
[13] Crocker, *op. cit.,* Aug 2, 1989.
[14] Warman , *op. cit.*
[15] *Ibid.*
[16] Retzlaff, Herbert, OHS sound recording 1311, Feb. 22, 1989.
[17] Killoran, Rollin, OHS sound recording 1308, Nov. 3, 1988.
[18] *Seattle Times,* April 28, 1971, p. 35.
[19] Crocker, *op. cit.*
[20] *Seattle Times,* May 5, 1971, p. 36.

[21] *Oregonian,* May 5, 1971, p. 25.
[22] Green, *op. cit.*
[23] Robertson, *op. cit.* March 3, 1989.
[24] Green, op. cit.
[25] Lawrence, Pauline, OHS sound recording 1309, Jan. 12, 1989.
[26] Crocker read some of the oral histories collected by OHS in 1988 and 1989. He later added a hand-written note to accompany the transcript of his interview, expressing surprise and dismay about any contention that he was involved in a plot against Meyer, or that he wished to see Meyer retire from the company.
[27] Crocke , *op. cit.*, June 11, 1989.
[28] Robertson, *op. cit.*
[29] Crocker, *op. cit,* June 13, 1989.
[30] Robertson, *op. cit.*
[31] Killoran, *op. cit.*
[32] Crocker, *ibid.*
[33] Crocker, *ibid.*
[34] Killoran, *op. cit.*
[35] Crocker, *op. cit.*, June 1, 1989.
[36] Statement included with the transcript of Crocker 's oral history interview, OHS sound recording 1304.
[37] *Oregon Journal,* Nov. 18, 1971, p. C4.
[38] Warman, *op. cit,.* April 27, 1989.
[39] Crocker, *op. cit.,* Aug. 2, 1989.
[40] Crocker, *op. cit.,* June 1, 1989.
[41] Retzlaff, *op. cit.,* March 1, 1989.
[42] Green, *op. cit.*
[43] Warman, *op cit.*
[44] Fred Meyer Inc., *Annual Report 1971,* March 15, 1972, p. 1.
[45] Green, *op. cit.*
[46] Experienced personally by the author while waiting in a courthouse hallway with Green in 1981 during litigation after Meyer's death.
[47] OHS Fred Meyer Collection 199, box 8, folder 6, April 1, 1970.
[48] Crocker, *op. cit.,* June 13, 1989.
[49] *Ibid.*
[50] Interview with the author at Virgil Campbell 's Lake Oswego residence, Aug. 19, 2013.
[51] *Wall Street Journal,* June 11, 1975.
[52] Warman, *op. cit.*
[53] One page with more than 20 examples of Meyer's penmanship exercises is in the OHS Fred Meyer Collection 199, box 7, folder 5.
[54] *Ibid.*
[55] Sadis, Jerry, OHS sound recording 1313, March 23, 1989.
[56] *Ibid.*
[57] *Ibid.*
[58] *Ibid.*

CHAPTER EIGHT

Full Speed Toward 90

Regardless of any physical complications from his stroke, Fred Meyer still showed his typical entrepreneurial spunk as he headed into the final years of his life. The months were filled with acquisitions, new store construction and new business ventures. Now keenly aware of his own mortality, the patriarch quietly built a management team that he hoped would succeed him, and drew up plans for the personal riches he would leave behind. He also entertained presentations from suitors interested in buying Fred Meyer Inc. Some showed up with fancy slide shows. Meyer would listen attentively and ask probing questions, but he never took sales pitches seriously. To Meyer, they were just another tool for finding a competitive advantage or some innovative practice. "And he told us, 'Always listen to everyone,'" recalled Pauline Lawrence, who spent parts of two days per week in Meyer's presence. "'Always listen. Get all the information you can.'"[1] Meyer treated visits by suitors like a game. The flow of information always went one direction. Jerry Sadis said Meyer's instructions were, "Don't tell them anything but find out what you can." Meyer clearly enjoyed those exercises. "Mr. Meyer was really in his element when people would come," Sadis added. "He liked to be the center of attention. It's not fair to say he had a big ego, but he did like the activity and the involvement."[2]

One visitor in the early 1970s was Sam Walton, the Bentonville, Arkansas, entrepreneur on his way to building an empire of 1,960 stores before his death in 1992. Walton was 32 years younger than Meyer, but in many ways the two men were kindred spirits. Both had a knack for hiring good people and making them work relentlessly. Both lived and breathed retail, visiting stores outside their own geographical trade areas wherever they traveled. Both strived to cut costs anywhere possible, and both embraced new technology ahead of their competitors. Despite their wealth, both men intentionally declined to live lavish personal lifestyles. At the time of his Portland visit, Walton had yet to expand his Walmart chain outside of the South, and he had not yet added groceries to his mix of variety, soft goods, housewares and hardware. Because he was not yet well-known, Walton often would introduce himself as "a little fellow from Bentonville, Arkansas" who just wanted to look around and ask some questions.3 Walton's requests to inspect stores and talk with their operators were not always granted. Fred Meijer, a Grand Rapids, Michigan, chain store owner and friend of Fred Meyer who had successfully merged groceries with general discount merchandise in several Midwestern states, refused to see Walton, thinking that Walton wanted to buy him out.

Meyer, by contrast, was always willing to talk with merchants who were not direct competitors. Regardless of whether Walton tried his country-bumpkin approach and whether Meyer saw through it, Meyer agreed to see him and to let him inspect Fred Meyer operations. "Sam Walton is a good friend of ours and a good friend of mine, and he came out here to take a look ....and he marveled at our type of store," said Oran Robertson, who was part of the conversation.[4] The talks between Walton and Meyer focused on issues of bulk purchasing, warehousing and transportation.[5] Like Fred Meyer Inc., Walmart was big enough to be buying much of its merchandise directly from manufacturers rather than through wholesalers. The competitive edge of both companies depended heavily on transferring goods from in-coming trucks to their own delivery trucks with a minimum of delay, handling and storage. Fred Meyer Inc. was outgrowing its big Swan Island warehouse, and Meyer and Robertson were in the planning stages for a huge new warehouse that would be erected in the next few years in Clackamas County. Walton had already built the first few of his warehouses that eventually would become national models.

Walton's visit to Portland whetted his appetite for adding groceries to the Walmart retail inventory. Like Meyer before him, Walton had believed adding groceries would lure shoppers who otherwise might not visit Walmart. He also knew that grocery customers went shopping more often than variety customers. Profit margins on groceries were lower than on other goods, but if grocery shoppers bought non-food items during the same shopping trips, Walton's bottom line would be bolstered on both counts. Making the transition would not be easy; shipping and storing fresh and frozen foods added new layers of complexity to Walton's warehouse and distribution system. Walton received welcome advice in the late 1970s from Dale Warman, Fred Meyer Inc.'s top grocery manager, who met Walton at meetings of the National Mass Retailers Institute, a trade organization based in Arlington, Virginia. In his autobiography written in 1992, Walton described Warman as "a very astute retailer from the Fred Meyer company out in Portland and now a good friend." [6] Wal-Mart started adding groceries in the 1980s.

On his way to becoming the nation's biggest retailer, a distinction Walton achieved in 1991, 13 years after Meyer's death, Walton experimented with several retail formats. In the late 1980s he tried his biggest version, called Hypermarket USA, in which a handful of stores exceeded 200,000 square feet. The Hypermarkets were not a success. Customers found them too big for comfort, and big-ticket items like large appliances and expensive furniture proved unprofitable. Walton eliminated the big-ticket items, scaled back the size of his future stores to approximately 150,000 square feet and re-named them Walmart Supercenters. It was no coincidence that the size and inventory of the Walmart Supercenters were reminiscent of the Fred Meyer stores he had seen in Portland. Two business scholars who studied Walton's long career found that the one-stop Wal-Mart Supercenter, Walton's most successful retail scheme ever, "was patterned after the Fred Meyer stores."[7] Unlike Walton, however, Meyer had no dream of expanding his retail vision nationwide. "There's no doubt he envisioned the company growing and expanding geographically," said Jerry Sadis, who joined the Fred Meyer finance team late in 1971. "I don't think he had any vision of it going nationwide, but there was a lot of room in the Northwest to expand, especially in Puget Sound area."[8] There also is little doubt that Meyer and Robertson would have been so friendly to Walton had they known that someday Walmart would be a direct competitor.

Early in 1972, Meyer added the final member of his inner circle that would help run Fred Meyer Inc. in Meyer's final years and then oversee management of Meyer's wealthy estate. At the end of February, the *Oregonian* published a three-sentence item noting the departure of Gerry Pratt as business editor and business columnist after a 17-year career with the newspaper. More notable than the small size of the announcement was the fact that the newspaper felt compelled to report it at all. The arrival and departure of newspaper journalists was never considered newsworthy, unless they had climbed high into managerial ranks. Pratt, by virtue of his writing prowess and effervescent personality, had made himself the exception. In 1966, he had simultaneously begun a television career, first as a panelist on a weekly public affairs interview program and then later as host. He also delivered a business news report on a Portland radio station. Pratt, well-aware of the success of Tom McCall, a former television journalist whose media familiarity helped him win positions as Oregon secretary of state and later governor, also spoke of having political ambitions. Branching into radio and television was risky for Pratt in an era when newspaper managers saw radio and television as fierce competitors; running for office simply wouldn't be tolerated by a reputable newspaper because of the appearance of political bias in its news columns.

Journalistic ethics also were changing at that moment. It was not unheard of in Pratt's era for business writers to invest in companies they wrote about. The Securities and Exchange Commission had become aware of a practice informally called "pump and dump," in which a journalist would buy stock in a small company, write one or more favorable reports, and quickly sell when the stock rose. A whole industry called public relations had arisen in the 20th Century aimed at gaining favorable coverage in the press knowing that the public would respond accordingly; reporters knew it, too. The same year Pratt left the *Oregonian,* the SEC accused a Los Angeles Herald-Examiner business writer of violating SEC rules by engaging in the pump-and-dump practice. Although the case involving Alex N. Campbell was settled quietly two years later without an admission of wrong-doing,[9] it reverberated strongly in journalistic circles. The days of a business reporter advising senior *Oregonian* editors on stock investments ended with Pratt's departure. Responsible journalists and newspapers recognized that personal enrichment should play no part in their journalistic mission of informing the public.

The small news item about Pratt's resignation said he planned to continue his radio and television programs and do some work for Fred Meyer. It quoted Pratt as saying that he had been "thinking about political plans for some time."[10] Since first meeting Meyer in 1957, Pratt and Meyer had developed a close personal relationship. Pratt was one of the people who helped fill the void Meyer felt after Eva Meyer's unexpected death in 1960. The two men dined weekly and traveled on trips together while Pratt was still working at the *Oregonian,* according to Meyer's secretary, Jean Webb.[11] By the time Pratt joined Fred Meyer

Inc., it struck some other Meyer intimates that Pratt filled the role of a son that Meyer never had, much as Pauline Lawrence could be seen as a daughter figure. "Mr. Meyer got to know him and Gerry was a boy that came up by his shoestrings—pulled himself up, what do they say, by this bootstraps?" Lawrence recalled. "Mr. Meyer fell for people like that quite good; and he did for Gerry. And Gerry thought an awful lot of Mr. Meyer, and first thing you know, Mr. Meyer was wanting to help him. He wanted to help the man because he came from a poor family; Canadian, nine children, the mother raised them all, the father left when he was young. And Mr. Meyer believed that Gerry had a lot to offer – and he has, believe me."[12] Then in his mid-40s, Pratt retained a boyish handsomeness. He dressed sharply and spoke well. His journalism work had introduced him to upper echelons of Oregon business and politics; his journalist's curiosity about how the world works and how it might work better no doubt appealed to Meyer's probing intelligence.

Pratt immediately joined the Fred Meyer Inc. executive meetings on Tuesday mornings, although his portfolio at the outset didn't warrant his presence in the minds of some of the others. "It clearly was a personal relationship as opposed to a business relationship," said Jerry Sadis, who joined the company only a few months before Pratt.[13] Meyer put Pratt in charge of routine dealings with the real estate companies that owned the stores and land, which consisted largely of paying utility bills and collecting rent from lessees. Pratt also acted as a public spokesman on rare occasions when necessary. Two years later, Meyer found a larger role for Pratt, one that led after Meyer's death to the most divisive split in Fred Meyer Inc. history.

In July, 1972, the company opened a 135,000-square-foot store in Albany, a city with only 18,000 residents, according to the 1970 census. The proposal had been a point of dispute between Meyer and John Davis, who felt the Albany area was too small for such a big store. Meyer's instincts proved good once again. "It turned out to be all right," said Cy Green, who had taken charge of the southern region after Jack

Crocker's departure. "Yeah, it was a little tough. We had a new competitor down there. Bi-Mart went in right across the street. Took us a little while to learn how to deal with them, but it became a very successful store."[14] Albany was the start of a new growth cycle, in which Meyer said the company intended to add 55 percent more floor space in three years. Construction had already started on a store in Longview, Washington, and two more in the Tacoma area. Meyer said plans were in the works for new stores in Eugene, Gresham and Oak Hills, an affluent Washington County suburb west of Portland.[15]

Meyer's aggressive expansion plans led one discount competitor to leave Oregon. The Weisfield family in Seattle, which had been operating discount stores for about a decade, decided to sell to Fred Meyer Inc. all five of its Oregon locations. Its Valu-Mart stores were located in Portland, Beaverton, Milwaukie, Salem and Eugene. Given the smooth transaction, Weisfield Inc. sold seven more locations, mostly in the Seattle area, to Meyer in 1975, as Weisfield decided to leave the discount store business and focus on its jewelry business. As the second deal ended, Bill Weisfield told Oran Robertson that Fred Meyer Inc. should take a look at its most successful store, located in Anchorage, Alaska. Meyer himself was not enthusiastic about Alaska, still having bad memories about his experience there more than six decades earlier as a hopeful gold miner. Still, Robertson, Dale Warman and Virgil Campbell flew to Anchorage to check it out. Although the distance from Portland was about as far as Chicago, prices in the less-competitive Alaska market could support the higher transportation costs. Fred Meyer Inc. went ahead with the acquisition. "And it was one of the best things we've ever done," Robertson said years later. "It's been a great store for us." Fred Meyer Inc. later added a second store in Anchorage and opened in several other Alaska locations. "So we owe Bill Weisfield a real big kudo for having talked us into that." [16]

At least once a year, Fred Meyer asked his executive team to suggest new retail categories the company might enter. Fred Meyer Inc.

had not been bashful over the years about trying new ventures and dropping them if they were not successful. The company had tried major appliances at two different times, both downtown and at Hollywood, but customers were more inclined to look for refrigerators and washing machines elsewhere. Draperies and carpeting? Didn't work out. Neither did fabrics or furniture. Gasoline, automobile servicing and tires were tried at different times and places, depending on circumstances. Home improvement turned out to be a hit, inspired by the belief that plumbers, electricians and carpenters had become so expensive, homeowners took on more repair and remodeling tasks themselves. Garden centers proved to be a success in a region where plants grew easily. An idea championed by Dale Warman before he resigned was a catalog store where customers could see merchandise and then order it for delivery or pick-up later. The company opened catalog outlets in two Portland Valu-Mart locations acquired in 1973, plus at stores in Seattle and Eugene. "They just didn't work," Robertson said. "We'd have a lower price on Coleman ice chests in our regular stores than the catalog business had, you know. It wasn't our cup of tea. And we should not be in the catalog business anyway, because we're supposed to have the lowest prices (in the stores) and how the hell can you have lower prices in a catalog?"[17] All was not lost in the catalog venture, however. Jewelry showed surprising strength in catalog sales. Always nimble, the company expanded into better-quality jewelry in Fred Meyer stores.

If Warman's idea for catalog centers wasn't a hit, another of his ideas was. He had a district manager in Seattle tell him about the manager's brother-in-law who worked at a health foods store. "He dresses funny and he eats funny and that place is just packed with people all day," the manager told Warman. Warman passed the suggestion along to Meyer. Meyer told Warman, "You know, if we could hire this kid and put in a test store, it might be a way to grow the business." The young man was Ronald K. Johnson, who came for a personal talk with Meyer. The concept may have struck a nerve with Meyer given his eating habits and belief in healthy food. Meyer agreed to let Johnson open a health foods section at the big Lynnwood store north of Seattle. "If you can make that successful, the first one, we'll let that mother a whole lot more," Meyer told Johnson.[18] The trial exceeded expectations. By late 1973, Fred Meyer Inc. rapidly added Nutrition Centers at many locations, selling products such as bulk grains, seeds, nuts, protein supplements, natural cosmetics, health books, teas and yogurt. Months before Meyer's death in 1978, Johnson was promoted to merchandiser of the Nutrition Center Division, meaning that he supervised the centers throughout the Fred Meyer chain.[19]

The success of the Nutrition Centers exemplified one of the lessons that Meyer often repeated at the management meetings. "He always explained the difference between merchandising and marketing, and said, 'Merchandising is selling to the customer what you want to sell, whereas marketing is having what the customer wants to buy,'" Warman said. "And what he always tried to keep us doing was be marketers, having what the customer wanted to buy, what they were looking for....And that was what Mr. Meyer was great at."[20]

Fred Meyer turned 87 in February 1973. On Meyer's birthday, Oran Robertson lost his temper with the patriarch after 23 years of near-daily contact, and told Meyer he was quitting. The spat was prompted by a presentation made to Meyer and the executive committee by one of Robertson's subordinates in the engineering department. The man spoke at length using convoluted sentences and big words. His presentation took too long, and he failed to sense frustration mounting in the room. Meyer, always motivated by efficiency, liked short, fact-based statements using small words. After the presentation, Meyer demanded that Robertson fire the employee. Though the man had an annoying way of speaking, he was a capable engineer, Robertson said, and did valuable work designing warehouses and production facilities. Meyer repeated that he wanted the man fired. Robertson said since the man worked in Robertson's department, Robertson as department head should make personnel decisions. Meyer still wanted the man fired. Robertson could stand no more. "You don't need my services any longer if you're going to fire all of my men," he told Meyer. He picked up his papers and stormed out of Fred Meyer Inc. headquarters. He returned later that night to clean out his desk.

When Robertson arrived, Cy Green was still at the office. He planned to leave soon for Meyer's birthday party downtown. The employees had bought Meyer a small color television for his apartment. Robertson informed Green that he had quit. "Please don't do it," Green said. The two men talked for half an hour and Robertson relented. Then he and Green headed to town. It was reminiscent of the incident years earlier when Herb Retzlaff quit in a huff and then showed up the next day and heard nothing at all from Meyer. "I went to the birthday party and it was as if nothing had ever happened," Robertson said. Later, Robertson heard that Meyer had made a comment after Robertson walked out in anger. "I wonder what's wrong with O.B.?" Meyer had said. "Maybe he needs a vacation."[21]

The rift was quickly forgotten. The verbose engineering employee kept his job, but never again appeared at Meyer's executive committee. Only weeks later, Meyer called Robertson to his office and said he wanted to create a new position in the corporate hierarchy. It would be vice chairman of the board of directors, and Meyer intended to recommend that Robertson fill the new post. The rest of the message was even clearer. If Meyer died or ever decided to step down, he wanted Robertson to be his successor as chairman. "And hell," Robertson said years later, "that was the farthest thing from my mind." Robertson had never been a candidate for president in Meyer's thinking, so far as Robertson knew. Before he accepted, Robertson wanted to talk with Earle A. Chiles. Though Chiles had been forced into retiring as president in 1968, he was still a member of the board of directors. The two men were driving to Medford when Robertson raised the subject. "Earle, I've got kind of a touchy thing that I've got to ask you," Robertson said. "Mr.

Meyer asked me this week if I would become vice chairman of the board. That puts me in kind of a tenuous position because you are Mr. Meyer's stepson; you've been president of the company; you've been here so long." According to Robertson, Chiles replied, "I think it's great. I don't want to work that hard anymore. I'm retired. I'm enjoying it. I think that's wonderful."[22]

One person did not think it was wonderful, however. Earle Meyer Chiles, the son of Earle A. and Virginia Hughes Chiles, apparently had grown up believing that the corporate mantle would fall to him someday. "He wanted to run the company," Robertson said. "There is no question about that."[23] After high school in Portland, Earle M. Chiles attended Menlo College in Menlo Park, California, a private junior college known to be favored by those who hoped eventually to make it into Stanford University. Chiles did well in his two years at Menlo and transferred to Stanford to finish his undergraduate degree. Fred Meyer wanted all his employees to start at the bottom and work their way up. Earle M. Chiles trained as a checker but was injured in an automobile accident. Later, he managed the new Garden Centers at Raleigh Hills and in Salem, but he quit when his father left as president in 1968. Meyer wanted his top executives to be completely devoted to their work. The young Chiles had other interests, and it would not have been a plus in Meyer's mind when Chiles showed up from time to time in newspaper society pages. "He (Meyer) tried to work with him like he would with me or anyone else," said Pauline Lawrence. "You don't know nothing so you got to start at the bottom and go up." Gerry Pratt, speaking in general and not specifically about the younger Chiles, said Meyer surrounded himself with people who were willing to struggle for survival and success. "It's very tough if you want to come into the company with accumulated wealth," he said. "Those who have (tried) are not in the company because there's a great emphasis on production. There's a lot of head-busting. If your facts are right and you are lucky, you might survive. There are no 'yes men.' He's so confident of himself he hasn't had to build those crutches."[24] The short answer is that the working relationship with the younger Chiles did not work out to Meyer's satisfaction.

By his rejection of Jack Crocker in 1971, Meyer had narrowed the field of possible successors as chairman of Fred Meyer Inc. Pauline Lawrence, who listened to Meyer's thoughts at their weekly dinners, believed that Jack Crocker was Meyer's first choice, until the events of 1971. "Jack was strictly business all the way. Oran was a wonderful engineer, a terrific person. Mr. Meyer was torn...which one of these men is my best man? Because it was down to those two, because he sure wasn't going to have his grandson (Earle M. Chiles) there." And now Crocker was out of the picture. "But, definitely Jack was the frontrunner first, and then it was Robertson. And Mr. Meyer said many times, 'I think we made the right choice, I think we made the right choice.' Well, I knew him so well, that when he brought up anything a second time, it was on his mind and he wasn't sure."[25] Robertson's new title as vice chairman became official in May, 1973.[26] It carried no extra pay and no additional duties.

A few months later, the company was hit with a new complaint from the Federal Trade Commission.[27] The agency's legal counsel, the U.S. Department of Justice, accused Fred Meyer Inc. of violating the consent decree that had emerged from litigation ending with the U.S. Supreme Court decision in 1968. The federal regulators sought a $900,000 penalty, on grounds that Fred Meyer Inc. had negotiated deals with several suppliers that gave Fred Meyer advantages over other buyers. Two of the instances involved manufacturers of small electrical appliances who allegedly paid Fred Meyer promotional allowances to be used for in-store product demonstrations, regardless of whether those events actually occurred. In another allegation, the regulators claimed that Fred Meyer negotiated a deal for its supplier of records and tapes to provide racks for the inventory and to service those racks on a regular basis. Fred Meyer Inc., according to the allegation, then cited fear of labor-union objections and asked the supplier to pay the company an equivalent amount of money for Fred Meyer employees to perform the chores, instead. In another instance, Fred Meyer Inc. allegedly negotiated a monthly payment from a food supplier to stock its pasta products.

Fred Meyer Inc. took steps to challenge the case, but after two years both sides decided to settle. Fred Meyer Inc. paid $200,000 in an agreement that did not involve any admission of wrong-doing. Gerry Pratt, acting as the company spokesman, said the deal made sense for Fred Meyer Inc. to eliminate the uncertainty.[28] It also was less expensive than taking the matter to trial and adding more legal fees. The settlement amount also suggested that the government's case may have been weaker than the regulators first thought. The company's attitude was that all the deals were made by willing participants who each saw advantages, or they would not have agreed to them. "The old man's basic philosophy," Pratt said, referring to his boss, "is that if the other guy can't make a profit, we're not interested in doing business. We may drive a hard deal, but if the supplier isn't making any money off of it, we don't want to do business with him."[29]

In the mid-1970s, Fred Meyer Inc. began seeing a demonstrable, sustained increase in apparel sales, notably on the men's side. Despite Jack Crocker's breakthrough with Levi-Strauss and the Fred Meyer Pant Kingdoms in 1971, men's apparel was still spotty with an undependable supply of close-out goods picked up on an as-available basis. "Nobody was doing soft goods the way Fred Meyer was doing it because it wasn't the right way of doing it," said Jerry Sadis, who was crunching the numbers.[30] That started to change in 1973 after the arrival of Alan Ferguson, who slowly but steadily improved the quality and stability of the menswear inventory. Meyer himself noticed the improvement in sales and once asked Cy Green, the new president, to explain why. Green worked his way through possible explanations: better fashions, faster turnover, fewer markdowns, better inventory control. All the while, Meyer thrummed his fingers impatiently on the conference table. "And when his fingers are drumming on the table, you know you are not giving the right answer," Green recalled. "And you just keep struggling, trying to come up with the right answer. Finally, Meyer slammed his fist into the table, and said, 'You put a good man in charge! You put a good man in charge! You put a good man in charge!'"31 It was another of Meyer's favorite lessons, memorably delivered. In a little over six years, Ferguson rose to the position of senior vice president for soft goods, and became one of several executives remembered with a personal bequest in Fred Meyer's will.

With nearly 20 years behind them at the successful Gateway location on the eastern fringe of Portland, Fred Meyer in the early 1970s started planning for a major expansion at that location. Construction was already underway on a new freeway called Interstate-205 that would loop around Portland's eastern edge. The new highway broke away from Interstate-5 just north of Wilsonville, swung to the east to pass Oregon City, then headed straight north to a new bridge across the Columbia River. The highway reconnected with Interstate-5 north of Vancouver, Washington. The new route was intended to ease traffic on the twin Interstate Bridges that carried Interstate-5 across the Columbia River and to allow vehicles a potentially faster route along the edge of Portland rather than through its center. The good news for Fred Meyer was that plans for an eight-lane freeway in Multnomah County included a big interchange that would route thousands of cars per day past his expansive Gateway property near Northeast 102nd Avenue and Halsey Street.

But much to Meyer's chagrin, the political sands shifted literally under his feet. In 1972, some politically-active citizens began objecting to freeways that had been inked on to planning maps after World War II. Freeways that had been comparatively easy to build in rural areas and smaller cities now faced public opposition on grounds of air pollution, lead poisoning, neighborhood disruption and dispersal of homes and businesses. Freeway opponents gained momentum in 1973 when a new federal law allowed regions to transfer federal highway funds from freeways to public transit options if state and local officials agreed. Although the state's plans for the new Interstate-205 called for eight lanes and eight interchanges in its nine-mile path through Multnomah County, construction wending its way south to north had not yet reached the county line. Late in 1973, three members of the Multnomah County Board of Commissioners asked state highway officials to reconsider the width and number of interchanges. Commissioner Mel Gordon, leader of the triumvirate on the five-member board, urged that the freeway be pared to four lanes and four interchanges.[32] One of the "deleted" interchanges in Gordon's plan was the Halsey Street exit that Meyer had counted upon to funnel thousands of cars per day adjacent to his proposed new Gateway complex.

One of the most influential figures in Oregon's freeway development from 1959 into the early 1970s was Glenn L. Jackson, the chairman of Pacific Power & Light Co. He was appointed to the State Highway Commission (later renamed the Oregon Transportation Commission) by a Republican, Gov. Mark Hatfield, reappointed by a second Republican, Gov. Tom McCall, and then by a Democrat, Gov. Bob Straub. Jackson had earned the nickname, "Mr. Oregon," and was ranked as one of the most powerful people in the state by the news media. He and Fred Meyer had become acquaintances, and had dinner occasionally over the years. In 1969, Glenn Jackson was elected to the board of directors of Fred Meyer Inc., one of the few outsiders to sit on a board dominated by Meyer executives. He was no push-over. "He was a rather outspoken person at board meetings," recalled Jack Crocker. "Most of us were a little afraid of Fred Meyer– you know, we had a certain fear of him. Like if he got real upset we weren't going to push it too far. And Glenn probably more than any would just say, 'Aw nuts, Fred,' or something like that."[33] Though Jackson had supervised some 700 miles of Oregon freeway construction during his 20 years on the transportation commission, the political sensitivity of Portland freeway development in the 1970s had removed the matter from the hands of appointed officials like Jackson. The key negotiations were handled at higher political levels by elected officials, including Gov. Straub and County Commissioner Gordon. Jackson, no doubt aware of a potential conflict of interest in serving as state transportation commission chairman and as a Fred Meyer director, resigned from the Fred Meyer Inc. board in 1975. His dinners with Meyer came to an end. If the two men ever communicated again, it was not evident to any of Meyer's closest associates.

After several public hearings, Gov. Straub and Commissioner Gordon reached a compromise in July 1975. The freeway would be trimmed from eight lanes to six, with space for a transit line to be built sometime in the future. There would be six freeway interchanges, not eight as originally planned and not four as sought by Gordon. The officials also agreed the freeway would be built at grade level and in some places below grade. There would be no elevated portions. [34] To reach Halsey Street, the original plan called for elevated sections as high as 80 feet. Fred Meyer Inc. would continue to have direct access from eastbound traffic on Interstate-84, but there would be no direct link to Interstate-205.

Frustrated by watching from the sidelines without any official role, Meyer still tried to influence the outcome. He and Robertson made front page news when they announced plans for a $22 million Gateway project – but said it wouldn't happen if they didn't get the Halsey Street interchange. "Let them build what they originally planned, and we'll be happy," Meyer said. For a man who had built his long career on speed and adaptability, the delays were irksome. "This whole project has been held up by the freeway controversy," Meyer said of his Gateway plan. "It was supposed to be completed in 1978, but it won't be completed until 1988 the way they are moving around." Robertson was blunt as possible: "If there is no access, the project will not be developed."[35]

The bluff by Meyer and Robertson did not work. Five months

later, city and county officials formally approved the compromise plan.[36] Despite Robertson's threat, the company eventually went ahead with a new 180,000-square-foot Fred Meyer store at Gateway. Ironically, its completion took almost as long as Meyer himself had feared. A hotel developer who planned a 150-unit building as part of Meyer's 1976 plan withdrew. Given delays for zone changes, sewer construction, planning for the Portland region's first light rail line that passed nearby and litigation arising from Fred Meyer's death in 1978, the new Gateway Fred Meyer wasn't finished until 1987. "We're very glad to get it built," Robertson said at the time.[37] Meanwhile, the new bridge carrying Interstate-205 traffic across the Columbia River was completed in 1982. It was named for Glenn L. Jackson, who had died in 1980.

In 1974, Fred Meyer Inc. ran into more citizen-driven opposition when it started pushing dirt with heavy equipment on a 28-acre parcel near Oak Hills on the edge of one of Portland's newest western suburbs. The Fifth Avenue Corp., one of the Fred Meyer real estate subsidiaries, had bought the land in 1964. It was zoned for general commercial development, which would have allowed for a large-scale Fred Meyer shopping center. But once the earth moving equipment arrived, residents of the tony new suburb protested. They didn't like the dust and the noise, but most of all they didn't want a massive one-stop shopping center erected literally at the front door of their neighborhood. In response to the public objections, the Washington County planning department said the Meyer development team had failed to obtain a permit for excavating in a flood plain. In typical aggressive Meyer style, the earth movers kept to their task. The county went to court asking for a stop-work order; Fifth Avenue Corp. asked for a court order stopping the county from interfering. It was the start of a legal battle that lasted four years.

Two months after the Oak Hills project had begun, Washington County commissioners approved a new comprehensive plan that changed zoning on the site. If the new zone survived a court challenge, the "neighborhood commercial" designation would allow small retail buildings but not the big Fred Meyer complex. Fred Meyer officials felt blind-sided and claimed they had received no notice of the potential change, which apparently had been under discussion in the county for almost a year. The company had spent $300,000 on excavation. "But then we were stopped and we came to discover that what they had been doing was lengthening the time out so that they could change the zone with a comprehensive plan, and so that we could not build," Oran Robertson said afterward. "We heard nothing of the change before it went through."[38] The Fred Meyer legal team attacked the new zoning, claiming lack of public notice and inadequacies in the order approved by county commissioners. But after a favorable ruling at the Oregon Court of Appeals,[39] the Oregon Supreme Court reversed, concluding that the company had been amply notified by newspaper advertisements and that the form of the commission's order complied with the county's home-rule charter.[40] All three courts that had considered the case, starting with the Washington County Circuit Court, threw out the company's claims for monetary damages based on diminished property value as a result of the zone change.

The Oak Hills case was still pending in court when members of the Oak Hills Homeowners' Association were invited to a wine-tasting event at the neighborhood's recreation center. The host was Fred Meyer Inc. After the residents had been drinking and chatting for about 90 minutes, a driver in a car with one passenger pulled to a stop, "and Fred G. Meyer totters out with his cane, bow tie and a smile," according a resident's account. Some of the residents had been part-time Fred Meyer employees in their teenage or college years, and some offered pleasant recollections of events at Meyer's stores. Finally, a resident asked the question on many minds. "Why are you here?" Meyer answered, "You are all customers. I don't want you mad at me."[41]

Meyer himself was only weeks from death when the final Oak Hills ruling was issued. In the Fred Meyer Inc. annual report of 1975, he had already voiced his frustration about zoning, freeway matters and new taxes such as the TriMet payroll tax for public transit. Meyer usually opened these reports with a one-page statement limited to successes during the year and plans ahead. Now, approaching his 90th year, his statement took a more bitter tone. "These government policies, as well as zoning and even highway design at a local level, have taken a great deal of time and costs, and it appears they will continue to do so in the future," he wrote. "The need to continue to develop maximum return from existing stores is more obvious as environmental regulations and a labyrinth of local and state bureaucratic bodies continue to make building and expansion more difficult."[42]

Corporate life was not on hold, of course, while land-use matters percolated slowly. Meyer's prescience as a real estate investor was proven again in 1976 when Fred Meyer Inc. opened its 155,000-square-foot shopping center in Gresham. Meyer had acquired 35 acres at East Burnside and Foster Road in 1955 when the acreage was farmland. "There weren't even sewers out there, but we knew it was– Meyer knew it was– a strategic location," said Herbert Retzlaff.[43] The company leased it to farmers until population growth, sewers and the big new streets were ready to accommodate development. The 90-year old patriarch pinned a green carnation to his lapel for the St. Patrick's Day opening. "We were a little slow in getting here," Meyer said, "but here we are."[44] The addition marked the 25th active location in Oregon, and increased the Fred Meyer multi-state total to 64.

As customary, Fred Meyer Inc. continued looking for new business opportunities. One arose in the second half of 1973. A small savings and loan with a single office in Tillamook was available for sale. According to Oran Robertson, the idea to buy it was brought to Meyer by Gerry Pratt.[45] Meyer had often rented space to branch banks near his shopping centers, not only as a convenience to his shoppers but as magnets to draw potential shoppers. It was an intriguing idea. Always wanting to investigate what was already out there, Meyer commissioned

Jerry Sadis to look at the Handy-Andy chain in Texas and at Smitty's in Phoenix to examine in-store branches. In October, 1973, Meyer personally bought a controlling interest in Fidelity Savings and Loan Association. He installed Pratt as president and later sold his 97 percent personal interest in the savings and loan to Fred Meyer Inc. at his cost. Meyer and Pratt agreed that the newly-renamed Fred Meyer Savings & Loan would operate with its own board of directors as a subsidiary of Fred Meyer Inc. It was a decision that would lead to a bitter split less than a decade later between Pratt and Robertson.

If the decision to enter the savings and loan business was a hasty one, Meyer wouldn't admit to it. "I've been thinking of something like this for a long time," he told a reporter in June 1974. Meyer said he envisioned a shopper making large purchases at a Home Improvement Center being able to get a home improvement loan at the same location. He said mortgage lenders could be available on evenings and weekends, making access much easier for working customers. Showing Meyer's ability to see the future, journalist Donald J. Sorensen added, "Looking further ahead, he foresees the day when a customer can go through the grocery line, hand the checker a plastic card and pay for the groceries from the savings account."[46] Meyer also took a more expansive view. "There are three basic things man has needed since he was civilized," he told a reporter for a business magazine. "He had to have food, clothing and a place to live. Even when people lived in caves, if you had a monopoly on caves you would have done quite well. Well, we're in the food business, the clothing business and now we have mortgages on the homes."[47]

The decision to buy the savings and loan also was influenced by the mutual desire of Meyer and Pratt to find a more significant role in the company for Pratt. "I'm just confident Mr. Meyer wanted to make a spot for Gerry, because he was already on Fred Meyer's payroll just as a p.r. guy," said Dale Warman. "And I think he saw that, hey, I'm not able to keep this guy busy, so I'd better create a job, find something for him to do."[48] Jerry Sadis said that, once the company decided to enter the savings and loan business, there was no other executive available to take it on. "It's safe to say Gerry's selection as president of the savings and loan was based on his personal interaction with Mr. Meyer, versus a checklist of qualifications that would have dictated it." The decision was made "almost 100 percent certain by Mr. Meyer, but certainly accepted by everyone else." [49]

After his many years as a business reporter, Pratt was no doubt happy to try taking a small enterprise and making it grow big. The fact that he knew little about the savings and loan business was not a deterrent in Meyer's mind. Meyer had a history of giving big responsibilities to employees he trusted, and the results were usually favorable. Meyer knew that a fresh eye in business sometimes was a good thing. According to Herb Retzlaff, "He told me, 'You know, I'm going to put Gerry in charge of the savings and loan because he doesn't know a damn thing about it so he doesn't have any preconceived notions."[50]

The savings and loan business shot from the gate, just as Meyer and Pratt predicted. By the end of 1974, in less than a year under new management, it had grown to five offices, with three located in stores. A year later, the total was 12. By late 1977, the total was 22. "Gerry was a great p.r. guy, great front guy with the public and a great salesman," Warman said. "That business really blossomed, really grew fast."[51] The new venture rocked Portland's banking world by being open from 9 a.m. to 9 p.m., Monday through Saturday. Its in-store branches had lower rental costs than free-standing buildings. The savings and loan opened new accounts for as little as $5, and offered premiums for new accounts ranging from steaks and smoke alarms to tools and microwave ovens, depending on deposit size. The number of account-bearing customers rose from 5,460 in 1974 to 39,222 in 1976 and 67,064 at the end of 1977.[52] Competitors were stunned and frustrated. "There wasn't a friend in the industry," Sadis said. "Everybody was hoping it would fall on its face, and all it did was grab more deposits and more deposits and more deposits. There may have been a tinge of jealousy." Meyer, of course, wasn't concerned about what any competitor thought. "He'd say, 'The competitors hate us but the customers love us. What's wrong with that?'"[53]

The bottom line for the savings and loan, nonetheless, was proving bumpy. It lost $240,000 in 1975 largely due to start-up expenses, but bounced back with a gain of $422,000 in 1976. A downside to all those new, often-small accounts was the on-going printing and distribution of monthly statements; postage cost the same whether the account was large or $5. The association's aggressive marketing campaign also far exceeded the industry averages for percentage of customers with long-term certificates of deposit, which paid higher interest rates than passbook accounts. Over time, that was a factor that would affect profits. The ability to generate steady, positive returns would be the true test of Pratt's ability in the minds of directors of Fred Meyer Inc. The company had a long history of trying new ventures, keeping the successful ones and jettisoning losers. The road ahead would get bumpier yet, thanks to national conditions over which Pratt had no control.

In 1975, the 89-year old Meyer made a personnel decision he'd made only once before in his long career: He took back a senior manager who had left him earlier. As a general rule, managers who left the company never heard from Meyer again. Dale Warman, like Rollin Killoran two decades earlier, was an exception. Killoran apparently had urged Meyer to communicate with Warman after Warman had left as marketing director to accept a senior vice president's job with Allied Stores in Detroit. About a year and a half after his departure, Warman started receiving occasional missives from Meyer, including suggestions on marketing strategies and advertising ideas. Warman found that living in Detroit was less pleasant than the Pacific Northwest he was used to; in fact, he'd never sold his Vancouver residence. During a trip to Portland in 1975, Warman met privately with Cy Green in a hotel room where the two men negotiated Warman's return as marketing director.

Warman was struck by the wording Meyer used in a welcoming memo: "It may be of interest to know that the staff looks with great enthusiasm on your return to the firm's executive staff."[54] Meyer, it seemed, couldn't admit his own enthusiasm lest it be construed as an error in letting Warman leave in the first place. Upon his return, Warman posted signs at the office stating, "Selling is our business." Meyer took them down and added his own personal scrawl to make them read: "Selling profitably is our business."[55]

Meyer's belief in Warman's abilities was demonstrated a year later when, with little warning, Meyer had him elected to the board of directors. The incident showed again how quickly Meyer could turn against someone. The seat filled by Warman was a director's position held by Melvin Smith, who was a member of Meyer's nine-person slate in the eventful 1971 meeting in which John Davis was ousted. Smith had preceded Rollin Killoran as advertising manager in the 1930s, but left the company when a seemingly-major health problem arose. In the end, Smith made a full recovery and had established a successful consulting firm in Los Angeles when Meyer nominated him as a director in 1971. Smith likely had rankled Meyer by advocating for additional outside directors on the board. There also were times when Smith could not attend board meetings because of conflicts. Meyer ousted Smith in a matter of minutes in March, 1976. According to Warman's recollection, "He just said, 'Mel, you're so active down in California, you've got so many things going on and you can't seem always to be at our board meetings, and we have Warman here now that's had a lot of experience back in Detroit and all around the country. And we're just going to accept your resignation. And I want Dale Warman to take your place. Can I hear a second for that?' …(T)hey took a vote on it and it happened just like that." Warman added, "It got awful quiet in there, I remember that. In fact, it was uncomfortable, I think to a lot of people. But Mr. Meyer always had plenty of votes. I mean, it was unanimous." Smith rose quietly walked out. [56]

In 1975, Fred Meyer Inc. announced its biggest building project ever, yet one few customers would ever enter. The company bought approximately 89 acres from Southern Pacific Railroad in Clackamas County to build a bakery, warehouse and distribution center that eventually would cover 600,000 square feet – the equivalent of 15 of Portland's downtown blocks. As usual, nothing proceeded as quickly as Meyer wanted. The county zoning regulations specified that a certain amount of the property needed to be preserved as park land. The requirement baffled Meyer, who saw no need for a park in a trucking hub. Clackamas County commissioners agreed to pare the green space almost in half, from 15 percent of the site to 8.1 percent.[57] Meyer balked at another proposal that he mitigate storm water runoff from the massive warehouse roof by planting what is now called an eco-roof. "One of those crazy people wanted us to put grass on the roof and we had to fight that," he said afterward. "A lot of these planning commission members are like children. They don't know what they are doing. They've never had any power before."[58]

The big complex was erected in stages, and was not finished before Meyer died in 1978. It was built, like all Meyer projects since the early 1960s, by Howard Andersen's construction company. During a news conference at a ceremonial ground-breaking, Meyer posed atop a bulldozer for photographers. Andersen couldn't resist calling out to Meyer that the big machine cost $125 an hour to rent. Meyer immediately ended the news conference and slowly clambered down.[59]

By March 1976, Meyer, who had just celebrated his 90th birthday, fully accepted the fact that he needed a managerial structure to replace him. That month he resigned as board chairman and nominated Oran Robertson to replace him as chairman and chief executive officer. Of course, Meyer had more than enough votes on the board to approve his plan. He would remain as chairman of the board's executive committee.[60] For a man of his years, Meyer's brain was still amazingly agile. But those closest to him realized that time was taking its inevitable toll, and so too, perhaps, did Meyer. Pauline Lawrence had started to notice a change in the early 1970s. "Because he was getting older, and he was not out in front of it. He didn't hear the things that us people would hear, or see, you know. But he'd get little parts of it. And then he'd ask us questions of so and so, are they getting along? Naming some of the people. 'Do they work together? Are they going to be a team? I want a good strong team after I'm gone to keep this thing going as it is.'" [61] Sadis, who had joined the company late in 1971, noticed the changes, too. "There was a gradual erosion of that closeness of authority he kept. It clearly was going on when I was there. The perception of Mr. Meyer quote 'running the business' is false. It was moving too rapidly for him to have the tight control he had in the late 60s or early 60s." In 1975, Meyer made the last of his annual trips to New York City to discuss prospects for Fred Meyer Inc. stock with Wall Street analysts. "That kind of a trip was very tiring on him, so we didn't push it," Sadis said.[62]

Later that year, Fred Meyer Inc. published perhaps the oddest newspaper advertisement in the company's long history. It occupied a full page in the *Sunday Oregonian*, the week's biggest and most expensive issue. The surprising aspect was that it did not attempt to sell anyone a single product or grocery item. Instead, the company offered its best measure of Fred Meyer Inc.'s impact on the Oregon economy. "Fred Meyer spends over $51 million annually on Oregon Products...and over $42 million for Oregon employment," it said. "What this means to you is: Fred Meyer is good business for Oregon...the money you spend at Fred Meyer helps build 'your' Oregon." The ad itemized $12.6 million paid to the state's farm industry, $10 million spent with Oregon manufacturing companies, $8.7 million paid for fish, meat and poultry, $4.3 million paid to Oregon dairy farmers, $3 million spent on transportation, and $17.5 million paid for Oregon construction projects. The advertisement said Fred Meyer employment in the state had hit 9,000, half of them women "who enjoy the benefits of an equal opportunity employer." More than 100 professional druggists were earning $22,000 per year. Thousands of others, the ad said, were earning up to $12,500 as checkers, stock clerks, waitresses, cooks, office workers, warehouse men and truck drivers. [63] The advertisement ostensibly was run in honor of Oregon Products Week. Given its size and expense, however, it was more a tribute to the elderly patriarch of Fred Meyer Inc., who believed deeply in supporting the local economy. In 50 years, Fred Meyer and his company had come a long ways from Yamhill Street.

Though Meyer ostensibly had transferred his corporate mantle to Robertson, at times it seemed there was little change in the management committee or board meetings. "I sat in several meetings where you'd still think Mr. Meyer was chairman," Pauline Lawrence recalled. "Robertson was there as chairman, and he sat at the head of the table, and he started the meeting, and he ended it and all like that. But Mr. Meyer was there, too, for a long time, until he got sick."[64] Warman noticed the same. "Well, whether we were talking about remodeling a store, or taking out a big mortgage or buying a piece of property or what have you, there was discussion, but I think everybody pretty well listened to Mr. Meyer because he had the most votes. He was going to win."[65]

It was clear to many corporate insiders that Meyer from the middle 1970s was setting up the structure that would replace him. One of those final acts was to add two more members to the board of directors who were important to him, Gerry Pratt and Pauline Lawrence. Robertson had lobbied for additional "outside" directors, and Meyer agreed to expand the total board roster from nine to thirteen. In addition to Pratt and Lawrence, the new directors were C. Howard Burnett, a Union Pacific Railroad vice president based in Portland, and Tod McClaskey, chairman of the Thunderbird/Red Lion upscale hotel chain.

Lawrence was reluctant to accept. She told Meyer she didn't feel qualified. Meyer disagreed. "He said, 'You'll learn just like you've learned everything else in life. And it's nothing strange or different, you can learn it the same as the rest of it.'" Meyer appealed to her instincts about women's equality. After all, Lawrence had quit the Mannings restaurant job as a young woman when she had been passed over for a promotion by a less-qualified man. She had broken ground late in her career as first female president of the Oregon Restaurant Association in 1975. "We have a little problem," Meyer told her. "Some of the fellows don't believe we're ready to have a woman on there." Meyer believed it

Shortly before his final hospital visit, Fred Meyer threw an opening pitch at a Portland Civic Stadium baseball game. (Oregonian)

was time for the company to have its first female director as a public company. Lawrence accepted.[66]

She found the meetings difficult. "Our meetings were so long. I dreaded them. And I told Mr. Meyer that I never felt I was qualified to be a board member. And he said the reason I was qualified was because I was a woman and he wanted a woman on there. Well, there was no discussion after that." Lawrence said little during her first board meetings. "I felt there was resentment with the other fellows of having a woman, when most of them had a friend or another man they would rather have had on there. So I felt a little bit like an unwanted person on that board." Yet it was difficult to pinpoint specific instances that led to her discomfort. "They all treated me nice, they all were very helpful to me...It was mostly my feeling that I felt this way." As Meyer had predicted, Lawrence's intelligence and adaptability prevailed. "But after I was there for awhile, it didn't take me too long...too many meetings 'til I began to feel a little bit sure of myself."[67] Pratt, in contrast, showed no reluctance at being a board newcomer. "When Gerry got on, he was a very good board member. He spoke out," Lawrence said. "Mr. Meyer backed him a hundred percent, see. Mr. Meyer loved the guy, he really thought a lot of him."[68]

Total Fred Meyer Inc. sales for 1977, the last full year of Meyer's life, hit $822.8 million. Over its 18 years as a publicly-held corporation, sales had increased every year. There had been no serious wobbles. For 72 consecutive quarters, the company had beaten sales for the corresponding quarter the year before.[69]

---

[1] Lawrence, Pauline, OHS sound recording 1309, May 25, 1989.
[2] Sadis, Jerry, OHS sound recording 1313, April 20, 1989.
[3] Walton, Sam, and Huey, John, *Made in America,* Bantam Books, 1993, p. 108.
[4] Robertson, Oran, OHS sound recording 1312...
[5] Sadis, *op. cit.*
[6] Walton and Huey, *op. cit.,* p. 111. Walton misspelled the last name as "Worman."
[7] Vance, Sandra S., and Scott, Roy V., *Wal-Mart: A History of Sam Walton's Retail Phenomenon,* Twayne Publishers, 1994, p. 132.
[8] Sadis, *op. cit.*
[9] *New York Times,* Sept. 19, 1974, p.63.
[10] *Oregonian,* Feb. 29, 1972, p. 15.
[11] Webb, Jean S., OHS sound recording 1316, July 11, 1989.
[12] Lawrence, Pauline, OHS sound recording 1309, Jan. 12, 1989.

[13] Sadis, *op. cit.*
[14] Green, Cyril K., OHS sound recording 1307, Feb. 27, 1989.
[15] Fred Meyer Inc., *Annual Report 1972,* p. 1.
[16] Robertson, Oran B., OHS sound recording 1312, March 28, 1989.
[17] *Ibid.*
[18] Warman, Dale, OHS sound recording 1315, May 17, 1989.
[19] *Oregonian,* July 15, 1978, p. F7.
[20] Warman, *op. cit.*
[21] Robertson, *op. cit.,* March 3, 1989.
[22] *Ibid.*
[23] *Ibid.*
[24] *Willamette Week,* March 28, 1977, p. 2.
[25] Lawrence, *op. cit.*
[26] *Oregonian,* May 17, 1973, p. C 12. .
[27] *United States of America v. Fred Meyer Inc.,* U.S. District Court, District of Oregon, 73-874.
[28] *Oregonian,* Dec. 17, 1975, p. 1.
[29] *Willamette Week.,* April 4, 1977, p. 7.
[30] Sadis, *op. cit.*
[31] Green, *op. cit.*
[32] *Oregonian,* Oct. 3, 1973, p. 30.
[33] Crocker, Jack, OHS sound recording 1304, June 13, 1989.
[34] *Oregonian,* July 26, 1976, p. A12.
[35] *Ibid.,* Jan. 20, 1976, p. 1.
[36] *Ibid.,* June 4, 1976, p. B1.
[37] *Ibid.,* Nov. 12, 1987, p. D15.
[38] *Willamette Week,* March 7, 1977.
[39] *Fifth Avenue Corp . v. Washington County,* 28 OrAp 485 (1977)
[40] *Fifth Avenue Corp . v. Washington County*, 282 Or 591 (1978)
[41] Recollection of Laurance Sitter, submitted to Fred Meyer Inc. in 2007. Located in Fred Meyer Collection 199, box 35, folder 11, OHS.
[42] *Fred Meyer Inc.,* Annual Report 1975, p. 1.
[43] Retzlaff, Herbert, OHS sound recording 1311, Feb. 15, 1989.
[44] *Oregonian,* March 18, 1976, p. D4.
[45] Robertson, *op. cit.,* April 4, 1989.
[46] *Oregonian,* June 9, 1974, p. F7.
[47] *Forbes,* "Nothing Really Changes," Jan. 23, 1978, p. 68.
[48] Warman, *op. cit.*
[49] Sadis, *op. cit.*

[50] Retzlaff, *op. cit.,* March 1, 1989.
[51] Warman , *op. cit.*
[52] *Fred Meyer Inc.,* annual reports of 1976 and 1977.
[53] Sadis , *op. cit.*
[54] Warman , *op. cit.,* April 27, 1989.

[55] Green, op. cit.
[56] Warman, *op. cit.*
[57] *Oregonian*, Feb. 24, 1976, p. A15.
[58] *Willamette Week,* March 6, 1977.
[59] Andersen, Howard, OHS sound recording 1300, Aug. 9, 1989.
[60] *Oregonian,* March 10, 1976, p. 1.
[61] Lawrence, *op. cit.,* May 25, 1989.
[62] Sadis, *op. cit.*
[63]*Oregonian,* Oct. 10, 1976, p. C1.
[64] Lawrence, *op. cit.,* Jan. 12, 1989.
[65] Warman, *op. cit.,* May 17, 1989.
[66] *Oregonian,* July 4, 1978, p. D5.
[67] Lawrence, *op. cit.*
[68] *Ibid.*
[69] *Oregonian,* March 1, 1978, p. A11.

CHAPTER NINE

The Final Days of FGM

Glen Day was admitted to St. Vincent Hospital in June, 1978, for transfusions necessitated by a bleeding ulcer. He had spent 26 years working for Fred Meyer, starting in 1932. At age 19 and with the Great Depression showing no signs of easing, Day considered himself fortunate to land a job in the little laundry and dry-cleaning storefront that was part of Fred Meyer's Alderway Building. As the years wore on, he managed several functions for Meyer, including the early days of automobile servicing and tire sales, and later the Fred Meyer bakery. In 1955, he was promoted to vice president in charge of warehousing and manufacturing. Three years later, Day left Fred Meyer Inc. to work with a company that produced wholesale specialty mixes for commercial bakeries. Now, 20 years later, Day found himself in a hospital room adjacent to one occupied by Fred Meyer, his former boss.

Meyer suffered from fluid on the lungs, which made breathing difficult. About two months earlier, not long after his 92nd birthday, he had encountered days when he felt too weak to make it to the office. Meyer knew this was his last visit to a hospital. "He indicated that he was going to get himself discharged from the hospital....and two days later he had gone back to his apartment," Day said. "He was a very determined man and they couldn't keep him in the hospital if he didn't want to stay there. He had been known to do that previously, and he'd get up and walk out of the place."[1]

Fred Meyer leaves St. Vincent Hospital for the final time in June, 1978. (Oregonian)

Meyer had no desire to die in a hospital, his body riddled with tubes and mechanical devices. He went home to his 19th floor apartment on Harrison Street. His doctor told him he should not go to the office. But there was still work to oversee and personal matters to take care of. Meyer hired a private nurse, Ann Thompson, who was experienced in end-of-life care, to be with him 24 hours per day in his apartment. He moved his office out of the second bedroom and into the living room to make room for her. He had his secretary of 20 years, Jean Webb, bring him papers every day from the Fred Meyer Inc. headquarters. "I think it kind of hurt his feelings or something like that" when the doctor instructed him not to leave the apartment, Webb said. "But as long as I would come each day and bring him his papers, pick up what he had done that day and sit and visit with him for a few minutes and discuss things that had gone on in the office that day, that seemed to satisfy him. I mean as much as anything could, when he knew he was limited." Webb quickly developed her own barometer to gauge how he was feeling any given day. "I could tell by the amount of work that came out that some days he was not feeling as good. And then towards the last, we knew – and he realized it, too, and admitted it. I mean, he admitted that there were certain things he wanted to get done before he left this world."[2]

Meyer's physician, Dr. Donald E. Olson, also had told Meyer to restrict the number of visitors to conserve his strength. Pauline Lawrence was an exception. She visited Meyer's apartment each morning on her drive from the Burlingame neighborhood to the office. "I used to bring him custard from the store because he loved our restaurant custard," she said. Lawrence believed that Gerry Pratt's feelings were hurt by the doctor's restrictions. "Gerry felt very lost about that and he wasn't able to visit with Mr. Meyer very much. In fact doctors didn't want nobody there except necessary people. I believe he (Pratt) felt like he was kind of pushed out. But he really wasn't, as far as I know."[3] Two visitors who did make a pilgrimage to Meyer's apartment in the final weeks of his life were Herb Retzlaff, Meyer's controller for three decades, and Roy Webster, a partner in a private accounting firm who served as the company's outside auditor. Retzlaff recalled, "He was quite mellow and I remember him saying to me, 'Well, Herb, we used to have a lot of good times together, didn't we?'"[4] Virgil Campbell, who was head of the company's northern division, also made a trip to see Meyer a final time. "He basically thanked me for the visit," Campbell recalled. "He said, 'You've done a good job. Keep on top of things for me when I'm gone.'"[5]

Meyer faced death without fear or outward signs of emotional distress. Jerry Sadis talked to Meyer by telephone in those final weeks. "I think he knew a year in advance or two years in advance. It's fairly evident he was getting things in order."[6] Meyer was never one to share personal feelings or to complain about physical ailments, and his last illness was no exception. "Well, of course, he was a person who could really hide his physical condition quite well, and he was a very personal individual, so he didn't want anyone ever feeling sorry for him or to help him in way, shape or form," Oran Robertson said.[7] Meyer's calm also was a reflection of his Rosicrucian religious beliefs, which suggested he would return to the earth again someday in a new physical body. Max Heindel, who had proven to be an inspirational influence when the two men met in Seattle seven decades earlier, had concluded that eternal heaven as a reward for a good life on earth made little sense. He believed that humans could benefit from past experiences and return to earth to help others. In perhaps his briefest explanation, Heindel wrote in his seminal book: "The Theory of Rebirth teaches that each soul is an integral part of God, enfolding all divine possibilities as the seed enfolds the plant; that by means of repeated existences in an earthly body of gradually improving quality, the latent possibilities are slowly developed into dynamic powers; that none are lost by this process, but that all mankind will ultimately attain the goal of perfection and reunion with God."[8] Meyer had made regular contributions to Heindel's Rosicrucian Fellowship throughout his adult life.

In his final weeks, Meyer worked with lawyer and good friend Paul Boley on a codicil to his will that had been written in 1976. Both versions called for establishment of a charitable trust that would receive most of Meyer's assets after his death. Meyer also worked on lists of valued employees that he would honor with gifts worth $3,000 before his death, the maximum allowed under federal rules at the time without incurring a gift tax. Webb said he made those gifts a priority "because he said he realized he had very few days left. He just knew, himself."[9] Meyer also had Webb bring him numerous files from his office, from which he purged an indeterminate number of personal items. Some of them, Pauline Lawrence said, were the unsolicited love letters he had received over the years from single women.

At least one inquiry arrived about the possible sale of Fred Meyer Inc. Any suitors were wasting their time. That was perfectly clear to Thompson, the nurse. She told Pauline Lawrence, "He ain't going to sell that company. He don't want to sell that company."[10] Another topic of discussion was how the chain of Fred Meyer stores should react upon his death. Should they close in his honor? "No, that was very specific, that he did not want that," Webb recalled. "He was emphatic about that."[11] Ever the merchant, Meyer knew that a day of lost sales was gone forever.

Meyer's condition worsened late in August, but there was no intention of taking him to a hospital. "That is his wish and my wish," Dr. Olson said.[12] Pauline Lawrence filled a prescription for morphine, in case it was needed for pain. On Sept. 1, Meyer told Lawrence that he wanted to see Oran Robertson, Cy Green and Gerry Pratt at his apartment bedside at 6 p.m. "He called and wanted to see us, and if you knew Mr. Meyer at all, you knew that he would know ahead of time when his time was up, if you want to call it that," Robertson said. "And I think he knew it and wanted to tell us how he wanted us to work together and what to accomplish and so on."[13]

Meyer told Lawrence that he had two things on his mind. "Number one, that we work together and get along, and not fight because there had been discussions between them, and little words and things like that. And then the other thing, that he had appointed three of us as his trustees. And he realized the importance of getting along." There was, to Lawrence's recollection, no mention about selling or not selling Fred Meyer Inc. Meyer had made his wishes known in his final years, already. "His whole idea was that he wanted the company to stay together," she said. "He handpicked the people that he put on his board and everywhere else, hoping that would keep the company going. Because what he wanted, was the company to continue on to operate just as it is, at that time. ..He was older, he knew he wasn't going to be there.

And he almost knew it was going to (be sold) but he didn't want it to happen."[14]

Oran Robertson, Cyril Green and Gerry Pratt showed up at Meyer's apartment on time at 6 p.m. Meyer was too weak to sit up, but he was still able to speak in a soft voice. Pratt held Meyer's emaciated torso upright and Meyer dangled his weakened legs off the edge of the bed. He spoke few words. There would be a disagreement later between Robertson and Pratt about Meyer's final thoughts, but the two agreed on this part: "Promise me, promise me, promise me that you will get along together."[15] Meyer's visitors soon left and went separate ways into the summer evening.

Early the next morning, September 2, Pauline Lawrence received a phone call from Ann Thompson, the live-in nurse. "You'd better come by real quick, because I don't think..." Lawrence rushed to the apartment, arriving not a moment too soon. She hurried into Meyer's bedroom and found that Thompson had propped up his head with pillows, because Meyer no longer had strength to hold it up himself. She reached for his hand. She said Meyer was alert and clearly recognized her, but he was too weak to speak. The edges of his lips curled into a gentle smile. "I was holding his hand when he died, and he was gone almost immediately after I got there," Lawrence said. "But he looked up and smiled at me, and dropped his head. And then, of course, she (Thompson) immediately said, 'He's gone.'" The morphine Lawrence had brought earlier had gone untouched.[16]

News of Meyer's death made the newspaper's front page the next morning, along with a second longer article in an inside section. Sometime before, Meyer had said, "After all, someday in the paper you're going to read that I didn't wake up that morning." [17] That day had arrived. The articles recounted the major episodes of his life, including the long-standing inaccuracies about being born in Brooklyn and opening the first Fred Meyer store in 1922. The same edition carried a quarter-page Fred Meyer advertisement showing a formal portrait of Meyer, taken in his late 80s. The photograph floated in a gentle sea of white space, surrounded with a black border. It showed Meyer looking straight ahead, with a winsome smile and wearing an oversized bow tie. "In his memory and at his request," the caption said, "the stores will remain open to serve you, the customer."[18] At his death, the company operated 63 stores in four states, Oregon, Washington, Alaska and Montana. Total employees numbered approximately 10,000. All stores opened as usual on Monday, the day after his death was reported. The company received some objections from people who felt Meyer's death warranted a day of respect. Oran Robertson received some of them. "He would not have wanted us to close those stores in any way, shape or form, because in Mr. Meyer's mind those stores were there for one purpose, and that was for the convenience of the customer."[19]

Clearing out Meyer's apartment was a simple matter. He had instructed that his furniture be given to Thompson, the nurse. His closet was virtually empty, since he had a habit of giving his old clothes to the Salvation Army whenever he acquired new ones. His personal effects amounted to a wristwatch of little value and a set of Eva Meyer's silverware. An inventory of his estate filed in Multnomah County Probate Court listed the personal assets in his apartment – furnishings, art, clothes, books and the silverware – with a total value of about $1,750.[20] The sparseness of his personal environment reflected values Meyer had expressed to Portland historian E. Kimbark MacColl in an interview just a few days after Meyer left the hospital in February. "Does not believe in living it up," MacColl wrote in a summary. "No need to have a home or property. Apartment living has always been his style. Not interested in an ego trip and a lot of embellishments. Many businesses have fallen on hard times because the executives became stuffed with their own importance, swelled heads, pretensions, etc. Keep simple and keep to basic principles."[21]

Meyer's funeral likewise was a simple affair, at his request. It was held at a Portland funeral home that allowed room for no more than

300 people. Many started showing up an hour early. In his will, Meyer had made his preferences clear. "I request that there be no lamenting at my funeral by anyone and that no flowers be given by anyone but that any amounts that anyone otherwise would wish to expend for flowers be given to the Salvation Army of Portland, Oregon, for caring for the unfortunates of Portland."[22]

Meyer's bodily remains, according to his wishes, were handled in the manner prescribed by the Rosicrucian Fellowship. His body was kept in a quiet room for 84 hours, giving time for what Max Heindel called the "seed atom" to advance from earth to a heavenly state, so it could be implanted later into a new human being. On the fourth day, Meyer's body was cremated and the ashes were strewn from the Arrah Wanna Bridge across the Salmon River near his beloved former recreation home called "Eva's Eden" near Wemme. Eva Meyer's remains had been placed 18 years earlier in a crypt at Riverview Cemetery; Meyer had kept the receipt.

Four days after his death, Fred Meyer's will was filed in Multnomah County Probate Court. It was significant for many reasons, perhaps the most being that it contained the seeds of legal and personal conflict that that eventually led to the sale of Fred Meyer Inc. The will also identified the most important people in Meyer's mind and created what would become Oregon's largest single charitable trust for many years to come. In addition, a four-page document accompanying the will laid out factors the trustees should consider in allocating money from the trust. Although grammatically cumbersome in parts, the "Memorandum to the Trustees of the Charitable Trust to be Created Under My Will" defined issues that are essential for understanding Meyer as a person and what he thought was most important in life.

Meyer had not been a generous charitable benefactor during his life in terms of giving cash. He had given large amounts of food to the Salvation Army at Christmas, and he supported the Portland Police Bureau's Sunshine Division with toys for children. He did not believe in handouts, especially to the young. When he received requests from Little League teams or children's organizations, he would give them opportunities to earn money themselves, by holding car washes in his parking lots or selling Girl Scout cookies at store entrances. His will, by contrast, included bequests to several organizations. The largest, amounting to $200,000, was to the Rosicrucian Fellowship, the religious organization to which he belonged for more than 70 years. Next in line was the Cascade Division of the Salvation Army, to which he gave $100,000. Other bequests were: $50,000 to the Shriners' Hospital for Crippled Children; $25,000 each to Columbia Christian College in Portland, the Oregon Graduate Center and the Police Bureau's Sunshine Division; $15,000 each to Dammasch State Hospital, the Masonic and Eastern Star Home and the Tucker-Maxon Oral School of Portland; and $10,000 each to the Toy and Joy Makers and the St. Vincent Foundation.

Individual bequests from Meyer were directed to 27 individuals, most of them being company employees. The bulk of his estate, estimated at $48 million by Meyer before his death, was earmarked for a new charitable trust that would allocate funds in perpetuity for religious, scientific, literary, charitable and educational purposes. The personal bequests ranged from $15,000 to $50,000. The largest three, at $50,000 each, went to Meyer's surviving sister, Sophie Wright, a New Jersey resident, and to Cyril Green and Virgil Campbell. Mary Chatfield Boyle, his sister-in-law, and Earle A. Chiles, his stepson, each received $25,000. Mary Grubmeyer, a niece who was the daughter of Meyer's late brother, William Grubmeyer, received $15,000. A total of 21 key employees received bequests ranging between $10,000 and $30,000, seemingly based on their tenure and rank in the company at the time of Meyer's death. Dale Warman, whose service was almost as long as that of Green and Campbell, but his bequest was $20,000 less than theirs. He thought Meyer might have penalized him for having left the company for three years to work for Allied Stores in Detroit.

Notably missing among the individuals receiving bequests were Oran Robertson, Gerry Pratt and Pauline Lawrence, the three people who likely were Meyer's closest associates. They were not ignored, however. Meyer named them as personal representatives of his estate and as trustees of his charitable trust, both positions which entitled them to recompense. Of course, all three were directors of Fred Meyer Inc., for which they also received remuneration. There was a fourth name on the list of personal representatives that was more surprising. Warne Nunn was a well-respected figure in Oregon political and business circles, but he lacked the long personal involvement with Meyer exemplified by Robertson, Lawrence and Pratt. Pratt had crossed paths with Nunn back in his newspaper reporting days, and no doubt knew him through political connections, as well. Nunn had graduated from Willamette University and joined the U.S. Air Force during World War II. Returning after the war, he began a long career in state government which included stops as an assistant public utilities commissioner and head of the motor vehicles department. In 1957, Nunn joined the staff of Oregon's new young secretary of state, Mark O. Hatfield. After Hatfield advanced to governor, Nunn spent the next eight years as one of Hatfield's top two administrative assistants, along with Travis Cross. During Hatfield's highly-successful gubernatorial tenure, Nunn and Cross were responsible for many of the operational decisions and behind-the-scenes negotiations of the state's top office. Nunn worked closely with the State Highway Commission and its influential leader, Glenn Jackson, the chairman of Pacific Power & Light Co. With Hatfield on his way to the U.S. Senate, Warne Nunn in 1968 joined Pacific Power, first as public affairs manager and later as manager of the utility's Portland district.

Nunn and Gerry Pratt tightened their personal bonds in 1974 when Nunn agreed to join the board of directors of the savings and loan association Meyer had purchased earlier that year. Since the John Davis fracas of 1971, Meyer had been urged to add more non-employee directors to the board of Fred Meyer Inc., and Nunn was elected, certainly with Pratt's approval, in 1975. By demeanor and political training, Nunn was a quietly affable person who seemed willing to learn from, and negotiate calmly with, a wide variety of people. From his years working with Hatfield and Glenn Jackson, Nunn knew how to achieve results and let others take the credit. When Meyer wrote the basics of his will in 1976, he had come to respect Nunn enough to include him as a personal representative of his estate and as a trustee of Meyer's charitable trust.

Meyer likely had been advised that it was legally untenable for Robertson, Pratt , Lawrence and Nunn to wear three hats at once – especially when each hat imposed the highest level of fiduciary responsibility upon its wearer to three different legal entities, the corporation, the estate and the trust. At his death, Meyer owned about 28 percent of Fred Meyer Inc. stock that would become the primary asset of the charitable trust. However, prudent trust management would require a diversification of assets. In addition, the trustees would seek a higher rate of return than the three percent dividend paid by the corporation at the time. The only way the trust could continue in perpetuity was to achieve stable, reasonable revenue from its assets. Meyer certainly knew that his shares would be sold to someone, and that the greatest value would be achieved if the sale involved corporate control. In essence, Meyer was asking Robertson, Lawrence, Pratt and Nunn to find a solution for which he himself had no realistic answer: how to fund the trust without selling its primary asset, Fred Meyer Inc.

Meyer could have chosen another path. Nearly 80 years before Meyer's death, another self-educated, hard-driving, fabulously successful entrepreneur faced a similar question about what to do with his vast wealth. Meyer had listed Andrew Carnegie's self-service libraries as one inspiration for Meyer's success in self-service grocery sales. Carnegie, like Meyer, felt a deep obligation to use his wealth to benefit the larger society. In an 1899 essay, "The Gospel of Wealth," Carnegie concluded that ultra-successful entrepreneurs during their own lifetimes should live unostentatiously and leave only moderate bequests to their heirs. He urged these business people to apply their wealth for community benefit without waiting until death. He believed that savvy entrepreneurs would make the best decisions about how their money should be spent. Carnegie expressed scorn for the ultra-wealthy who chose to die without spending their riches. "Men who leave vast sums in this way (at death) may fairly be thought men who would not have left it at all, had they been able to take it with them," he wrote. "[23]

Carnegie sold his vast steel industry holdings at age 65, and oversaw the funding of more than 2,500 public libraries in North America and the United Kingdom. Like Carnegie, Meyer lived without ostentation and gave modest gifts to the few relatives who survived him. However, because running Fred Meyer Inc. was his only real interest in life, Meyer could not bring himself to sell it. There was another significant difference in the intervening years between the deaths of Carnegie and Meyer: There were no federal income or estate taxes in Carnegie's era. Had Meyer sold Fred Meyer Inc. during his lifetime, his tax liabilities would have been paid at the expense of funding the trust. The goals of Meyer's trust, however, fell firmly in line with the recommendation of Carnegie, who wrote: "In bestowing charity, the main consideration should be to help those who will help themselves; to provide part of the means by which those who desire to improve may do so; to give those who desire to use the aids by which they may rise; to assist, but rarely or never to do all."[24]

Meyer attached a four-page document advising trustees how he would like to see trust money spent. Knowing that he could not foresee all uncertainties of the future, his advice was offered as suggestions as opposed to binding directives. Dated March 29, 1976, it was a document of sweeping scope, showing that Meyer's mind remained fertile and deeply curious at age 90. "In general," he wrote, "I suggest that the trust favor programs which promote useful knowledge concerning the production, distribution and consumption of wealth and the various related factors of the economy, which foster scientific research, which tend to increase the power of mind over matter, and which serve the needs, conveniences and pleasures of life."

On business matters, Meyer asked his trustees to consider projects that would improve the production, processing, packaging, transport and distribution of "all kinds of goods, wares and merchandise." He also urged research into employee training and personnel relations aimed at improving efficiency and employee well-being. Among social services, Meyer asked the trust to support "agencies which relieve and assist sick, needy, aged disabled and handicapped persons," as well trying to remedy alcohol and drug addiction. However, Meyer's most-detailed instructions concerned his life-long interest in a connection between science and religion. He asked the trust to "aid and encourage scientific research regarding the origin, evolution and future possible developments of man, from both the scientific and spiritual aspects, seeking out the purpose and mysteries of life and being, all in a scientific way and in harmony with religion – not regarding the intellectual understanding of the Universe and God as an end in itself, but in order that men may believe, know and live that civil and religious life which will aid to build true fellowship among all peoples."

Meyer also recognized that money alone wouldn't provide all the benefits he desired. There always would have to be room for human ingenuity. His last words in the memorandum to his trustees were, "Finally, in all giving, give thought. With thoughtful giving, even small sums may accomplish great purposes."[25]

To the surprise of some, Fred Meyer Inc. continued operating profitably and without noticeable change in the early months after Meyer's death. Some customers expected changes to occur quickly, and some perceived changes that didn't exist. One woman complained that the number of raisins in the MY-TE-FINE raisin bread had declined immediately after Meyer's death, and she was she sure that Meyer would not have approved. With the exception of Pratt at the savings and loan, there was little public awareness of the people running the company. Meyer had enjoyed the limelight late in his life, and the other managers always pushed him to the forefront whenever the television cameras showed up at grand openings. Those were fun occasions for Meyer, and the others understood the importance of remaining in his shadow. "It hurt us in the long run because the buying public of the stock really thought the day he drew his last breath that that would be the end of Fred Meyer Inc.," Robertson said later. "They didn't realize that there were a few of us around who'd been doing the things, really running the company, even though he was here."[26]

Approximately a month after Meyer's death, Robertson and a handful of top company executives held a private retreat in Port Ludlow, Washington. Robertson wanted to introduce a more collaborative style of leadership. Those attending included Cy Green, Dale Warman, Jerry Sadis, Virgil Campbell, Pauline Lawrence and Gary Baker. It was, according to Sadis, the first time all of them had talked together outside of Meyer's presence. The purpose of the meeting was to set goals for the year, review management and discuss any sensitive matter anyone wanted to raise. Robertson set the ground rules: They were all equals, they were free to discuss anything they wanted. But he repeated Meyer's death-bed plea that they all work together. If anyone walked away from the retreat feeling animosity toward anyone, Robertson said, that person should quit the company. Sadis said tension in the room soon melted, leading to free-flowing discussions. When it ended, there were no hard feelings.

Gerry Pratt was not invited to the Port Ludlow retreat. The savings and loan was a subsidiary, and Pratt ran it with a separate board of directors, as Fred Meyer had intended. The focus of Robertson's retreat was on retail, and the fast-growing savings and loan was not considered a "retail" operation in his view, although it operated under the same roof with many stores. Pratt's absence also may have reflected a view that he was not a Fred Meyer Inc. team player like the others. Most of the senior executives had started as young men and worked their way up the ranks, often feeling the wrath of Fred Meyer along the way. Their lives were dominated by their work and they had few outside interests. Pratt, albeit personally close to Fred Meyer, essentially had entered at the top. He dressed fashionably, socialized in high political and social circles, and was a well-recognized television personality. He was still talking about running for high political office.

Earle A. Chiles later told Robertson it was a mistake not to have included Pratt. Pratt was invited to the second retreat, held a year later at Black Butte. According to Sadis, Pratt left some meetings early and interrupted his participation at times by taking phone calls. Overall, the event was less successful than the first one, Sadis believed.[27] By the time of the second retreat, the savings and loan was experiencing internal and external difficulties that would lead to a highly-publicized blow-up in just a few months.

Pauline Lawrence was the first of Meyer's closest associates to retire. She left her position as vice president of the Eve's Restaurants in 1979, but remained as a member of the board of directors and as a trustee of Meyer's charitable trust, which had yet to be funded. Lawrence noted that her blood pressure quickly dropped back to normal levels. But she also noted the restaurant operations started to fade soon after she left. "As long as she was there we made money," Robertson said. "Never, ever did we lose money with her there."[28] That changed with her departure. There had been an explosion in the world of fast-food dining options, and perhaps buffet-style eating was going out of style. For whatever reasons, the company concluded it could not run the restaurants profitably. Some were leased to other operators, but they couldn't make profits, either. Gradually, the restaurants were phased out and their floor space was devoted to other uses that would generate better returns.

Of course, Lawrence was disappointed to see the restaurant

chain she had built fall to ruin. "I think Mr. Meyer would be very, very unhappy if he knew," she said. "Because he loved the restaurants. He ate all of his meals in them. And the girls all knew him. They all waited on him. He thought it was the greatest thing in the world. He was so happy with it. If he hadn't been happy with it he wouldn't have kept me around. Because he expected me to do the job that he wanted done, and told me and discussed it with me many, many times."[29]

Approximately eighteen months before Meyer's death, two perceptive journalists from Portland's *Willamette Week* newspaper, Ron Buel and Steve Forrester, published a three-part series about Fred Meyer Inc., touching on elements of its history and trying to look ahead to the post-Meyer era. Meyer himself agreed to sit for an interview. When he was asked about his will, he said, "The will will be designed to keep the company running the way it is." Robertson expressed optimism. "We have a great team now. I never felt better about what will happen to the future of this company than I feel today." Gerry Pratt told the journalists, "Oran B. Robertson will run this company and he'll run it as long as he wants to. Unless I'm mistaken, I think he's got the full loyalty of people like Green, Dale Warman and Jerry Sadis." The two journalists came away with a different feeling. After Meyer's death, they wrote, "other top managers are expected to cut each other up after he is gone." [30]

---

[1] Day, Glen, OHS sound recording 1307, June 27, 1989.
[2] Webb, Jean S., OHS sound recording 1316, July 11, 1989.
[3] Lawrence, Pauline, OHS sound recording 1309, Jan. 12, 1989.
[4] Retzlaff Herbert, OHS sound recording 1311, March 1, 1989.
[5] Interview with author at Campbell 's Lake Oswego home, Aug. 19, 2013.
[6] Sadis, Jerry, OHS sound recording 1313, April 20, 1989.
[7] Robertson , Oran, OHS sound recording 1312
[8] Heindel, Max, *The Rosicrucian Cosmo-Conception,* The Rosicrucian Fellowship, Oceanside, Calif., p. 148.
[9] Webb, *op. cit.,* July 18, 1989.
[10] Lawrence, *op. cit.*
[11] Webb, *op. cit.,* July 18, 1989.
[12] *Oregonian,* Sept. 1, 1978, p. B1.

[13] Robertson, *op. cit.*
[14] Lawrence, *op. cit.,* May 25, 1989.
[15] *Willamette Week,* June 2, 1980, p. 1.
[16] Lawrence, *op. cit.,* Jan. 12, 1989.
[17] *Oregonian,* Sept. 3, 1978, p. D10.
[18] *Ibid., p. A3.*
[19] Robertson, *op.cit.,* April 11, 1989.
[20] *Oregonian,* March 21, 1979, p. 1.
[21] MacColl, E. Kimbark, box 14, Portland State University Library Special Collections.
[22] Will of Fred G. Meyer, Multnomah County Probate Court, p. 1.
[23]http://carnegie.org/fileadmin/Media/Publications/PDF/THE_GOSPEL_OF_WEALTH_01.pdf, accessed Aug. 4, 2013.

[24] *Ibid.*
[25] Meyer, Fred G., *Memorandum to the Trustees of the Charitable Trust to be Created Under My Will,* March 29, 1976, Multnomah County Probate Court.
[26] Robertson, *op. cit.,* Dec. 8, 1988.
[27] Sadis, *op. cit.,* May 2, 1989.
[28] Robertson, *op. cit.,* March 28, 1989.
[29] Lawrence, *op. cit.*
[30] *Willamette Week,* April 4, 1977, p. 8.

CHAPTER TEN

Cleaning Up

Long before his death, Fred Meyer knew he would be leaving behind complicated, unfinished business. Foremost was how the shares in his personal estate would be managed by the charitable trust he had created in his will. He knew the trustees probably would have to sell those shares to diversify trust assets and to generate a higher annual return than the stock's 3 percent dividend. Meyer couldn't bring himself to sell the shares before his death, because it would have meant abandoning the enterprise that for five decades had been virtually the sole focus of his life. Nor would Meyer have wanted to pay the federal and state taxes that would have come due on a sale.

The strategy Meyer created to resolve the problem, however, was problematic. He named four board members of Fred Meyer Inc.– Oran Robertson, Pauline Lawrence, Gerry Pratt and Warne Nunn– as personal representatives of his estate and as trustees of the charitable trust created by his will. It is unlikely that his estate planners, lawyers Paul Boley and John McMurchie, recommended the plan because it posed a potential conflict of interest for the four people involved: A deal that would be in the best interests of the trust in selling its Fred Meyer Inc. shares might not be a deal that would be in the best interest of Fred

Meyer Inc. The inverse was also true: What was best for the company might not be the best deal for the trust. Yet under Meyer's will, all four individuals owed fiduciary responsibilities – meaning the utmost levels of honesty, diligence and full disclosure – to all three entities, the trust, the estate and the company. Nevertheless, Meyer wanted it that way, Pauline Lawrence testified later in court. "Mr. Meyer tried to make a team of people. He wanted us to work together."[1] As far as Meyer was concerned, "They knew what he wanted and could carry out his wishes."[2] She added that Meyer was well-aware of the potential conflicts. "He told me there would never be a conflict so long as I got court approval of what he wanted me to do."[3]

Meyer knew he was leaving behind another messy problem. In the last ten years of his life he had tried to clean up the legal tangle involving the nine real estate companies that had been created over the years to buy and then lease the land under several of his shopping centers in Oregon. Although Meyer had often manipulated the real estate companies to achieve his corporate purposes for decades, they technically were independent corporations, not subsidiaries of Fred Meyer Inc. After a change in generally-accepted accounting principles in 1968, Meyer had started buying stock he didn't already own in the real estate companies with Fred Meyer Inc. shares, thus merging the properties into Fred Meyer Inc.

Meyer's attempt to consolidate the real estate companies into Fred Meyer Inc. hit a major snag, however, in the person of Earle A. Chiles. Chiles had inherited some real estate company stock from his mother, Eva Chatfield Meyer, and he had purchased more shares from the charitable trust created by his mother at her death. Although Meyer had minimized Chiles' involvement in Fred Meyer Inc. for many years and had pressured him out as president in 1968, Chiles no longer gave in quickly when Meyer wanted to purchase Chiles' real estate shares. Chiles refused to sell without appraisals that would determine their contemporary value. Meyer, knowing that he had been paying what amounted to inexpensive rent for many years, rejected the appraisal request. Instead, Meyer sold his own interests in the real estate companies to Fred Meyer Inc., leaving it for others to sort out later. Resolving it took teams of high-powered lawyers from two of the Portland's largest law firms more than seven years of litigation including a protracted trial, a complicated appeal and a second round at the trial court it. Earle A. Chiles died in the meantime, not knowing what the outcome would be.

There was a third matter on the horizon at Meyer's death. It was less significant than the other two in the grander scheme of Fred Meyer Inc., but it turned into the sort of fight that a business never likes to see play out on the pages of daily newspapers. The public battle over Fred Meyer Savings and Loan likely never would have happened had Meyer been living; the force of his strong personality had always managed to hold together the team of disparate personalities working just under him. Trouble was on the horizon at Meyer's death; the nation's inflation rate that posed a massive challenge for the entire savings and loan industry was creeping from 6.5 percent in 1977 to roughly 8 percent in the month of Meyer's death.[4] Pratt's skills as a business manager had never been tested in hardship. Whether it was because of inflation or for other reasons, Meyer in his last year told Pauline Lawrence, "I can't go on doing the job for him. We have to let him see what he can do on his own."[5]

In the end, the savings and loan drama was interwoven with the first two strands of potential conflicts. All three of these legacy problems proved to be vital factors in the sale of Fred Meyer Inc. Difficulties at the savings and loan led to animosities between Oran Robertson and Gerry Pratt, thus quickly sundering the team that Meyer had called to his bedside on the eve of his death. It was precisely the kind of warfare that the Willamette Week newspaper had predicted shortly before Meyer's death.

By Meyer's death in September, 1978, Pratt had grown Fred Meyer Savings & Loan to 28 branches with two more in the offing that year. The business had added $976,000 to Fred Meyer Inc. earnings in 1977, and more than doubled that to $2,071,800 in 1978. But there were signs of trouble. Each new branch took time to reach profitability, so the association's fast expansion had its drawbacks even in the best of times. The longer hours of weekly operations were a convenience to customers, but added to staffing costs. Employee turnover was high, driving up administrative costs. In addition, the enterprise was installing a $3 million in-house computer system that was intended to cut costs in the long run, but which had trouble producing reliable information in its first year. As the accounting year neared an end, the association reported that its 1979 results would be somewhere between a profit of $200,000 and a loss of $400,000.[6] The final number turned out to be a loss of $239,000.[7] Worse yet, a continuing rise in national inflation was putting a painful squeeze on the "spread" between what the savings and loan had to pay savers and what it was receiving in return from fixed-rate borrowers. Pratt's aggressive marketing of six-month deposit certificates paying 10 percent or more added to those pressures. The association's spread between yields received and rates paid had dropped from a healthy 2.22 percent in 1978 to an average of 1.19 percent in 1979.

At year's end, the rate spread had worsened to 1.06 percent and showed little sign of abating. "This adverse trend continues into 1980 and the Association anticipates that the spread will continue to decrease and will be negative, at least during a portion of 1980," Pratt advised Fred Meyer Inc. shareholders. He estimated a possible loss in 1980 of $1 million to $1.5 million. "As a result, Fred Meyer Inc. is planning to make capital contributions to maintain the Association's net worth at levels sufficient to meet its operating and regulatory requirements." In a clear reference to the crushing vise of inflation, Pratt added, "However, many of the problems confronting the Association and the entire thrift industry derive from national economic conditions which are beyond their control."[8] Losses were never well-received at Fred Meyer Inc., regardless of reasons. The company preferred to be celebrating its first year of $1 billion total sales in 1979, when net earnings amounted to $22,380,000, or just over 2.2 percent of gross sales.

Oran B. Robertson, the second board chairman in the history of Fred Meyer Inc., opens the new Clackamas store in 1979. (Oregonian)

While the noose at the savings and loan was tightening, Pratt in 1979 was still thinking of running for the U.S. Senate against the Republican incumbent, Bob Packwood. Pratt never had held any elective office, but his prominence as a television public affairs host and his Fred Meyer ties gave him wide name recognition throughout the state. In September, 1979, at a meeting of the savings and loan board of directors held in Anchorage, Alaska, Pratt asked that Fred Jensen be elevated to president of the association, to operate the business if Pratt left to run for the Senate. Jensen, who had taken the position of vice president for marketing in 1974, was elected by a 5-to-3 vote. One of those opposing Jensen was Oran B. Robertson, chairman of Fred Meyer Inc. Robertson, believing that the savings and loan needed more experienced management, wanted a broad executive search. Pratt knew the significance of Robertson's vote immediately. Since Fred Meyer Inc. owned 97 percent of the savings and loan stock, Robertson could put himself in the driver's seat any time he chose. It was the start of a bitter split between Pratt and Robertson, two of Fred Meyer's favorite people.

Pratt surrendered his political aspirations in January, 1980. He calculated he would need to raise more than $500,000 to challenge Packwood, who had a history of compiling large political campaign chests. Pratt had a campaign fund at the time of $14,000, which he intended to return to the donors. At the same time, Pratt decided to give up his weekly public-affairs television show. "I got tired," he explained. "It's a seven-day-a-week job, and I've been doing it for a long time." Although details were not yet public, the financial picture was continuing to deteriorate at the savings and loan, and Pratt's career there was on the line. "The business needs me today," Pratt told the *Oregonian* political reporter.[9]

Top managers at Fred Meyer Inc. were arriving at a different conclusion. Whether based on faulty data from the new computer system or other internal reports, there was concern about the accuracy of information provided to the board of directors. Losses from the savings and loan were mounting. Robertson met with Pratt in February 1980, and proposed that Jerry Sadis become chief executive of the savings and loan. Pratt would remain as chairman but relinquish managerial powers. His salary would be reduced from $85,000 to $50,000 per year. "The implication was that I could go and wind my watch," Pratt said at the time. He asked to think it over, but the Fred Meyer Inc. directors approved the plan before Pratt responded. The change did not sit well with the directors of the savings and loan. In early May, Warne Nunn, a director of the savings and loan, called for Pratt to be reinstated. He believed that Sadis knew even less about the savings and loan business than Pratt and that Pratt had been responsible for the association's earlier growth and success. Warren McMinimee, another association board member, put a more pleasant spin on it. He said Sadis had cleared up the problems he had been sent to fix. After an hour's discussion, the savings and loan board reinstated Pratt, over opposing votes from Robertson, Sadis and Rollin Killoran.[10]

In response to Pratt's reinstatement, the Fred Meyer Inc. board less than a week later called for a special meeting of the savings and loan stockholders to replace the association's board. Since Fred Meyer Inc. owned 97 percent of the savings and loan stock, the result was be a foregone conclusion. Yet, it was not without messiness. Fred Meyer Inc. tried to replace the savings and loan board in May, but failed to comply with legal requirements for giving timely notice. On July 16, the old savings and loan board was ousted and replaced by a slate of Fred Meyer Inc. directors. Some of Pratt's supporters made pleas on his behalf, though Pratt himself was not present. *Oregonian* business reporter Donald Sorensen was frustrated by limitations placed on him. He captured it thusly: "Complete with such tactics as meeting behind closed doors, barring the press, walking out backdoors and down hallways and being evasive in their comments, Fred Meyer Inc. directors elected themselves as the new board of the savings and loan, repeating the actions of the ill-fated meeting of May 23. This time, however, it looks like the election will stick."[11] It was a bitter pill for Gerry Pratt, who still wanted to prove himself as a successful entrepreneur. His friend, Pauline Lawrence, wondered aloud at an earlier meeting as to why he still wanted the challenge. "I said, right in front of everyone, 'Gerry, why are you wanting to stay so bad, when you have already said that you wanted to walk out of it because it was getting too much?' And he said, 'I can tell you why I want to stay, because I feel I built the business. And I want to run it; and I'll straighten it out.'"[12]

Pratt did not get that opportunity. Financial conditions at the savings and loan were worsening. It had expanded to 39 branches, with 29 in Fred Meyer stores, but the spread between interest rates earned

Financial troubles beset Gerry Pratt at Fred Meyer Savings & Loan after the death of his mentor. (Oregonian)

and interest rates paid had declined even further to .16 percent. Because of high interest rates, new loans had plummeted by 75 percent, costing the association approximately $3.1 million in reduced loan fees. The association reported a net loss of more than $4.6 million in 1980. Overall, the savings and loan had lost $1.64 million since its purchase in 1974. Deregulation of the industry approved by Congress offered new opportunities but also new risks. The Fred Meyer directors had seen enough. They looked for a buyer. "In our judgment, the savings and loan industry faces an uncertain and volatile future in this type of environment," Robertson and Cyril Green wrote in the Fred Meyer Inc. annual report. "We believe your company's capital can be used more effectively by concentrating on retail growth."[13] The company also sold its Roundup wholesale company that year, allowing Fred Meyer Inc. to pursue retail opportunities in Central and Eastern Washington without the hard feelings of competing directly against its own wholesale customers.

Pratt did not accept his ouster quietly. He hired business lawyer Henry Carey to file a lawsuit attempting to halt the sale of Fred Meyer Savings & Loan. The suit also included a list of alleged other improprieties by Fred Meyer Inc., involving company bonuses, construction procedures and purported dealings with a relative of Oran Robertson.[14] Robertson had tried to downplay any suggestion of a power struggle with Pratt, but the day after Pratt's suit was filed, Robertson responded with an uncharacteristic blast in the news media. Robertson said Pratt had threatened the suit earlier if he didn't get his job back as chief executive at the savings and loan. Robertson said Fred Meyer Inc. officials believed it would be improper to negotiate with Pratt for the sole purpose of protecting themselves from his lawsuit. "Pratt's assertions and their timing make it clear to us that the only real intent of Mr. Pratt's complaint is to damage the credibility of Fred Meyer management and that Mr. Pratt is motivated to this intent out of vindictive retaliation for his removal," Robertson said.[15]

Of course, the rancorous split between Pratt and Robertson contradicted the death-bed plea by Meyer that his top associates "get along together." Pratt contended that Meyer's final statement the night before his death included another promise, "that you will let Gerry run the savings and loan."[16] Robertson had no recollection of such a comment. He insisted that the decision to replace Pratt was made for business reasons, not a personal vendetta. "He asked us to please work together, and that is what we did," Robertson said of Meyer's final wishes. "But I could not help it if an individual of that group did some things that were not in keeping with good business principles, and just because of what he (Meyer) might have said, I would not have done it differently." [17]

Meanwhile, Robertson had other concerns on his mind. Two prospective bidders had shown interest in the savings and loan. That was a good sign, because it offered the chance to eliminate further losses and an opportunity to capture value from Pratt's six-year tenure presiding over rapid growth at the association. More significant in the long run, however, was a private missive received from Kohlberg Kravis Roberts & Co. (KKR), a New York-based private equity firm that was pioneering a new strategy in acquiring, expanding and then reselling mid-sized companies. KKR often focused on companies struggling with ownership and management succession issues. The firm generally invested some of its own money in its deals, but the bulk of the purchase prices came from borrowed money that would have to be repaid from company profits. KKR liked to call its strategy "bootstrapping," but it came to be known more commonly as a leveraged buyout– the leverage being the borrowed capital.

Jerome Kohlberg, the head of KKR, was a Yale Law School graduate who had come to Portland in the early 1950s as a law clerk for U.S. District Judge Gus J. Solomon. He already was a little familiar with Portland because he had a grandmother who had been born there. He had first-hand knowledge of Fred Meyer's aggressive expansion in the Portland region in the early 1950s while working in the U.S. Courthouse, which ultimately was renamed in honor of his boss, Solomon. Kohlberg subsequently went to work in the corporate finance office of the Bear Sterns & Co. investment bank in New York City. According to one account, Kohlberg on more than one occasion stopped at Fred Meyer Inc. headquarters during Meyer's later years to ask if Meyer was interested in selling his company. Meyer had always listened carefully to see what he could learn, then said he wasn't interested. [18] Kohlberg and two younger associates at Bear Sterns, Ben Kravis and George Roberts, had put together leveraged buyouts of privately-held firms at Bear Sterns before forming KKR in 1976. The KKR offer to Fred Meyer Inc. in September, 1980, was estimated at $45 per share for all of the company's 6.9 million shares outstanding. The number was significant because Fred Meyer Inc. shares were trading just below $30 at the time, and Meyer reportedly had never been offered more than $35 per share during his lifetime.

Fred Meyer Inc. referred the offer to its own investment banking adviser, Kidder Peabody & Co. Within a week, Fred Meyer directors voted to reject the offer without discussing it in person with any KKR representative. Yet Fred Meyer Inc.'s future was definitely in play. The charitable trust, now two years after Meyer's death, needed to convert its shares into the best deal it could find. Two Portland companies hinted about buying the company, but never made firm offers. A French retailing giant, Carrefour S.A., was a serious suitor, but it failed to gain approval it needed from the French national government. Jerry Sadis, the Fred Meyer finance director, put together a plan in which the company could borrow enough money to buy the trust's shares at $45 per share, matching the KKR offer. But Earle A. Chiles, who was now the largest individual Fred Meyer shareholder, quashed that plan when he declined to support it.

Near the end of 1980, Gerry Pratt settled his suit against Fred Meyer Inc. out of court. Some company directors had wondered all along whether Pratt thought he could get his job back or perhaps had dreams of replacing Robertson as Fred Meyer chairman. If so, an inflammatory lawsuit was the wrong tool. All the accusations of improperly dealings by Robertson and Fred Meyer directors were dismissed. Pratt received three years of salary as savings and loan chairman, amounting to $255,000. The company also paid Pratt's legal fees of $35,700. As part of the deal, Pratt resigned as a director of Fred Meyer Inc. He remained as a personal representative of the Meyer estate and as a trustee of the charitable trust. Neither side commented on the outcome.

Pratt's departure as a Fred Meyer Inc. director removed him from any perceived conflict of interest he had as a corporate director and as a personal representative of the estate. That opened the door for Pratt and Warne Nunn, who had also resigned as a director, to file another suit in January, 1981. This one sought the removal of Oran Robertson and Pauline Lawrence as personal representatives. Pratt, still represented by Henry Carey, alleged that Robertson and Lawrence had not kept him and Nunn apprised of offers to buy Fred Meyer Inc. and had failed to listen to offers from qualified buyers. Pratt said in an affidavit that Kohlberg, who hadn't lost interest in Fred Meyer Inc., in late December, 1980, sought a meeting with the four personal representatives, and that Robertson declined without telling the other representatives.

In Kohlberg's view, Fred Meyer Inc. was exactly the kind of company that his firm liked to acquire using the leveraged buyout strategy. The company already had good management and a steady revenue flow from products consumers need on a regular basis. The business was not likely to be revolutionized by unexpected breakthroughs in technology. Although most money KKR used to acquire companies came from lenders, Kohlberg required managers to put up a percentage of the obligations so they would have an incentive to generate profits. However, Fred Meyer Inc. was novel target for KKR in that it was a publicly-traded company; all earlier deals had involved privately-held firms. As a company, KKR did not want to be snared in public controversy. Normally, if a company didn't like a proposed deal, KKR would back away. But in the case of Fred Meyer Inc., if management, Earle A. Chiles and the trust favored a leveraged buyout, there would be no risk of controversy. The remaining shareholders wouldn't be able to stop the sale.

Kohlberg, however, had yet to get a foot in the Fred Meyer door. Help came in the form of a call from his old boss, Judge Solomon, to Gerry Pratt. "Gus encouraged me to bring Jerry Kohlberg into the deal," Pratt said several years later. "I met Kohlberg over breakfast one day. My perception of him was that he was meticulous, guarded, and careful. I finally persuaded them (company directors) to meet with Kohlberg privately, and he made them an offer." [19] Robertson disliked the KKR proposal at the outset, but he, like Pratt, over time also came to admire Kohlberg.

For a full year starting in January, 1980, the Pratt suit aimed at removing Lawrence and Robertson as personal representatives played out sporadically in Multnomah County Circuit Court, while private talks unfolded under intense secrecy between Fred Meyer Inc. and KKR. As it turned out, the only personal representative to testify was Pauline Lawrence. She spent 21 hours over five days facing aggressive questioning from Carey. Later, she called them the worst days of her life. During one, she became physically ill and had to leave the witness stand. Multnomah County Circuit Judge James R. Ellis presided over the trial without a jury. Since a judge has more discretion in separating relevant from irrelevant testimony than jurors, Ellis allowed Carey wide leeway in his interrogation of Lawrence.

Carey was at once one of the most respected yet controversial lawyers in the Portland legal community. The former World War II fighter pilot had built a reputation for representing small "underdog" plaintiffs in complex legal battles against banks and large institutions. Carey was creative in developing his legal theories, aggressive in his questioning and undaunted by whatever legal opposition he faced. Seemingly quiet and mild-mannered out of the courtroom, this gaunt and balding lawyer was one of Portland's fiercest tigers at the counsel's table. Perhaps he called Lawrence first, thinking the high school graduate from Neelyville, Missouri, whose career had been devoted to cooking and restaurants, would be easy to intimidate.

If that was the reason, Carey misjudged Pauline Lawrence. Though clearly uncomfortable on the witness stand, she waded carefully through Carey's complex questions. She answered clearly and calmly. She did not lose her temper, even when Carey tried to imply some impropriety concerning the proximity of her desk to Fred Meyer's in the corporate office. Was she a friend of Pratt's? "At one time, I thought so," she replied.[20]

Carey probed the relationships between Pratt and Meyer, Meyer and Robertson, and the removal of Pratt from the savings and loan.

Lawrence revealed that Meyer had loaned money on several occasions to Pratt and had canceled meetings to talk Pratt out of deep fits of depression. "He was trying to help Gerry become one of the team of people," she testified. Carey tried to show that Pratt was removed from the savings and loan for personal reasons, but Lawrence pushed back. "We had auditing to show there wasn't good management," she said. "We felt we had to make a change because it was getting worse all the time." On a personal note, Lawrence testified that Pratt once asked to move his own desk into Meyer's small personal office, "but he didn't because Mr. Meyer didn't want anybody in his office."[21]

During Lawrence's testimony, Carey revisited the September, 1979, savings and loan board meeting at which Fred Jensen was elected president, over the objections of Robertson. "He (Pratt) was thinking of running for office and we had to have someone to run the savings and loan," Lawrence said. She added that Robertson wanted to look beyond the association's own staff for a candidate, but Pratt won the vote favoring Jensen. Carey contended that "the whole crisis started when Mr. Robertson couldn't have his way and objected to the election of the president." He asserted that Pratt was squeezed out later by Robertson's vindictiveness, not by "business judgment." Lawrence replied that the Fred Meyer board took over because of poor performance at the savings and loan, not because of personalities.[22] Another line of questions touched on Meyer's thoughts about Robertson. "He felt that Mr. Robertson was one of the most honest men he had worked with," Lawrence said. "He thought he was an honest man who did a good job."[23]

At the end of Lawrence's testimony, Carey had made no progress in impugning her integrity as a personal representative of Meyer's estate. Judge Ellis found no reason to remove her. A few other witnesses were called in the ensuing months, but the case largely was put on hold. Nobody explained why at the time, but it was because the bigger story was unfolding behind closed doors.

Jerome Kohlberg finally got his chance to make his case for a leveraged buyout in March, 1981. Fred Meyer directors had begun thinking seriously about the buyout proposal. There were three major concerns: raising the overall price per share above $45, a recommended 10 percent contribution by top managers who would continue at their jobs, and structuring the large debt load so it would not slow or eliminate additional Fred Meyer expansion. One strategy for paying down debt in leveraged buyouts was to sell off assets, but Fred Meyer Inc. had little that it wanted to sacrifice. Maintaining stores to keep them attractive and adding new stores required capital. "We were very concerned about that," said Sadis, who was a key figure in the talks. "In order to be successful in retail, it takes a lot of ingredients."[24]

After Kohlberg's initial pitch, George Roberts, a KKR partner who preferred to work from San Francisco, went to work on the details. Roberts was a cousin of Henry Kravis, and the two had attended Claremont Men's College together in the early 1960s. Henry's father, Ray Kravis, helped his nephew land a job at Bear Sterns where Roberts first met Kohlberg. Roberts' financial analyses always were detailed and careful. He convinced Fred Meyer directors that a buyout might only slightly slow potential expansion. He also recognized the undervalued assets represented by the buildings and land owned by the real estate companies. Roberts realized that those assets could be used in increasing the total purchase offer. He proposed a two-pronged structure with a new Fred Meyer Inc. as an operating company to run the business, and Fred Meyer Real Estate Properties Ltd., a limited partnership to lease the buildings at full market rates to the operating company. Under the proposed deal, store rents would climb from $7 million per year to $41 million. The operating company could deduct the higher rents against its earnings, and the limited partnership could claim depreciation credits. "In this way the proposal would 'unlock' the value in the beneficial leases for the profit of the investors at the expense of the federal and state governments."[25] It was yet another plum courtesy of federal tax laws. By nature of its structure, the Fred Meyer deal would take advantage of the most common tax loophole in the leveraged buyout scheme, an exchange of stock equity for corporate debt. Interest on the debt is deductible, whereas dividends paid out to stockholders are not.

While George Roberts was preparing a new offer for all Fred Meyer Inc. shares, he also was working on a novel plan for borrowing money to fund a substantial portion of the buyout. To date, most financing for leveraged buyouts had come from major insurance companies and commercial banks. Roberts had his eyes on a new funding source: billions of dollars tied up in state-funded pension plans. His "partner" in this part of the project was a man with deep roots in Oregon retailing and money management, Roger S. Meier. Meier was a fourth-generation Oregonian whose great grandfather, Aaron Meier, was a founding partner of the historic Meier & Frank department stores. Roger Meier had grown up in retail operations and served as board secretary of Meier & Frank from 1961 until 1966, when the company was acquired by The May Department Stores Co. As a youngster, he grew up with the competitive battles between Meier & Frank and Fred Meyer during the years that Meyer had several smaller stores almost encircling the big Meier & Frank department store in downtown Portland. For years, Meier & Frank enjoyed the reputation of being the biggest department store west of the Mississippi River. But unlike upstart Fred Meyer, Meier & Frank didn't foresee growth opportunities in Portland's suburbs. The downtown department store sat quietly while Meyer scouted prime suburban locations years in advance of store construction. After the sale to May Department Stores, Roger Meier concentrated on managing the family's wealth, and, since 1970, he had served as a member of the Oregon Investment Council.

The Council was the first of its kind in the nation. It had been created by the Oregon Legislature in 1967 at the instigation of State Treasurer Robert Straub, but it didn't begin operations until after it survived a legal challenge in Oregon state courts. Straub, who became a close associate of Roger Meier, was the son of a prominent San Francisco corporate lawyer and was more sophisticated about money management than his somewhat shambling public image suggested. After serving in World War II and graduating from Dartmouth College, Straub settled in Springfield, Oregon. He worked briefly for Weyerhauser Corp. before starting his own business as a home builder. After serving as a Lane County commissioner and state senator, Straub was elected state treasurer in 1964 on a platform that included creating a system to generate better returns on money collected by the State Accident Insurance Fund and the Public Employees Retirement System.[26]

The five-member investment Council, appointed by the governor, was created to choose private investment specialists to make "prudent" investments with money placed in trust with the state government. By 1980, funds managed for the benefit of state-employee pensions amounted to more than $600 million. Unlike other members of the Council, Roger Meier worked full-time meeting, talking and socializing with securities investors, brokers and deal-makers. Many of his investment recommendations as Council chairman went unchallenged by other Council members. After talking extensively with George Roberts, Meier was prepared to recommend that the Oregon pension system invest roughly 8 percent of its assets in the Fred Meyer leveraged buyout.

George Roberts finished putting together details of a new leveraged buyout proposal in a letter dated June 2, 1981, to Fred Meyer directors. KKR offered $53 per share if the purchase included Fred Meyer Savings & Loan, and $55 per share without the thrift.[27] In essence, KKR agreed with Fred Meyer Inc. management that there was scant value in retaining the savings and loan. Fred Meyer Inc. already was in negotiations with Daniel K. Ludwig, a reclusive billionaire who had made his money primarily from the shipping industry and who was interested in adding to his American Savings and Loan operations based in Utah. Fred Meyer directors agreed to hold talks with KKR. The company also referred the offer to its own adviser, Kidder Peabody, to include in its evaluation.

Barely two weeks after the new KKR offer, Fred Meyer Inc. received approval from the Federal Home Loan Bank Board to sell its savings and loan for $24 million.[28] The sale to Ludwig more than recouped all losses from Fred Meyer Savings & Loan operations, leaving the parent company with a modest profit after its seven-year venture into the thrift business. There was no additional financial benefit to Pratt, who had been eliminated from the management picture and from the Fred Meyer board of directors.

Concerns about the buyout proposal for top-level managers at Fred Meyer included the amount of their own investment positions in the buyout, the management structure and potential impingement on the company's expansion plans. Kohlberg and Roberts fielded the questions. They were looking for 10 percent of the purchase price to come from top managers; for many of those, the investment would be tantamount to their personal net worth. KKR liked the management structure as it stood, and pledged that KKR's role would be akin to a board chairman. KKR had no interest in nitpicking daily managerial decisions. As for expansion, Kohlberg and Roberts wanted Fred Meyer to continue its rising trajectory by looking for acquisitions. Confidence grew on both sides of the proposed deal. Kidder-Peabody decided that the $55 per share offer was on the lower side of reasonable.

The proposed buyout created yet another potential conflict of interest for several current Fred Meyer Inc. board members, including Robertson, Green, Campbell and Sadis. They couldn't exercise independent judgment on behalf of the corporation in agreeing to the sale if they had personal interests in the acquiring company. The solution was to find new "outside" directors for Fred Meyer Inc., who could sit on a committee to evaluate the KKR deal and make a recommendation to the full board. The new outside directors were: John M. Fluke, the founder of Fluke Manufacturing Co., an Everett, Washington firm that made computerized testing and measuring equipment; Edward S. "Ted" Smith, chief executive officer of Omark Industries, a Portland-based firm that manufactured cutting chain for power saws; and Jill S. Ruckelshaus, a political activist who had worked in the Richard Nixon and Gerald Ford Administrations, and who had been appointed to the U.S. Civil Rights Commission by President Jimmy Carter. Fluke and Smith also served as directors of Pacific Northwest banking institutions. To avoid yet another potential conflict of interest they could not be seated on the Fred Meyer Inc. board until after the sale of Fred Meyer Savings & Loan. The independent directors reviewed the KKR proposal and concluded that it was a fair one for Fred Meyer Inc. shareholders. Seven weeks after the $55 offer was received, Fred Meyer Inc. announced that it would proceed with final details toward a leverage buyout for $420 million.[29]

There was one remaining glitch. Earle A. Chiles and his son, Earle M. Chiles, believed that the KKR deal did not give them adequate value for their interests in the five real estate companies in which they held at least partial ownership. They met with Jerome Kohlberg on August 25, 1981, in an attempt to settle their differences.[30] The meeting was not successful. Kohlberg apparently held firm to the view that leases owned by the real estate companies were assignable to the proposed new Fred Meyer Inc. without changes. Since both of the Chiles were members of the board of Fred Meyer Inc., they found themselves in a legal conflict of interest if they asserted their rights on behalf of their real estate company shares. The two men resigned from the Fred Meyer board. Earle A. Chiles said he would not interfere with the leveraged buyout to KKR, but he reserved the right to file suit later on behalf of his real estate stock. Chiles didn't want to pass up the opportunity of the $55 per share offer. Given his holdings in Fred Meyer Inc., his own payout would reach $22 million.

The leveraged buyout closed in mid-December, 1981. The deal included $178 million from the State Accident Insurance Fund and Oregon Public Employment Retirement System. Banks, insurance companies and private investors joined top Fred Meyer managers in the $420 million transaction. Approximately a dozen senior Fred Meyer managers bought into the deal, including Oran Robertson, Jerry Sadis, Dale Warman and Virgil Campbell. It was the largest deal in the history of KKR and the first leveraged buyout of a public company. It also marked the first time that funds held in a public pension system had bought into a leveraged buyout. Not everyone was pleased, however. The Portland Federation of Teachers, whose members were covered in the state pension system, filed suit hoping to stop the deal. So did several Fred Meyer competitors, including retailers PayLess Drug Stores, Bi-Mart, Emporium and G.I. Joe's. The teachers association claimed that the leveraged buyout put too much pension money at risk in one investment. The retailers alleged that state government shouldn't be helping one business at the expense of others.[31] The case was settled with a promise that state officials would not be involved in company management.

A few days after Fred Meyer stockholders approved the deal, Multnomah County Circuit Judge James R. Ellis approved a negotiated settlement in Gerry Pratt's lawsuit aimed at removing Pauline Lawrence and Oran Robertson as personal representatives of the Meyer estate. With the buyout deal finished, Robertson agreed to resign as a personal representative. The final estate matters would be handled by Lawrence, Pratt and Warne Nunn. At the same time, Meyer's longtime friend and attorney, Paul Boley, resigned as one of the five trustees of the charitable trust created in Meyer's will. He cited health reasons. The Meyer estate, valued at $120 million as a result of the buyout, was the largest ever admitted to probate in Oregon, Ellis said. The long delays in Pratt's case had been imposed by the judge, who had been kept apprised of the KKR negotiations. Ellis said he did not want infighting by the personal representatives to jeopardize the sale and the value it added to the charitable trust. The judge added that difficulties in administering the estate may have been instigated by Meyer himself. "He gave each the benefit of his ideas on what should be done (with the estate). I suspect he did not give exactly the same ideas to each."[32]

After the sale closed in December 1981, Oran Robertson took a final look at three huge volumes of acquisition documents. He found that some of the terms did not accurately reflect the oral agreements that had been reached with KKR. Since the deal was signed and done, he held little hope of negotiating changes, but Robertson raised the issues with Kohlberg, anyway. He was surprised by Kohlberg's response. "And I'll be damned if they didn't come forward and say, 'Let's revise this thing. Let's do it the way it was supposed to have been done,' even though it was all done. You know, I don't know of anybody that would really do that."[33]

Earle A. Chiles, Meyer's stepson, died in December, 1982, one year after the buyout. He had never carried out his threatened legal challenge over his interests in the real estate companies. However, his wife, Virginia Hughes Chiles, acting as his personal representative, and their only child, Earle Meyer Chiles, who also owned a smaller amount of the stock, filed suit on behalf of his estate in September 1983. They sought tens of millions of dollars on grounds that current and former executives of the "old Fred Meyer" and the "new Fred Meyer" companies had failed to negotiate fair-market leases for 15 Fred Meyer stores in the Portland region. They also sought punitive damages, a form of civil punishment for egregious violations of law intended to deter others from similar behavior.

For most of 1986, the trial played out in the courtroom of Multnomah County Circuit Judge R. William Riggs, who heard the case without a jury. It was perhaps the most complex litigation in state history, generating 20,000 pages of testimony and some 2,000 exhibits. Teams of lawyers from the large Miller Nash law firm represented the Chiles' interests, while Stoel Rives, another large Portland firm, represented the Fred Meyer Properties Limited Partnership. Aside from the parties and troops of lawyers, however, the case held little public interest. The long trial confirmed the strong-handed and domineering managerial approach that Fred Meyer practiced throughout his long business career. The handful of real estate companies loaned money back and forth among themselves as needed, often without supporting documents. Meyer's firm control over all aspects of his operations and his disregard for some legal formalities was demonstrated by the following exchange between a lawyer and Gerry Pratt on the witness stand.

Q. Incidentally, on these minutes of the Real Estate Companies, it was Mr. Meyer's practice, wasn't it, to circulate those to the directors and have each director sign them?

A. Yes. Sometimes you signed them before they were done.

Q. I take it you wouldn't sign a document if its recitations were-n't accurate to your satisfaction, would you?

A. You would if you worked for Mr. Meyer.[34]

Critical testimony in the real estate trial focused two "leeway" provisions in the KKR offer that were never disclosed to the Chileses. One provision involved the offer of up to $4 million per year in additional rent or mortgage payments to lessors and mortgage lenders for all properties to gain consent for the buyout. The other stipulated that the KKR deal could close even if consents had not been obtained on properties where obligations amounted to no more than 7.5 percent of operating profits, so long as those consents were obtained later. Fred Meyer Inc. officials believed that the leases were assignable to the new entity and that such assignments could not reasonably be withheld. Judge Riggs disagreed. He held that the majority shareholder in the real estate company had a legal obligation, known as a fiduciary duty, to disclose all facets of the proposed KKR deal to minority shareholders. Because that did not happen, he ruled that the transfer to the new limited partnership was the equivalent of a sale. After hearing testimony from numerous real estate appraisers, the judge established a value of $12 million owed to the Chiles' holdings. Interest over the intervening years would have raised that amount to more than $18 million.[35]

Both sides appealed to the Oregon Court of Appeals. The Chiles estate argued that Judge Riggs should have awarded pouniti8ve damages.

The defendants refused to concede a breach of fiduciary duty. After oral arguments in February, 1988, the appeals court took nearly a year to issue its lengthy opinion, yet another indication of the case's complexity. The court cleared the KKR defendants, noting that as buyers they had no fiduciary duty under law to the Chiles' interests. However, the three-judge appeals panel confirmed the fiduciary duty breach by the Fred Meyer-controlled property interests. In the end, the appellate court decided on a different method of determining damages. Writing for the panel, Appeals Judge Edward Warren said the measure should be the difference in value from the date of the KKR buyout to the end of the leases, whenever they were set to expire. It sent the case back to the trial court to calculate the amount based on the new formula. The court found no malicious intent that would justify punitive damages. On that point, the court touched on Meyer's management style, and how relationships were altered by his death.

> Defendants' failure to recognize their duties was the result, ultimately, of the years of Meyer's domination of both Old FMI (Fred Meyer Inc.) and the RECs (real estate companies). The individual defendants had spent much of their careers watching Meyer manipulate the RECs in ways that he thought best suited his interests and Old FMI's needs and seeing Chiles either acquiesce or make generally ineffective protests. They had learned from those experiences that the RECs were the tools of their majority owner, that the minority had little to say about what happened with them and that the primary purpose of the RECs was to serve Old FMI's needs. Even the negotiations surrounding the Real Estate Company Proposal did not change those longstanding habits of thought. Defendants simply failed to adjust to a situation in which the interests of the minority shareholders of the RECs were no longer the

> same as those of the majority shareholder and in which the minority was no longer willing for the RECs to subordinate themselves to the majority's interests or to tie themselves without reservation to one company. The majority had always had fiduciary duties to the minority in theory, but those duties had never had any practical significance during Meyer's life....
>
> "We do not....believe that their actions were sufficiently egregious to require judicial punishment. The long-standing subordination of the RECs' interests to those of Old FMI, and Chiles' almost equally long acquiescence in that relationship, contributed to defendants' insensitivity to their fiduciary duties to Chiles and the RECs. Defendants did not willfully harm Chiles but only failed to fulfill their duties to him. Punitive damages would not serve any useful purpose."[36]

The Chiles case returned to Multnomah County Circuit Court after the Court of Appeals ruling. A different trial judge, Lee Johnson, ruled in November 1990 that the various Chiles interests were due more than $22.3 million from the new Fred Meyer Properties limited partnership under the formula set by the appellate court. The final total included $2.5 million that the judge said could have been negotiated from the "leeway" provisions in the KKR offer, had the Chiles known of them.[37]

Twelve years after Fred Meyer's death, the litigation over his tangled business affairs was finally complete. "If he was alive today, I think he would say, 'You did a good job selling,'" Pauline Lawrence said in 1989.[38] Though Meyer had always refused to sell during his lifetime, Lawrence added that he never specifically told her not to sell. In the end, the sale achieved his primary goals. His own management team, headed by Oran Robertson, Cyril Green, Virgil Campbell and Jerry Sadis, remained intact running the company. The value created for the Meyer charitable trust, some $120 million, more than doubled what

Meyer had expected in his lifetime. And stores throughout major cities of the Pacific Northwest still bore the name Fred Meyer. That would have pleased him. Meyer was not a man who cared for plaques or awards, Lawrence said. "He liked his name on the stores all the time because that was his business."[39]

---

[1] *Oregon Journal,* Jan. 23, 1981, p. 13.
[2] *Ibid.,* June 17, 1981, p. 9.
[3]*Ibid.,* June 18, 1981, p. 30.
[4] www.inflationdata.com., accessed Aug. 13, 2013.
[5] *Oregon Journal,* June 13, 1981, p. 15.
[6] *Oregonian,* March 4, 1980, p. A7.
[7] Fred Meyer Inc., *Annual Report 1979,* p. 1.
[8] *Ibid.* p. 15.
[9] *Oregonian,* Jan. 22, 1980, p. B5.
[10] *Ibid,* June 8, 1980, p. E3.
[11] *Ibid,* July 17, 1980, p. A13.
[12] Lawrence, Pauline, OHS sound recording 1309, Jan. 12, 1989.
[13] Fred Meyer Inc., *Annual Report 1980,* p. 1.
[14] *Oregonian,* July 16, 1980, p. 1.
[15]*Ibid.* July 16, 1980, p. E7.
[16] *Willamette Week,* June 2, 1980, p. 1.
[17] Robertson, Oran, OHS sound recording 1312, April 11, 1989.
[18] Bartlett, Sarah, *The Money Machine, How KKR Manufactured Power and Profits,* Warner Books, 1991, p. 104.
[19] *Ibid,* p. 104-105.
[20] *Oregon Journal,* June 12, 1981, p. 19. The author was a reporter for the *Oregon Journal* at the time and sat through many hours of Lawrence's testimony.
[21] *Ibid,* June 13, 1981, p. 15.
[22] *Ibid,* June 16, 1981, p. 13.
[23] *Ibid,* June 17, 1981, p. 9.
[24] Sadis, Jerry, OHS sound recording 1313, May 2, 1989.
[25] *Virginia H. Chiles, Executrix of the Estate of Earle A. Chiles , Deceased; Virginia H. Chiles; Earle M. Chiles , v. Oran B. Robertson ; Cyril K. Green ; Jerry Sadis ; Virgil Campbell ; C. Dale Warman ; Jerome Kohlberg Jr.; Henry R. Kravis ; George R. Roberts, et al.,* 94 Or.App. 604, 1989.
[26] For an account of Straub's victorious treasurer's race and reasons for creating the Oregon Investment Council, see Johnson Charles K., *Standing at the Water's Edge, Bob Straub's Battle for the Soul of Oregon,* OSU Press, 2012, Chapter 5.
[27] *Oregonian,* June 4, 1918, p. D1.
[28] *Ibid.,* June 17, 1981, p. F1.
[29] *Ibid.,* July 23, 1981, p. 1.

[30] *Chiles v. Robertson, op. cit.*
[31] *Oregonian,* Dec. 8, 1981, p. A12.
[32] *Oregon Journal,* Dec. 22, 1981, p. 11.
[33] Bartlett, Sarah, *op. cit.,* p. 105.
[34] *Chiles v. Robertson, op. cit.,* footnote 5.
[35] *Oregonian,* Nov. 6, 1986, p. E11.
[36] *Chiles v. Robertson, op. cit.*
[37] *Oregonian,* Nov. 8, 1980, p. E2.
[38] Lawrence, *op. cit.,* May 25, 1989.
[39] *Ibid.*

CHAPTER ELEVEN

Epilogue

The leveraged buyout of Fred Meyer Inc. turned out to be a financial success, years before the conclusion of the complex legal case involving the Chiles' real estate interests. Between 1981 and 1986, the company expanded from 63 stores at Fred Meyer's death to a total of 93. Sales climbed from $978,000,000 the year Meyer died to $1.58 billion in 1986. The increase in stores included 11 newly-constructed Fred Meyer centers and acquisition of the Grand Central chain based in Salt Lake City, Utah.

Grand Central had been founded by Maurice Warshaw, a contemporary of Fred Meyer. Both men had immigrated to the United States as children. Warshaw opened his first discount department store in Salt Lake City in 1930. Like Meyer, he prospered during the Depression by offering self-service and low prices. The two founders knew one another and exchanged merchandising ideas from time-to-time over the years. Grand Central offered soft goods and variety departments but never ventured into full-line groceries. A large expansion shortly before Warshaw's death in 1979 left the company with stores in five states but strapped for cash in the recession of the early 1980s. After lengthy negotiations, Grand Central accepted a $26.4 million buyout offer from

Fred Meyer Inc.[1] Fred Meyer kept the Utah and Idaho stores but sold others to Walmart.

The transaction called for the Grand Central name to remain on those stores. But reminiscent of Fred Meyer's difficulties in landing Levy-Strauss bluejeans in the 1960s, problems arose when some suppliers who sold to Fred Meyer didn't want their products offered under Grand Central's "discount store" format. Oran Robertson, Fred Meyer's chief executive, discussed the dilemma with Don Mackey, a grandson of Maurice Warshaw, who had been a key figure in the Grand Central deal. Mackey understood the problem. "It's very clear to me," he told Robertson, "you have to change the name to Fred Meyer."[2] Over time, Fred Meyer Inc. added food to the Grand Central stores and hoisted its signature big red Fred Meyer signs.

Two notable deals occurred in 1986. Kohlberg Kravis & Roberts issued new shares of public stock in Fred Meyer Inc., raising about $98 million in new capital. In a related transaction, the Fred Meyer properties branch sold 35 stores and its huge Clackamas warehouse to Metropolitan Life Insurance Co. for approximately $400 million with a long-term lease-back arrangement. The two deals established a total company market value of roughly $800 million, nearly double the leveraged buyout price of 1981. The return on state-managed funds invested in the controversial leveraged buyout amounted to 53 percent,[3] far surpassing returns available under the state's earlier practices. Yet the investment's success "may have led governments and union leaders to imprudently rely upon a continuation of the unsustainable extraordinary returns of the 1980s and 1990s,"[4] according to Mark Henkels, a public policy and administration professor at Western Oregon University. Investment returns earned by the Oregon Investment Council cratered during the recession beginning in 2008, leading to protracted maneuvering in political circles and the Oregon Legislature over funding for the Public Employees Retirement System.

Though the Fred Meyer buyout was the largest at the time it

was consummated, it soon became a piker compared to larger deals devised by KKR. Founder Jerome Kohlberg decided that he preferred to work with smaller deals, so he separated from Ben Kravis and George Roberts in 1987. Kravis and Roberts went on to structure deals involving tens of billions of dollars. As time went on, contention arose: Did leveraged buyouts helped the national economy and the companies involved, or did they primarily generate large fees for the deal-makers? The subject emerged as a broader public debate in 2012 because the Republican candidate for president, Mitt Romney, had been a leveraged buyout deal-maker for Bain Capital, a firm engaged in the same type of deals as KKR. There seemed to be no clear answer to the underlying question during the election campaign.

The decision by Fred Meyer Inc. to sell Fred Meyer Savings & Loan in 1981 proved to be wise. Financial difficulties arising from inflation, deregulation and changing accounting rules plagued the industry for the rest of the decade, leading to forced mergers or the demise of several large Oregon thrifts such as Willamette Savings, Far West, Benj. Franklin, Pacific First Federal and Equitable Savings. Yet some of the innovations pioneered by Fred Meyer Savings & Loan endured. The in-store branches remained popular, whether operated by Willamette Savings, Washington Mutual Bank or Chase Bank. Evening and Saturday hours survived as operational staples from which there appeared to be no likely retreat.

The Fred Meyer Charitable Trust, created by Meyer's will in 1978, finally opened for business in 1982 with assets of $120 million. Paul Boley, one of the five trustees named in Meyer's will, resigned for health reasons soon after Meyer's death. The other trustees, Oran Robertson, Gerry Pratt, Warne Nunn and Pauline Lawrence, filled the vacancy with Travis Cross, a health care administrator who had worked with Nunn in Gov. Hatfield's office. By 1990, the trust had approved grants totaling $77 million in accord with guidelines Meyer had specified. The requests for help were daunting, despite the trust's large size.

"Trying to respond to all the needs is like sprinkling holy water on the farm," Gerry Pratt said. "You can't irrigate everything."[5] The trust changed its name in 1990 to Meyer Memorial Trust to eliminate confusion about a connection between the company and the trust. ``Many people mistakenly believe that the trust is the philanthropic arm of the Fred Meyer retail chain," Robertson said. Pickets had shown up at some stores, objecting to grants provided by the trust to Planned Parenthood.[6]

Original Meyer trustees were, from left, Travis Cross, Gerry Pratt, Oran Robertson, Pauline Lawrence and Warne Nunn. (Oregonian)

As trustees, Lawrence and Pratt managed to restore a friendship strained by Pratt's lawsuit aimed at removing her as a personal representative of the Fred Meyer estate. Lawrence resigned as trustee in 1995 and died in 1997. Robertson remained as chairman of the trustees until his death in 1999. Nunn resigned as a trustee in 2006 and died the following year. Pratt, the only surviving original trustee, resigned in 2013. He was the last member of the trust and its staff to have had any personal experience with its benefactor, Fred Meyer. Always a facile writer, Pratt turned to fiction and short stories later in life. His brief promotional biography makes no mention of working at Fred Meyer Inc. or Fred Meyer Savings & Loan.

Oran Robertson was the only person on Meyer's management team to lead the company after Fred Meyer's death. A decade after the patriarch's death, few of Meyer's top managers remained. Virgil Campbell retired as chief of operations and Jerry Sadis departed as chief financial officer in 1987. Dale Warman retired in 1990 as vice president in charge of strategic marketing, store planning and engineering. Cyril Green was the last of Meyer's inner circle to retire, leaving in 1996 after nearly 50 years with the company. Robertson retired as chief executive officer in 1988 at age 70, with the chain comprising 99 stores. The board of directors went outside of Fred Meyer Inc.'s ranks to hire Frederick M. Stevens as chairman and chief executive after Robertson. Stevens had risen through the ranks in 29 years at K Mart, based in Troy, Michigan. In 1991, Robert G. Miller, another outsider, left Albertson's as vice president in charge of retail to replace Stevens as chairman and chief executive at Fred Meyer Inc.

During his eight-year tenure as chief executive, Miller led Fred Meyer Inc. on an aggressive buying spree. He bought two jewelry store chains with 89 outlets, many of them free-standing stores in large shopping malls. He turned his attention back to food in 1997 in a $2 billion acquisition of 152 stores under three names owned by Smith's Food & Drug Centers, based in Utah. The following year, Miller added 89 Quality Food Center stores, mostly serving the Seattle region. He also reached into Southern California again to acquire Food 4 Less Holdings Inc., which operated 264 Ralphs stores and 80 Food 4 Less warehouse outlets.

The deals left Fred Meyer Inc. in control of 824 stores in 12 states from Alaska to Texas. The total included an assortment of one-stop shopping formats and a variety of smaller food-and-drug, warehouse food and jewelry outlets. ``We knew we were going to be acquired or acquire someone," Miller said in mid-1998. ``We chose to acquire."[7]

Miller's acquisition spree ended in 1988. A bigger fish in the grocery waters, Kroger Co., offered $13 billion for Fred Meyer Inc. The

Cincinnati, Ohio-based chain had its own claim to grocery retailing history. Bernard Kroger, the son of German immigrants, opened his first small grocery in Cincinnati in 1883, three years before Fred Meyer's birth. He, too, was an aggressive retailer who quickly built a chain of small stores. In 1901, Kroger opened what is believed to be the first in-store bakery. He calculated, as did Fred Meyer years later, that he could sell more bread at cheaper prices and make better profits if he baked bread himself rather than buying it from another bakery. Barney Kroger, as he was better known, was still running his chain in 1930 when one of his employees in Cincinnati, Michael E. Cullen, wrote a long memo outlining his plans for larger stores offering full self-service, high-volume sales and aggressive advertising campaigns. An intermediary disposed of the letter without giving it to Kroger. Cullen then went on to establish his first King Kullen store in Queens, New York, which earned the title as the first American supermarket.[8]

Fred Meyer Inc. directors and shareholders quickly approved the Kroger Co. offer. The transaction produced a company with more than 2,200 stores in 31 states, and put Kroger in the top echelon of American food retailers. The Fred Meyer stores, averaging 165,000 square feet, were the largest in the Kroger chain and were the only ones to offer one-stop shopping with food, drugs, variety, hardware and other departments.

Kroger Co. left the Fred Meyer name on those stores and retained the Fred Meyer Inc. headquarters for its Pacific Northwest operations in the same building Meyer acquired in Southeast Portland in 1963. Kroger still runs a Founder's Day sale every spring, but the pictures of Fred Meyer – a jovial-looking old man in glasses and a bow tie – appear to grow smaller as years pass. As new generations of customers rise and old ones die off, the value of the Fred Meyer name may well diminish. There was a time, after all, when Portlanders believed that the city's landmark department store, Meier & Frank Co., would always be called Meier & Frank no matter who owned it. Eventually, Macy's changed the name.

It is conceivable, even probable, that Fred Meyer stores await a similar fate. An executive sitting in a distant city in some future year might decide that standardization and using a single name for all stores in the national chain would save money and bolster identity. If so, the big Fred Meyer signs will come down, and the Meyer name will linger only as a dynamic chapter in Pacific Northwest retailing history. As a firm believer in efficiency and standardization, the man known to all employees during his long life as Mr. Meyer no doubt would understand.

---

[1] *Oregonian,* March 27, 1984, p. D7

[2] Robertson, Oran, OHS sound recording 1312, March 28, 1989.

[3] Bartlett, Sarah, *The Money Machine, how KKR Manufactured Power and Profits,* Warner Books, 1990, p. 118.

[4] Henkels, Mark, professor, Western Oregon University, in Epilogue to Johnson, Charles K., *Standing at the Water's edge: Bob Straub's Battle for the Soul of Oregon,* Oregon State University Press, 2012, p. 287.

[5] *Oregonian,* Dec. 11, 1983, p. C6.

[6] *Oregonian,* April 21, 1990, p D2.

[7] *Ibid,* June 21, 1998, p. R4.

[8] McFadyen, Tevere, *The Rise of the Supermarket,* American Heritage Magazine, vol. 236, issue 6, 1985.

CHAPTER TWELVE

Some Final Thoughts

"Business is always good for good merchants –adopt, adapt, adjust – and try to do business the way the customer wants it done." –FRED MEYER[1]

"He didn't have a good life, a good family life, because I don't guess any genius does. They've got so much out there, that any person that did what he did, there's no way he could have it all, you know. And he just didn't have time for a family life." – PAULINE LAWRENCE[2]

"He had a magnetism about him, that you either worked for him and was devoted to work for him, or you got out—I mean the top people. And we'd get so angry at the man because of his temperament, you know. But we were still devoted to our jobs, trying to please in every way. I think every one of the top people tried hard as they could to please. They didn't like it, sometimes, the way it was going, but they tried because of one thing...they all respected him. He could have been the greatest teacher in the world because he had so much."—PAULINE LAWRENCE[3]

"He was always doing what was best for Fred Meyer Inc., always. And I think it always took priority over his personal interests." – CYRIL GREEN.[4]

"He was a very hands-on manager. When he went in a store, I mean he didn't just walk through it. No, he saw what was going on and he'd raise hell if it wasn't what he thought it should be." – HERBERT RETZLAFF [5]

"Keep learning, keep earning." – FRED MEYER[6]

"I think his philosophy of life was positive. He wanted to do something worthwhile in life and he did it. And he wanted to do good things for people, which he did by building up his business which provided jobs for many people, both in the business and outside the business. He was very action-oriented. And what he wanted to accomplish was something good. He wasn't self-centered or egotistical about it. In fact, amassing money for the sake of money didn't mean anything to him. He was very, very simple in his own wants and he didn't smoke or drink." – HERBERT RETZLAFF[7]

"Money as such meant little to him. But he wanted to make money in order to be able to expand the business, to build new stores, to put more people to work and thereby help the communities in the areas where these stores were being built. He was a builder in that sense. He wanted to build economic value that would aid the communities." – HERBERT RETZLAFF[8]

"I couldn't tell you a light side that I've ever known in the man. His mind was business. And he wanted business. He thought only of business....At the beginning you sensed that he wanted everybody to have the same motivation, wanted them to perform and think like he did. But it isn't humanly possible to think with Mr. Meyer. He's a breed all his own." –RAY CHIRGWIN[9]

"The man was always going in one direction. Everything else was a waste of time." – RAY CHIRGWIN[10]

"A self-made man, he liked to have self-made men around him, but he doubtless knew more about economics, real estate and merchandising than anyone in Oregon. He could lecture for hours on such subjects as the gold standard, inflation, foreign currencies, taxation questions and every other facet of trade and money." – DOUG BAKER[11]

"He could be very grandfatherly when he wanted to be, and he could be a mean old tyrant when he wanted to be. And I mean he could go from one to the other." – GARY BAKER.[12]

"I can surmise, but no matter how much education any of them had, they still weren't as smart as the old man. He read so much that he had enlightenment on just about any doggone subject." – RAY CHIRGWIN[13]

"I don't think I ever heard the man ever, ever apologize or ever say he was wrong." – RAY CHIRGWIN[14]

"A nimble dime is better than a lazy dollar." – Fred Meyer[15]

"Mr. Meyer should go down in history as being the most aggressive merchandiser, most knowledgeable merchandiser, that ever hit this town. I think he's head and shoulders above anybody else in the city of Portland. For money, he used the word beans, and he said in a meeting one time, 'If I lost all my beans tomorrow, it wouldn't make any difference because I could make it up right way.' Now, that's how much confidence he had in himself." – RAY CHIRGWIN[16]

"Well, some of the people, some of the employees were scared to death of him. Because they had heard some of his little tirades that he tied into one person or another. I think the majority of the employees had a very high respect for Mr. Meyer as a very influential leader and for his ability to organize an organization that he did develop."—GLEN DAY[17]

"You don't want to catch him on a day when he is frustrated or mad about something else. You can tell when you work with (someone) all the time. But Fred Meyer always tried to teach us, if you would get the facts on whatever you are talking about, not make assumptions, not make up something yourself, you generally speaking come out fine.....You generally would win a few battles. He'd always win the war, it seemed. But along the way you at least got to express yourself. He said he encouraged that. He did up to a point, before you disagreed with him."– ROLLIN KILLORAN[18]

Sign near Fred Meyer's desk: "There's nothing as devastating as the death of a beautiful theory by a gang of brutal facts." –Recalled by GARY BAKER[19]

"He had that austere frugality that was so common among men of his breed. He lived alone in a simple, two-bedroom apartment, with one room converted into an office to work at home right up until he died. There was never hired help, except for a woman who did the laundry a couple of days a week and dusted the place. You had to struggle to get him to shop for a suit, and his friends kept him in bow ties. Yet he delighted in good things, and delighted in saying of Eve: 'She could go into a store and by instinct walk to the most expensive thing in the place.' He used to say that's why he worked so hard: 'She was a good woman and I had to work hard to keep her.'" – GERRY PRATT [20]

"He never made a mistake in his life that he knew about. Somebody else always did."–Oran Robertson.21

"That man had vision and he could see things that nobody else could see and he always picked great locations. He always knew where the freeways were going to go. He would have made one of the greatest engineers that ever came down the pike if he had gone that direction. He really would have because he could imagine things." –Oran Robertson [22]

"I hope what he's remembered for is a man that came here with nothing, started something and created something out of nothing...That he built an organization and not just a company, but an organization to continue it...and that he left 99 percent of his estate to the citizens of the communities where he operated. I mean, I am extremely impressed by that. And I don't give a damn what he was personality-wise, or what his idiosyncrasies were or whatever. The bottom line is, he created – just think how many people were able to support themselves, support their families, send their kids to college, get them out of high school, provide careers for people, make money for people. And then to take everything that he earned and give it back to everybody...pretty remarkable, I think." – Gary Baker[23]

"When you're green, you're growing. When you're ripe, you're rotten." – Fred Meyer[24]

"He didn't care how much (money) you lost. But don't you ever hide behind a veil or curtain of any kind and try to blame it on someone else or some other condition or something like that. Boy, that was death." – ORAN ROBERTSON[25]

"If you wanted to talk Shakespeare, he'd sit and talk Shakespeare by the hour. Music, any form of music—you want Gershwin? He'll talk Gershwin. You want to talk Mozart? He'll talk Mozart. You want to talk the Bible? He'll talk about the Bible." – JACK CROCKER[26]

"We always saw that he was the one front and center in all situations like that (store openings). It was interesting with him because you can't say he had many friends. He was not an outgoing individual. And yet he loved to get up like that and in so doing he had a real sense of humor. And he talked to people with a very basic, fundamental manner. He always told me, 'If you have a choice of two words, use the smaller one and don't talk *to* people, talk *with* people.' And he was very effective at that." – JACK CROCKER[27]

"If it was good, it was his idea. And if was bad, it was somebody else's idea." – HOWARD ANDERSEN[28]

"You very seldom got by with anything that he didn't know about, because he had a pipeline. He had a way of finding out every darn thing that goes on in this company. I don't know who....sometimes I think he had rooms bugged and everything. I don't know. But he always just knew."–DALE WARMAN [29]

"You know, you never got a lot of strokes from Mr. Meyer. You just didn't. He never complimented anybody that I know of. But you grew as a result." – DALE WARMAN[30]

"I knew him when he was 84 to 92. That's not a young man, but he was a young thinker and a very active person." – JERRY SADIS[31]

"Mr. Meyer ran it like the navy and like the army. Everything was very rigid, very disciplined. He was a Patton. He really was." –DALE WARMAN[32]

"He was a very peaceful man, and a very confident man. And there's no question in my mind that when he died he didn't have a fear or a question or a concern or anything. I mean, he always reminded me of an extremely confident guy. I never saw Mr. Meyer 'down.'" –GARY BAKER[33]

"The hallmark of Mr. Meyer was that he was all business. Even in a personal relationship, he was probably thinking of how he could improve the business." – JERRY SADIS[34]

"The record is replete with other evidence confirming Meyer's complete domination of the business and of all who worked with him. Those who would not bow to him simply left." – OREGON COURT OF APPEALS[35]

"He who steals my time steals my money." – FRED MEYER[36]

---

[1] *Oregon Journal,* Nov. 4, 1932, p. 11.
[2] Lawrence , Pauline, oral history interview, Oregon Historical Society, sound recording 1309, Dec. 8, 1988
[3] *Ibid.*
[4] Green, Cyril K., OHS sound recording 1307, Feb. 27, 1989.
[5] Retzlaff, Herbert, oral history interview, Oregon Historical Society, sound recording 1311, Feb. 22, 1989.
[6] *Oregon Journal,* Nov. 4, 1932, p. 11.
[7] *Ibid.*
[8] *Ibid.*
[9] Chirgwin , Ray, oral history interview, Oregon Historical Society, sound recording 1303, July 24, 1989.
[10] *Ibid*

[11] Baker, Doug, was a popular newspaper columnist for the *Oregon Journal.* Baker and Meyer talked many times over the years. *Oregon Journal,* Sept. 5,1978, p. 15.
[12] Baker , Gary, oral history interview, OHS, sound recording 1301, May, 16, 1989
[13] *Ibid.*
[14] *Ibid.*
[15] *Oregon Journal,* Feb. 13, 1961, Sec. 2, p. 10.
[16] *Ibid.*
[17] Day, Glen, oral history interview, Oregon Historical Society, sound recording 1306, June 27, 1989.
[18] Killoran , Rollin, oral history interview, Oregon Historical Society, sound recording 1308, Nov. 3, 1988.
[19] Baker, *op. cit.*
[20] *Oregonian,* Sept. 5, 1978, p. B7.
[21] Robertson, Oran B., OHS, sound recording 1312, Dec. 20, 1988.
[22] *Ibid.*
[23] Baker , *op. cit.,* June 23, 1989
[24] *Ibid.*
[25] Robertson, *op. cit.*
[26] Crocker, Jack, oral history interview, OHS sound recording 1304, June 1, 1989.
[27] Crocker, *op. cit.,* Aug. 2, 1989.
[28] Andersen, Howard, OHS sound recording 1300, Aug. 9, 1989.
[29] Warman, Dale, OHS sound recording 1315, April 20, 1989.
[30] Warman, *op. cit.,* May 17, 1989.
[31] Sadis, Jerry, OHS sound recording 1313, April 20, 1989.
[32] Warman, *op. cit,* April 20, 1989.
[33] Baker, *op. cit.*
[34] Sadis, *op. cit.*
[35] *Virginia H. Chiles, Executrix of the Estate of Earle A. Chiles, Deceased; Virginia H. Chiles; Earle M. Chiles , v. Oran B. Robertson ; Cyril K. Green ; Jerry Sadis ; Virgil Campbell ; C. Dale Warman ; Jerome Kohlberg Jr.; Henry R. Kravis ; George R. Roberts, et al.,* 94 Or.App. 604, 1989, footnote 5. .
[36] Attributed to Meyer by Imogen Robbin, who preceded Jean Webb as Meyer's secretary. Found in OHS Fred Meyer Collection 199, box 9, folder 11.

Credits

The suggestion for this book came from my wife, Barbara Coleman. We were having coffee late in 2012 in the newly-remodeled Fred Meyer Hollywood store where a mural-sized photograph of the original Hollywood Fred Meyer taken in the 1930s graces a wall in the eating area. "Has anybody ever done a biography of Fred Meyer?" she asked.

My preliminary exploration soon revealed that the Meyer Memorial Trust in 1988 and 1989 had funded a Fred Meyer oral history project conducted by the Oregon Historical Society. Oral historians James Strassmaier and Clark Hansen engaged in lengthy interviews with approximately a dozen high-ranking company officials who had had first-hand involvement with Meyer. Funding for the project was terminated before the project was completed. Fortunately, Strassmaier and Hansen had already finished with most of the major figures. The interviews were sealed until 2010.

Human memories are not perfect, especially about specific years. Newspapers, company documents and court records proved helpful in pinning down accurate times of events. Trial court records are not always kept as perfectly as one might wish. Despite several efforts, Multnomah County Circuit Court clerks were unable to locate litigation between Fred Meyer and his brother, William Grubmeyer , in the 1920s that likely would have revealed the reason for their split. Microfilm reels are missing that should contain records of Meyer's allegations of conspiracy against Portland bakeries for refusing to sell him bread. Dedicated, persistent searching by Tracy Martinez-Williams in Baker County Circuit Court led to a brief summary of Eva Chatfield 's divorce from Ira Chiles in 1908. Carol K. Reis of the state Appellate Records Office helped me track down the 1928 litigation between Fred Meyer and Henry Meyer.

Other helpful stops along the research path included the Multnomah County Library, Seattle Public Library, Baker County Public Library, Oregon State Archives, the Multnomah Law Library and United States District Court in Portland. Other helpers included Mary Hansen of the Portland Archives & Records Center; Cristine Paschild, archivist at the Portland State University Library, and Tony Green and Peter Threlkel at the Oregon Corporation Division. The Internet played a major role as well, especially through the digitized archive of the *Oregonian.* Therese Bottomly of the Oregonian Publishing Co. graciously allowed me to examine the newspaper's photographic archives. Drew Vattiat provided technical assistance to get the *Oregonian* images safely to my computer. Jennifer Keyser and Scott Daniels were patient and helpful at the Oregon Historical Society Research Library.

Earle M. Chiles through his staff declined to be interviewed for this book. Gerry Pratt did not respond to an interview request. He also declined to be interviewed by the OHS historians late in the 1980s. Virgil Campbell, who displayed a framed photograph of Meyer in his den, graciously shared time and interesting recollections. Campbell died shortly before this book went to press.

Meyer's public statements are always interesting but often not reliable. As a consummate salesman, any comment he made publicly was intended as a "sell," not necessarily as an honest expression of his thoughts or history. A good example is the renovation of his final corporate offices. He vented angrily in private about the carpets and other "frills," while boasting in the newspaper that the carpeting was a money-saver. We owe deep thanks to those company officials who participated in the oral history interviews for allowing an intimate, fuller view of the man. Many of Fred Meyer's longstanding employees are no longer living. Rollin Killoran died in 1990; Pauline Lawrence in 1997; Ray Chirgwin in 1998; Herbert Retzlaff and Oran Robertson in 1999. Without participation by them and others in the oral history project, this book would not have been possible.

I deeply appreciate the help of my sister, Susan M. Leeson, of Salem, Oregon, who read the manuscript and guided me out of some nasty editorial sinkholes. My brother, George Leeson, of San Francisco, California, read an early version and offered vital suggestions for improvements. James Strassmaier also offered helpful comments. Jim Pierson did an expeditious and meticulous final edit that greatly improved the book's internal consistency. Fred Meyer Inc. kindly allowed me to use its trademarked "MY-TE-FINE" phrase in the book title. Courtney Roby-Sage designed the cover. I must add that no one at Fred Meyer Inc. or the Oregon Historical Society played any role in planning or writing this biography. Any errors or misinterpretations are mine alone.

Because incessant remodeling is a component of modern retailing, it is difficult to get a feel for any stores as Fred Meyer knew them. Perhaps the best opportunity is at the Hawthorne Boulevard store in Portland. There, the surface of the ground floor has been returned to its original green concrete and the angled concrete interior pillars still support a portion of the original rooftop parking. Though the building has been remodeled and expanded since his death, Meyer could walk into the old portion of Hawthorne and feel quite at home. And so can we.

FRED LEESON, 2014

Index

A

B

C

D

E

F

G

M

N

O

P

T

U

V

W

Y

ABOUT THE AUTHOR

Fred Leeson is a journalist and author who has lived in Portland, Oregon, almost steadily since his arrival as an adolescent in 1961. He holds a bachelor's degree from Stanford University and a J.D. from the Lewis & Clark Law School. Leeson was a reporter at the *Oregon Journal* from 1972 to 1982, and at the *Oregonian* from 1982 to 2007.

In the 1960s and 1970s, Leeson shopped at Fred Meyer stores at Hawthorne, Rose City, Walnut Park and Hollywood. Today, he lives close to Hollywood West, which he visits frequently. In 1973, Leeson, then 24, spent about an hour interviewing Fred Meyer, who was 87. During those minutes, Meyer displayed many of the traits reflected in this book.

Leeson's earlier books are *Rose City Justice,* a history of the Portland legal community, and *Multnomah,* a history of Multnomah County written with Jewel Lansing.

At the time of this writing, Leeson was president of the non-profit Bosco-Milligan Foundation, an architectural preservation education and advocacy organization. The foundation owns and operates the Architectural Heritage Center in Portland.